1st American.

OP 10⁴

WEIZMANN

WEIZMANN

Last of the Patriarchs

by

Barnet Litvinoff

G. P. PUTNAM'S SONS
NEW YORK

First American Edition 1976

SBN: 399-11718-0

Library of Congress Cataloging in Publication Data

Litvinoff, Barnet.
    Weizmann: last of the patriarchs.

    Bibliography: p.
    Includes index.
    1. Weizmann, Chaim, Pres. Israel, 1874–1952.
DS125.3.W45L58   1976   956.94′05′0924 [B]   76-22549

PRINTED IN THE UNITED STATES OF AMERICA

To my wife, Sylvia, who shared with me
this journey through another man's life,
and immeasurably lessened the distance.

A Note on Sources

HISTORICAL RESEARCH IS, AMONG OTHER THINGS, AN EXERCISE in compromise. Chaim Weizmann conducted his leadership of the Zionist movement on a dimension calling for negotiations with governments the world over, and I do not claim to have seen all the documentation thus generated. Fortunately, the Weizmann Archives in Rehovot, the Central Zionist Archives in Jerusalem, and the American Zionist Archives in New York embrace between them almost every primary source of importance, including copies of relevant governmental records from British, French, German and American state archives. This material, consulted together with the papers, published and unpublished, of the many personalities and lesser-known individuals who shared the stage with Weizmann, helped to produce as comprehensive a picture as might be required, for student and general reader alike.

I have not seen it as part of my task to scatter references throughout the text; or support the narrative with bulky footnotes, a historian's practice that does not always strike this author as wholly meritorious. Weizmann's own extensive records began with his period in Geneva, and have been cherished and amplified by Mr Meyer Weisgal, Chancellor of the Weizmann Institute, over the years. It is with profound gratitude that I acknowledge my debt to Mr Weisgal, and to the directors of the archives referred to above.

Contents

Illustrations

Acknowledgments

Pictures reproduced by permission of the Weizmann Archives, Rehovot; Central Zionist Archives, Jerusalem; Government of Israel; and 1. Central Office of Information, London; 2. Associated Press Ltd.; 3. Keystone Press Agency.

I

A Kind of Nation

THEY WERE A PEOPLE OF EXTREMES. SOME, THROUGH THEIR WEALTH
and initiative, held the reins guiding a corrupt and reluctant Imperial
Russia into its industrial dawn. The mass were so poor they lived by
trading their mean skills and second-hand goods for kopeks, and subsisted
on black bread and herrings, a diet varied only to honour the Sabbath day.
Between the extremes lay a small middle-class, with its intellectuals, its
pietists, its atheists and revolutionaries.

The people were the Jews; the period the later half of the nineteenth
century. Serfdom was a recent memory, and in such a society the Jews
were like their neighbours: docile, and submissive to a communal
hierarchy in which the man who could bribe a petty official was king.

They received no privileges of citizenship, and expected none. By conversion to the Church they could attain whatever Holy Russia offered by
way of education, and status, and a place in the public service. It was a
course sometimes thankfully embraced. But for the vast majority employment meant the cobbler's last, the tailor's bench, the peddlar's pack. They
occupied entire towns, and sprawling villages. Not a few were unlettered,
even illiterate.

Their ancestors had originated in Palestine and the Levant – they knew
exactly how (or thought they knew), through the scraps of the Bible they
learned by rote – and wandered along the seaport towns of the Mediterranean all the way to the Atlantic. By the Middle Ages they had reached
the heartland of Europe. Aliens everywhere, unwanted though not unused,
they were driven towards the east as protectors died or were deposed. They
came to untamed forests, where warring chieftans were establishing their
domains and fathering aristocratic lineages. Then Russian conquerors

advanced westward, and by the beginning of the nineteenth century possessed a great land-mass in Eastern Europe, and with it the millions of Jews it contained.

What to do with such people? Despite famine and disease they spawned large families. They had brought a language from the Rhenish provinces, but their culture was based on nostalgia for the Holy Land and a society two millenia past, while their law was an accumulation of regulations that had remained unquestioned for 1,500 years. Still, they were adaptable, and performed tasks which others despised but which were nevertheless essential to slow-moving Russia. Persecute them, move them out of their villages, drive them from the land, send missionaries among them, suborn their leaders, press them into long years of military service, stigmatise them as an accursed race of Christ-killers, and still the herd remained.

As the century drew to its close Imperial Russia was an ailing Leviathan suffering from Jewish indigestion. Edicts were introduced in the hope that a third of this nation of sorts would die off, a third would depart and join their brothers now Europeanised in the West, while the residue would at last become Russified. In the meantime they must be taxed to the hilt for their money-lending and liquor-purveying, prevented from crowding true Russians out of the universities, and confined, unless they had a singular contribution to make to the country at large, within a Pale of Settlement stretching from the Baltic to the Black Sea.

In this universe of wretchedness the Jews could still find elements of happiness. For many it lay in the belief that nothing was real except the certainty that one day the Messiah would arrive – he could be in the shape of a prince, or a pauper stumbling through the muddy streets of their village – and lead them back to the Promised Land. It was all there in the texts, to be repeated over and over again as an exercise towards the speeding of the day. Or happiness could be found in the peace of the Sabbath and the cycle of the seasons, with the faces in the family circle lit by the candles separating a sacred day from the profane. Or in making money by serving the creature needs of the *goy* and giving a portion to support a poor co-religionist; or at the card-table; or in some secret place where fellow-conspirators were planning to defeat the great oppression; or in flight. For a fourteen year old boy in the town of Pinsk, in what had a hundred years before been part of Lithuania, happiness was discovered in observing a test-tube warming over a jet of flame.

Chaim Weizmann and his elder brother Feivel had been sent from their home twenty-five miles from Pinsk to gain a modern-style education.

There was no secondary school in their native village of Motol, nor, for that matter, much else, and their father believed the times warranted better training for his children than could be provided in the stale rooms of the local ghetto schools, presided over by scholars convinced that all the world's wisdom reposed in the Talmud. Adequate though these might be for the sons of artisans and the indolent, they hardly measured to the needs of Ozer Weizmann's family.

He was a merchant, and employed tree-fellers to cut the forest lumber and move it down-stream through the thawing ice to Danzig. Ozer had inherited the business from his father-in-law, whose daughter he married while a poor free-boarder of the house. He was fifteen at the time, his bride Rachel fourteen, and he had come from a neighbouring village to study under the local rabbi. Now Ozer was well-to-do, and the children were coming fast. His rabbinical education notwithstanding, he had forward-looking ideas, was known to smoke openly on the Sabbath, and planned to give his daughters, as well as his sons, a schooling. He welcomed the idea of travel for them, for the present no further than Pinsk, but the world was vast with promise and Ozer wanted all his children (there would be twelve surviving to adulthood) to have a share in it.

The boy scrutinising the test-tube in Pinsk was born in 1874. By entering the school laboratory he had demonstrated his proficiency in the Russian language. And he had decided much more than to follow a career in chemistry. He had subconsciously accepted a role in the search for a new interpretation of his people's destiny.

Most Jews were ignorant of Russian, needing it but rarely. Like them, Chaim customarily spoke in Yiddish, and had pursued his earliest studies in Hebrew. But Ozer Weizmann insisted upon his children learning the language that would earn them a career in the world beyond the ghetto. The Jews loved Yiddish, which had a lilt that conveyed the pathos of their condition. It was the intimate code of the people in their introvertive state, expressing their rootlessness, improvisation, the life of exile. Its base was tenth century Germanic, but it retained some Hebrew and picked up Slavonic on its journey to the Pale. At the time of Chaim Weizmann's birth Yiddish had still not standardised its syntax nor completed its vocabulary, and had only begun to produce a literature. Hebrew, on the other hand, was already the literary medium of an aristocracy of pioneers determined to make the language of the Bible express once more the national sentiment of the Jewish people. Russian, however, was on a different plane. It was the key to social and economic emancipation.

The Jews of Imperial Russia were a century behind the stage of development their brothers had reached in the West. This was a dark continent; there, the so-called Enlightenment had spread its glow into the smallest ghetto. Even before their legal emancipation cultural release had begun, and was now proceeding side-by-side with an urge to adapt. Germany was the nerve-centre of it all. Frederick the Great was still on the throne of Prussia when Moses Mendelssohn, Berlin philosopher in the mould of the English rationalists and French Encyclopaedists, became the mediator between the Jews and Christendom. He translated the Hebrew Bible into German, and founded a periodical in the Hebrew language. By the time Napoleon had covered Europe with his standard, the ghetto walls had fallen.

Slowly, the winds of change travelled East. Here resistance was stronger, for the rabbis, observing in emancipation a peril to their preserve, classed the new ideas as heresy. The Jews were few in Germany, France and England, but in the Russian Empire they proliferated, and religion invested life with a fatalistic mysticism that denied man the right to disturb the divine pattern of existence.

Ozer Weizmann believed in the new trends. He termed himself a *Maskil*, follower of the Hebrew renaissance, and as such was moved by the need to bring his people into the modern world. This started with the premise that the Jews were not only unloved by others; they barely loved themselves. They had always produced thinkers and able leaders, but these had invariably moved away from their own, to give service to the wider world, where appreciation brought greater rewards and was not tinged with the cynicism brought by excessive familiarity. In Russia too. While the millions were chained to the mediocrity of the Pale, some thousands had put Judaism behind them and enjoyed privileged status as lawyers, government officials and journalists in Moscow and St Petersburg, cities that sounded august in the dark Jewish corners of Warsaw and Odessa. Ozer wanted the Jews to modernise without forfeiture of their soul.

His son lodged in Pinsk with the Luries, a banking family with ramifications in Western Europe, and in exchange for his board Chaim was tutor and companion to Saul Lurie, their youngest. His eyes were opened in that sophisticated household. He heard for the first time of Disraeli, a Jewish Prime Minister of England, and of Karl Marx, a Jewish prophet followed even by gentiles. Did this not reveal that beyond Russia lay a world of limitless opportunity, even for Jews? Here they were conscripted to serve the Tzar but none could rise beyond the status of noncommissioned officer; yet long before, in the American Civil War, the Union army alone had nine Jewish generals and scores of other officers of high rank.

When Chaim was seven years of age Tzar Alexander II was assassinated. Jews were found to be among the conspirators, and in the subsequent repression hostile demonstrations took place in the ghettos. The assassination had occurred in St Petersburg; the revolutionaries were found primarily among students in all the big cities. So despite the quota system to keep them out of the universities, and the Pale of Settlement confining them to their territorial prison, the Jews, it seemed, were everywhere. This prompted the government to introduce the May Laws, in 1882, which increased Jewish disabilities still more. Pogroms and rioting in the countryside sent the Jews scurrying to the safety of their larger towns, with Ozer Weizmann himself contemplating the removal of his family and business from Motol to Pinsk. The May Laws shook the Jews out of their torpor. The *Maskilim* had hoped to effect a spiritual change in their condition; the new regulations inspired a geographical change.

A movement ensued, soon to assume vast proportions, for emigration. Where to go? There was a golden land of promise across the Atlantic, and the great majority of those leaving decided to make their way there. To be sure, very few of the well-to-do would entertain such a prospect. They had their property, their comforts, their belief that they too were Russians of a sort, to keep them at home. America was for the *Lumpenproletariat*, and let them take their baggage off if they wished to that uncharted new world. It was here, in the old, that the innate cleverness of the Jew would find a surer way. And while the discussion proceeded in the ghetto, whether to go or whether to remain, a few hundred made a third choice: not to a land of promise across the Atlantic, but to *the* Land of Promise.

Mainly, they rose from the Ukraine and South Russia, most of them sons and daughters of *Maskilim*, with the wild dream of giving physical shape to the national regeneration of the Jews and make a new life for their people in the desert expanse that was Palestine. On their intrepid departure, their sympathisers at home saw the importance of keeping in touch with them, sustaining them, reinforcing them. An organisation, calling itself in Hebrew 'Lovers of Zion', was born. The Weizmann family, like the Luries, were drawn in their direction. Chaim the schoolboy was given a formula that was to summarise his life's purpose.

Religion was the culture of the Jews, and Palestine was central to their religion. There had been frequent attempts at a return to the ancestral homeland since the beginning of the Exile. Indeed, they were recorded as inhabiting that land without a break. For long periods they barely numbered in their hundreds there. In 1880 some 50,000 of the strictly pious were clustered around the synagogues of Jerusalem and other towns.

The Lovers of Zion craved something more, secular rather than religious. They wanted to be counted among the nations of the world in the way that many small peoples had just recently won the right. This pre-supposed a peasantry, a legal system, their own language employed for all purposes – in a word, autonomy. Could it be achieved? In many ways the concept was outlandish, utopian. Palestine was a neglected province of the Ottoman Empire, it was inhabited by ten times as many Arabs as Jews. The Christians too regarded it as sacred. But above all, were the Jews ready? What did they know of agriculture? The People of the Book were people of the market-place, not the soil; the thought rather than the deed. And most of their talented and more energetic sons aimed to escape from Judaism, not become enslaved to it.

The talk was endless, but there was action also. The Lovers of Zion convened a conference in Kattowitz, in Upper Silesia. This was a year before Chaim's arrival in Pinsk. Messengers brought reports from Palestine of the new colonisers eating the bread of their own toil as, they said, 'all other nations who dwell upon this earth do'. Yes, they were encountering difficulties; of course they needed financial help. But they were *home!* The Lovers of Zion went off to set up their headquarters in Odessa, which was as near as the Pale of Settlement could get geographically to the Holy Land, and made it their task to provide what resources they could, and to help establish further colonies. The movement not yet known by the name of Zionism was launched.

The creation of the Lovers of Zion was in its way a minor declaration of independence for Russian Jewry. Hitherto most of the charity and other good works for the Jews in Palestine had been initiated in the West, for a half-century by the English Jew legend spoke of as the friend of Queen Victoria – Sir Moses Montefiore. His portrait, in faded print, adorned almost every Jewish dwelling in the Pale, and the Kattowitz Conference had in fact been summoned in honour of his hundredth birthday. With great age his mantle had passed to Baron Edmond de Rothschild in Paris, who consented to act as patron to the new Russian settlers. The Lovers of Zion appreciated the act but resented the condescension. They determined to help their own.

At sixteen years of age, in 1890, Chaim regarded himself as a Lover of

Zion in Pinsk. The organisation had expanded with the inauguration of branches in Western cities also, including London. For once sleepy Russia had been the pioneer. The Turks then began to take fright at the flow of Jews coming 'home'. They put a stop to the immigration, technically at least. It meant that a little extra bribery was required to disembark at Jaffa; but it was enough to diminish the flow of newcomers to a trickle, though not before some Pinsk acquaintances of young Weizmann had made the move to Zion.

Pinsk had grown large enough to deceive itself into thinking it was a White Russian metropolis. Three quarters of its 28,000 population were Jews. During Chaim's stay at the Luries the railway was laid to connect the town to Brest–Litovsk and Warsaw in the west, and to the Luninetz junction in the east, offering alternatives to the river-route, which was frozen over during the long winter. This opened new horizons for the Lurie enterprises, and they established a chemical works where the youth, recognised by now as a young blood of the community, spent fascinated hours. The industrial revolution was at last making inroads in Mother Russia. Chaim was reading Gogol, and Turgenev, and Dostoievsky, and it seemed to him that each time he returned to Motol for the holidays a new baby was screaming away in its crib. The railway was tempting him to move on.

A decision would have to be made soon, for the Tzar's 'snatchers', as they were called, would be along to enrol him in the army. In the meantime, as the son of one *Maskil* and the house-guest of another, he did what was expected of him for the spirit of revival. He belonged to a young group of part-time, semi-professional teachers who penetrated the elementary schools and, in the teeth of the rabbis' opposition, taught that there was more to being a Jew than was found in the biblical commentaries. He told the children about the new Jewish farmers in the Holy Land, and showed them newspapers now being produced in the Hebrew language. Their people, he declared, were on the march.

But even the dress of some of the children belied his words: they were still clad in the white stockings and caftans that marked the Jews off as an anachronism. The charity schools of Russia seemed to epitomise the backwardness of the Jewish race east of the Vistula. Chaim found reasons in plenty for wishing to be rid of Pinsk. Shortly he would describe the place as 'God-forsaken – not a town but an enormous rubbish-heap, with hundreds of Jews pushing and hurrying through the streets, their anxious faces marked by great suffering, and moving as in a daze'. This was committed to writing after he had come to the West and made the humiliating comparison between existence in the Russian Pale and life outside.

He was now in Germany, a nineteen year old on a pre-university course in the chemistry department of the Darmstadt Polytechnic. Chaim had not so much effected a leap across a continent as a transition in time. Germany was at its industrial and cultural zenith. Every Jew coming from the East was dazzled. What could Germany not achieve with its scientific and mercantile inventiveness! The music to be enjoyed there, the theatre! And to young Weizmann, how exciting to frequent the student cafés, and receive the student wisdom, and what wonderful walks to be enjoyed by lakeside and in the hills!

Yet it all left a slightly bitter taste. He was paying his own way now, through a residential post at a Jewish boarding school adjacent to Darmstadt. He was teaching Hebrew and Russian to the sons of the gentry, and he discovered how emancipation in the world at large had given his people a split personality.

In their secular education the Jews of Germany demanded, and received, the very best. Everything was accessible, and with education came acceptance as Germans, albeit of the 'Mosaic persuasion', as some affected to call it. But as to Mosaic education, what had been good enough in the ghettos of old was good enough today. Teaching was as doctrinaire in the Jewish courses as Chaim had found it in Russia, rabbis as unbending in their orthodoxy. Here it was again, Chaim thought dispiritedly, the stifling tradition that all the Jews need offer to mankind was wrapped in the decaying bindings of their sacred books; as though centuries of civilisation since the Dark Ages had passed them completely by, and the Renaissance had come and gone with themselves still on the wayside, petrified in time.

He was only too well qualified to teach in this tradition. And here he was taking the fidgety boys through the commentary on the Bible and Talmud written in the eleventh century by Rashi; but he ached to initiate them into the revival, and the literature now being produced in a vivid Hebrew closer to Leviticus than were the works of that great sage.

He knew very well that the German Jews around him, intoxicated with their so-called emancipation, regarded his native Yiddish with contempt. They would stifle it if they could. But why shouldn't their children learn that this too was a language of the Jews, a minor language perhaps but not inferior in its poetry to Flemish, or Ukrainian? Weizmann knew he would have been dismissed if he dared to teach it to them.

Manfully, the youth laboured on in that school as the obedient dominie. He found escape in his studies, and buried himself in the formidable scientific literature to be found in the Polytechnic library, mastering the chemical formulae so reminiscent of the Cabbalistic symbols of the Jewish mystics. But one year was enough. Impatient to get on, he set his sights on the noted chemistry schools of Berlin.

Carl Liebermann, famous throughout the scientific world for his work in the synthesis of the dye-stuff base alizarine, directed the organic laboratories at the Charlottenburg Technical College. Weizmann applied for entry there, and was accepted. Liebermann assigned his new student to the care of Alfred Bistrzycki. Exploration of coal-tar, from which alizarine had been released, was providing clues to the molecular structure of an almost limitless range of products for which industry hungered. Weizmann's initiation into this school determined the life-time path of his career. He joined a group of young men who saw prospects of rich reward in supplying the factories of Germany and the world.

Luckily, Chaim had no longer to pay his own way as a student, so there need be no more of that depressing teaching. Ozer Weizmann was now installed in Pinsk, and had joined forces with a new son-in-law married to his eldest daughter, Miriam. Ozer was gradually handing over the reins to his son Feivel, but it was Miriam's husband Chaim Lubzhinsky who set the pace and took the old-fashioned business in hand. It prospered as never before, and the family scholar was made an allowance of a hundred marks a month. As a full-time student he was now officially exempt from military service, and if he stretched his allowance it would give him modest sustenance without too much worry. Chaim was conscious of being the fortunate one, away from the miserable Pale of Settlement and beyond his father's beck and call, while Feivel had to stay put, and forego this stimulating and privileged life in Berlin.

It was the city Moses Mendelssohn had made the Florence of the Jewish revival just a century before. What had become of that great dawn? Where were the bearers of the flowering that had transformed German Jewry into the most passionate devotees of Goethe and Beethoven, bestowing upon the Fatherland its greatest lyrical poet, Heine, and pamphleteers by the hundred, and salons conducted by Jewesses with the *esprit* and inheritences to open their fine houses to the cosmopolitan intelligentsia of the day? Many could be found in the bosom of the Church. Others constituted the vanguard of a new liberation, which saw the Jews dissolved, with all differences of race and creed, in an ocean of social change.

In the eyes of the newcomer from Russia, if this was emancipation it was also spiritual abnegation. And beneath the German–Jewish skin he detected a secret fear that this most civilised of worlds, which accepted them and offered them a share in promoting the inexorable march of Germany across the globe, was, in the ultimate, hostile. Antisemitism was an open fact of daily life in Russia, practised as government policy. Here, in the focus of Europe, it was a subtle human reflex.

A foreign Jew in the Berlin of the nineties was just another foreigner to the gentiles, but to the local Jews he was an *Ostjude*, relic of times best forgotten, when the race was overtly different and overtly despised in Western Europe too. Privately such people would still be acknowledged, given a meal perhaps, or sent to the charitable organisations for the dole that would keep them off the public charge. Outwardly they were spurned. Many *Ostjuden*, recognising their inferior caste, struggled to shed their skins and become like the others. And what of the students, like Chaim Weizmann recent arrivals from the world of the *Ostjuden*? Thankfully, he found some, like himself, protagonists of another, more positive attitude towards their people.

They too had a bourgeois family background in the Russian Pale. Their homes also subscribed to the Hebrew periodicals, and were in touch with relatives or friends planting slender roots in the ancient soil. Weizmann encountered young men and women in contact with the Odessa head-quarters of the Lovers of Zion, who could reel off the names of the new colonies in Palestine with text-book accuracy. Berlin abounded in student clubs, some for the purpose of drinking and duelling, some for the sterner pursuits of political debate. Socialism was the catchword of the hour. But there was a club for students of Weizmann's mind: the Russo-Jewish Academic Society. It met on Saturday nights under the leadership of Leo Motzkin, a mathematician from Kiev who had been at the foundation of the society while Weizmann was still a schoolboy.

Motzkin towered over the other members of the Russo-Jewish Academic Society by virtue of his seniority of residence in Berlin – he had arrived twelve years earlier than Weizmann, at the age of fifteen, according to his friends an infant prodigy. He already had a fiancée, the spirited Paula Rosenblum, once of Minsk. She recruited to their society the shy girls who came out of Russia to pursue the medical studies for which they could not gain access in universities nearer home.

To the young Weizmann this man represented the vindication of all he believed in. Motzkin shared his resentment of the religious incubus, and

also yearned to transform the class-rooms into nurseries not so much of
Jewish conformism as of Jewish pride. Under Motzkin's guidance the
Russo-Jewish Academic Society took on practical tasks, among the old as
well as the young. Berlin in the nineties was a staging-post for the great
migration westward. The haughty charitable bodies needed the students'
intercession as Yiddish interpreters and welfare assistants to speed the
passing *Ostjuden* on their way, and to the Germans of the Mosaic persuasion the sooner the better.

Motzkin found in the new member an eager volunteer in all this, and
expressed his appreciation by extending his friendship to Weizmann. He
was switching from mathematics to economics, and invited the younger
man to give him lessons, doubtless in elementary science. A small fee was
agreed. Sometimes he was good for a loan to tide Weizmann over till the
end of the month.

This was Weizmann's first grown-up friendship, and Motzkin found
his eagerness a little over-powering. Chaim returned to Pinsk for a few
months in 1895 and regaled the other with long letters about his boredom
in the old place, and demanded information about their society's activities.
'It's in your power to pull me out of this slough, and give me the chance
to transport myself into your circle and your life,' wrote Weizmann. The
fulsomeness was not reciprocated. Indeed, Motzkin rarely sent a reply. In
the end the friendship cooled, though the paths of the two men were
frequently to cross in the years to come.

All over the continent the sparks of a new Jewish consciousness were
igniting. The people were some eight million strong in Europe, and so
compact in the East that the question was being posed with ever greater
urgency: are they a nation? If so, where do they belong? Christians, some
of them realistic men of state, some novelists and poets like Byron and
George Eliot and the younger Dumas, had spoken, with more bravura
than the Jews themselves dared, of a re-born national life for this race in its
cherished homeland. The Jews were still approaching the subject on a
plane of dialectic which told more of their timidity of action and ignorance
of political agitation, than of their subtlety of argument.

The Lovers of Zion had been founded as an antidote to self-contempt,
and its leading member when Weizmann came to maturity was Menahem
Ussishkin, who had studied engineering at Moscow, and had chosen to
make a trip to Jerusalem for his honeymoon. With some justification,
Ussishkin regarded Odessa as the Hebrew capital of the world, and himself
as enjoying the prescriptive right to make the Lovers of Zion headquarters

the fount of all activities concerning Palestine. Odessa's intellectuals were a highly competitive group. Writers with little esteem for Jewish nationalism abounded there; others supported Ussishkin, and in exchange they benefitted from his patronage. He made their work known to Jews at home and abroad, and turned them into the cultural mid-wives of the re-birth.

Ussishkin attached great importance to such student cells as the Russo-Jewish Academic Society in Berlin. He provided them with an address where they could direct their demands for news about developments in the Holy Land. He sent them small sums of money for their expenses. He also expected them to raise funds, if only as a gesture.

But he was an organiser, not a theoretician. This role was filled by the essayist Asher Ginzburg, better known by his pseudonym Ahad Ha'am ('One of the People'). Arguments poured from his pen to fortify the students at their café chatter. Ahad Ha'am concentrated on a single theme: 'Don't rush things in Palestine, or we shall create little of permanent value there. Develop Hebrew culture in the Diaspora first, so as to make the people worthy of nationhood.' And it mattered little if a large Jewish settlement did not materialise. Better, let a spiritual centre arise in Palestine as in days of old, to radiate throughout the Jewish world. Its power would regenerate the people as a whole.

This philosophy was wholly commendable to Weizmann and his comrades. By their lights, little could be usefully done for the moment except to launch a cultural campaign among cynics, opponents and ignoramuses, leaving political activity to more propitious times. Ahad Ha'am was a man burdened with the hesitations of an intensely analytical mind, and he refrained from assuming the intellectual leadership of a movement that was his for the asking. He founded a body for public Jewish service, called *B'nai Moshe* ('Sons of Moses'), to which Weizmann belonged. Strangely, he insisted upon its operation in complete secrecy.

Ahad Ha'am preached spiritual rather than physical colonisation, through a doctrine of self-awareness. Naturally, his ideas attracted a counterblast from more practical men. And while the discussion waxed furiously among the Jews, the gentiles who believed in their cause wondered why there was no grasping at the nettle, with a full-scale effort to achieve the early restoration of the Israelite nation.

Thus Weizmann lived his dual life. His evenings were for association with his fellow-Russians, either transient or permanently in Berlin. An important meeting of his society, particularly one that challenged socialist opponents to debate, would attract the presence of 'personalities', towards whom he would as yet maintain a respectful distance: Jacob Bernstein-Kohan, already specialising in the tropical diseases he would one day need to treat in Palestine; Shmarya Levin, reluctant student of the theological seminary, for he was due to join that most despised of professions, the Rabbinate; Nachman Syrkin, a 'Lover of Zion' certainly, but torn with guilt lest he was not doing enough also for the social revolution; Victor Jacobson, a name to conjure with among the students, and secretary of their society. The young Viennese Martin Buber would occasionally turn up, though he seemed a drifter, and Samuel Pevsner, who was courting Ahad Ha'am's daughter.

Chemistry had its excitements during the day. The laboratory could perform nature's miracles, and in the late nineteenth century scientific man felt he was the ultimate civilised man, commanding all. Weizmann learned how Liebermann and his colleague Carl Graebe had been spurred on by the kings of German industry, and given every encouragement to develop their alizarine while a lone Englishman, without help, was closing in on the process in London, and how they had won the race to register the patent by a single day. Weizmann would have occasion to recall that Englishman, William Perkin, sooner than he realised. Synthetic dyes for textiles were the chemical call of the hour, and beside Weizmann in the laboratory another young chemist, Christian Deichler, was determined to fulfil the need. The two decided to collaborate.

Deichler did not share Weizmann's intensity of purpose, for he was free of pressure for the professional attainment that compensated the Jews for their social disadvantages. Nevertheless their collaboration was fruitful, and after three years together under Bistrzycki's guidance they were led to original research in the preparation of naphtha derivatives. Of course, they were too inexperienced to impress German companies with their work, but Weizmann, a protégé of the Luries, knew of the possibilities for making a mark on the infant chemical industry of Russia. They could conquer the West later, but if they were to strike upon a successful process now, why shouldn't he take it to his native land and utilise his Jewish contacts to effect a sale in that neglected market? Bistrzycki was impressed by Weizmann's enthusiasm. He was contemplating a move to Fribourg, in Switzerland. Perhaps his student would join him there? His Berlin semesters could be credited as part of his course, now leading to a doctorate.

These expectations were swimming in Weizmann's head by 1895, when he was twenty-one years of age. Ozer and his wife Rachel seemed at last to have terminated their practice of producing a child almost annually. Chaim invariably returned home for the Passover, remaining for part of the summer, and 'that year, with sister Miriam and her family joining them, they were sixteen at the festive table. As always, Ozer conducted the Passover service, punctuated with songs, morality tales and humour, to make the *Seder*, as it was termed, an occasion for jollification, and hope, but never without a tinge of sorrow. When the herbs were brought in by the old family servant they were eating the bread of affliction; when they broke the *matzo*, unleavened bread (and doubtless observed with deep distaste by the servant, for hadn't he, a gentile, been told that it was made with the blood of a Christian child?), it was the manna of hope, inspiring them all to chant 'next year in Jerusalem!'

Millions of Jews everywhere chanted the prayer as a mechanical rite. Not so the Weizmanns. Perhaps not next year literally, but even the youngest of them knew he was destined to exchange hated Russia and its oppressions for their real home, as He had promised. And as they relaxed at table news was exchanged of their acquaintances already settled in Palestine. Then the newspapers were passed around: *Hashiloach*, which came from Odessa and was edited by Ahad Ha'am, and *Hatzefira*, produced in Warsaw by the Hebrew journalist Nahum Sokolow, and then the Russian language *Voskhod*. The family read them for reports of a pogrom in a distant province, and for their stories from the colonies, and never an issue appeared but gave generous space to a speech by Ussishkin, and an account of the month's remittances sent off by the Lovers of Zion. If Kharkov or Minsk had suffered an exceptionally severe winter they would not have known of it. The periodicals told them of places in the Holy Land more familiar, and whether or not Jaffa had received adequate rain: a crop failure in Palestine was felt as a personal loss.

The scholar-son of the family learned of Pinsk friends who had disappeared, and how intimation followed that they were in Siberia, banished for seditious activities. It would mean a visit to their parents, as though for a bereavement. Letters were waiting to be read, some from across the Atlantic, and bearing addresses with strange street names, such as Delancey, and Rivington. Dispersal was a chronic condition of the Jews, but here, thankfully, around Ozer Weizmann's table, the family was united.

It could not be for long. The children spoke of their aspirations. Moses, just sixteen, intended to be a chemist like his brother. Little Minna, though only seven, chattered of becoming a doctor, and seemed ready then and there to go abroad to study. Gita wanted a career in music – there was only one place for that, the Conservatoire in Warsaw. Samuel had ambitions of entering the school of engineering at Kiev. Chaim felt desperate to earn some money very soon, to help pay for it all. Ozer Weizmann would deny his children nothing, but his more wordly son knew better the cost of education and lodgings. His contribution was needed for the youngsters' future.

Talk, talk, talk, the perennial Jewish disease. Suddenly, it was stilled. In the year 1897, to the stupefaction of the Lovers of Zion in Odessa, and the Pinsk bourgeoisie, and the Jewish world everywhere, the Messiah indeed arrived! He came in the form of a Viennese sophisticate, Paris correspondent of the *Neue Freie Presse*, and he had experienced a revelation. Theodor Herzl summoned the Jews to a great Congress, for the purpose of devising a programme leading to statehood. Some of the old guard, like Ahad Ha'am, shook their heads dubiously. Others, including members of the Lovers of Zion in London, took fright. But Ussishkin responded, and many students, and merchants, and not a few rabbis, all welcoming Herzl for the man he was: the first true leader the Jewish people had produced in centuries. And the young men and women of the Russo-Jewish Academic Society in Berlin were ready for his command.

Or most of them. When the call went out to meet in Basle for the First Zionist Congress, Weizmann was not available. In 1897 Bistrzycki obtained his professorship at Fribourg, and Weizmann was making his arrangements to follow him there that autumn. His decision to quit Berlin was made easier by a rift that had developed between himself and Motzkin. The hero of his adolescence had now turned completely against him, and Weizmann saw Motzkin as a man of superficiality, the eternal student, and infatuated with German *Kultur*. There was a more immediate cause: a debt of thirty marks outstanding to Weizmann. The young chemist was not in funds, and he pressed for it. Motzkin could not or would not pay.

This was painful, for friends were important to Weizmann, not so much for companionship but because he needed their intellectual stimulation, and frequently their reassurance. He could make quick decisions, but needed to try them out on others before acting on them. He had a fear of living in a vacuum, unappreciated, and the wit that flowed so easily from him in the company of others turned to morbid introspection when he was left to himself.

A significant piece of work had been completed at the laboratory with Deichler, and before moving on to Fribourg Weizmann fulfilled his promise to take the process to Russia and offer it for sale. He left Berlin at the end of August, 1897, hoping to be back within the month in time for the Congress – it was to be a foundation conference informally organised, and delegates required no special authorisation. Armed with a letter of introduction to a dye-stuffs company in Moscow, he took off with his formula, arranging to stay with an old Pinsk acquaintance now established in the capital. He had no permit to be in Moscow, so he would remain for a day or two only, without registering with the police.

The formula did not impress the Moscow company and remained unsold. But it was now impossible to get back to Basle in time for the Congress. Weizmann had to learn of the historic decisions taken there, and of the transformation Theodor Herzl now effected in the movement of national regeneration, from the lips of others.

The occasion had its magic. When Theodor Herzl rose to speak on the opening evening (dress clothes mandatory, for the Congress was a Central European creation) a rabbi cried from the body of the hall, 'Long live the King!' It was no extravagance. The wandering tribes of Israel were, with the dying century, at last taking some initiative towards their re-birth.

Herzl wrote in his diary: 'At Basle I founded the Jewish State.' He may have simplified the issue, but such is the prerogative of the prophet. The magic would have a curious effect upon the Jews. Many became spellbound by Herzl; others saw him as a charlatan. Chaim Weizmann, as an absentee, and a scientist, suspended his judgment. He must follow this man, so much he knew. But not blindly, not before Herzl revealed his hand.

Yet the emergence of Herzl's movement compelled the young Russian to face the critical choice of his life. His personality was divided by two worlds, the ghetto of his Russian origins, the Europe of his aspirations. Should he abandon the old for the new – it would be so easy – or should he seek a bridge between them? Family loyalties tugged at him, as did the friendships forged at the Luries' in Pinsk; and he felt a responsibility towards the deprived and despised people in whose culture he was formed.

But the West presented opportunities at every turn: the promise of total acceptance, recognition of his talents, good living and the freedom to enjoy the companionship of men and women of all nationalities away from the scrutiny of prying convention. These were privileges not lightly to be surrendered.

Nevertheless he decided that he must not abandon the ghetto. The new Zionism could have no meaning without connection with the Jewish past, cherished in that old world of the East. Perhaps this man Herzl understood that his movement would endure only by the interaction of the two worlds. If so, he had gained a disciple.

2

Into Battle

MYTHOLOGY COULD NOT HAVE INVENTED THEODOR HERZL. Confronting the 200 delegates of the First Zionist Congress stood a celebrated European journalist and man of the theatre, thirty-seven years of age. He had witnessed the trial and degradation of Captain Dreyfus, and had once advocated mass conversion of the Jews to Christianity. The religious-minded saw a suggestion of Moses in his piercing eyes and full black beard. He had forgotten the Hebrew he had learnt as a boy, was the spoiled son of indulgent parents and the neglectful husband of a superficial wife. He not only wept for his people; he mocked them. Herzl knew nothing of the Lovers of Zion, and to a large extent Paris had become his Jerusalem.

He had the Jewish affectation of professing ignorance of his people's culture, and was vague about their history. While writing *The Jewish State*, the tract that brought the revolution, he thought of calling it 'An Address to the Rothschilds', so he was evidently aware of the realities: that to do something in Jewish life you needed first of all to flatter a rich man.

Herzl got nothing from the richest Jews, nor from the great Jewish charities. The intelligentsia, with important exceptions, shunned him. He exhausted his small personal fortune in hiring staff and founding a newspaper in Vienna, and in assigning representatives to various capitals. When he opened his Second Congress in 1898, with Chaim Weizmann present, the number of delegates had doubled, and by electoral make-believe almost every Jewish community in the world was represented, Herzl himself being the delegate of Limerick in Ireland! By then the Jews were reproaching him for not bringing them Palestine in his travelling-case. He would be dead in six years, bequeathing to the Zionists an offer from the British government to give the Jews a country – in Africa.

Between drafting his historic pamphlet in 1895 and convening his Congress two years later, Herzl lost two of his illusions: that the Jews would readily work for an independent state of their own; and that it could be located anywhere suitable in the world. In fact, his Jewish State, once openly proclaimed as an aspiration, sounded forbidding to men who were, thankfully, nationals of various countries, not excluding those semi-citizens of Imperial Russia and the cautious Jewry of the Ottoman Empire. So the Zionists retracted, and devised a platform, called the Basle Programme, of a 'home secured by public law'. And he learned that no such region could exist other than Palestine, which was already the spiritual homeland of the people and the only reason for their persisting separate identity.

A third illusion Herzl cherished to his dying day. He believed little could be achieved by stealthy penetration of the country in yard-by-yard colonisation. He remained the passionate contender for a treaty, or Charter, with Turkey, whereby the large-scale settlement of immigrants could be openly organised and paid for by a great fund. The money would go to Turkey's crippled exchequer so as to clear the 'Sick Man's' national debt.

A small circle of admirers, mainly in Central Europe, principally in Vienna, sustained Herzl in his efforts to win the Charter. They constituted an Executive, or 'Smaller Actions Committee', to do his bidding. A more extended body, the 'Greater Actions Committee', was created from spokesmen of the various national federations of Zionists. The majority were of course from Russia and Austro-Hungary, with a handful more to speak for Zionists in countries where the movement only attracted small coteries. But this committee could meet but rarely. Work was conducted by Herzl, giving his all, and his small Executive.

What work? Almost exclusively, tortuous negotiations with the Porte, and bids for intercession in other centres of power – the Zionists called it their diplomacy. That, and fund-raising, to create the Jewish Colonial Trust as a banking instrument to cover Zionist tasks and, when opportune, to 'purchase' Palestine. All this seemed logical enough to the new adherents brought to the ideal by the Zionist Congress. But in Russia organised Zionism pre-dated the Herzlian movement. Its members were raising money for cultural and propaganda activities, and for colonisation in Palestine. This gave individual involvement to all, as contrasted with 'diplomacy', which Herzl pursued in secrecy and regarded as his personal prerogative. Hence the polarisation of Zionism into 'politicals' and 'practicals', and the confrontation of Herzl by Menahem Ussishkin.

Weizmann did not have far to travel for the Second Congress, for he was in Fribourg, on the point of completing his post-graduate studies. He now observed to what degree a virtually static movement had assumed impetus. Leo Motzkin was a prominent figure, having undertaken an official mission to Palestine to report on the condition of its existing Jewish settlement. Other student comrades recognised in the annual Congress a valuable public forum, with the Press taking down their speeches, and this gave them a sense of maturity and importance.

Though feeling something of an outsider, Weizmann gained election to the Congress Steering Committee, twenty strong, and intervened in the debate on the formation of the Jewish Colonial Trust. The Zionist bank aimed for a starting capital of two million pounds, and he demanded that its statutes specify control by the Zionist Congress, as they did not propose 'creating a bank for the capitalists'. His brief speech was delivered partly in Russian, partly in German.

He was in happy mood, for the delegate seated beside him was the girl of his choice. Sophia Getsova had been seen and approved by the family in Pinsk. A childhood friend of Paula Rosenblum, soon to be married to Motzkin, Sophia was studying at Berne, and her ambition was to practise medicine in Palestine. It was to all intents an ideal match, and had the effect also of reconciling Motzkin to Weizmann. Once more the eager letters flowed to Motzkin, about Congress affairs, and plans for evangelising the students, or merely gossip.

Now twenty-four, Weizmann had completed a dissertation on the action of electrolysis for the reduction (that is, the de-oxygenation) of nitro-anthraquinones so as to produce the amino-anthraquinones from which dye-stuffs are made. This won him his doctorate *magna cum laude*. Every spare minute was spent with Sophia in Berne. Also, he found his voice as a public speaker, and his name began to appear in the Russo-Jewish newspapers and in Herzl's weekly *Die Welt*. A European reputation was being born.

His personality expanded in the care-free intimacy of Switzerland, and he became a competent French-speaker. To his delight, Professor Liebermann's colleague Carl Graebe offered him a post in the organic chemistry department at Geneva University, of which he had been appointed head. It was to be as non-stipendiary lecturer, or *Privat-Docent*, with fees paid by his students. Weizmann could still continue his collaboration with Christian Deichler, so the arrangement suited him eminently. Geneva, Zurich, Berne, Basle – they formed a ring in which he

Pinsk, 1911. The last family gathering before Ozer Weizmann's death. Chaim is standing behind his father.

Left Vera and Chaim on their marriage, 1906. *Above* Vera with their sons, Benjamin and Michael, 1917.

Baron Edmond de Rothschild aboard his
private train in Palestine, 1914.

Theodor Herzl.

Ahad Ha'am, Weizmann's mentor.

Weizmann with Ussishkin, left, and Sokolo
at an early Zionist Congress.

could conveniently enjoy his role of student agitator. Weizmann's Geneva lodgings just beside the chemistry school, and the Café Landholt that he frequented in the city, and the laboratory itself, constituted the setting of a mild bohemia in which the future glowed with promise.

Herzl was a man in a hurry. A cardiac complaint frequently laid him low, but there was to be no respite from what he regarded as hack journalism for the *Neue Freie Presse* as he pursued his holy grail. He contrived to be in Constantinople in 1898 when the German Emperor arrived for a triumphal progress through the East, and was able to gain audience both there and in Jerusalem. He staged a roadside encounter when the royal caravan was moving out from Jaffa. It was all to remind the Kaiser to promote the Zionist cause with the Sultan, an idea not unfavourably taken up by Wilhelm, as the colonists would doubtless come under the protection of Germany, and even advance the cause of Germany.

Such meetings with the great confirmed to ordinary Jews everywhere that in Herzl they indeed had a leader. But the financiers continued to regard him almost with derision, and the Zionist bank remained a skeleton. Herzl made veiled promises of financial help to Turkish officials; they responded with guarded hints of allowing mass immigration. There was no tangible progress. Herzl thought a great demonstration in London would bring Zionism notice in the heart of the British Empire, and in 1900 he shifted the Congress away from Basle, to the Queen's Hall near Oxford Circus, with a garden party in Regent's Park. Many delegates, stuck in the new tube trains, which were not yet operating efficiently, were not seen for an entire day.

He had dedicated followers in London, notably the writer Israel Zangwill, and Moses Gaster, scholar and Principal Rabbi (*Haham*) of the aristocratic Sephardi community. Worried Jews from the East End interrupted their sonorous speeches to remind the Congress of the pogroms then taking place in Rumania. This underlined the impotence of Zionism, despite its glories, and an air of frustration hung over the meeting-hall.

Talk rather than achievement was turning the Congress into an annual repetition of itself. The London proceedings began, as always, with an extended *tour d'horizon* by Max Nordau of the world Jewish situation. Nordau, like Herzl of Hungarian birth, was the most considerable of the leader's converts. Writer, physician and polymath, he created a fresh sensation with each new book. But his words, and Herzl's own report hinting at negotiations on the point of fruition, fell on impatient ears. The Russian delegates brought the discussion down from the stratosphere by demanding the adoption of an immediate role: cultural activities, and such practical work as was feasible in Palestine.

It was the younger generation really making itself heard for the first time, and more strident than the rest was the voice of Chaim Weizmann. He produced an interesting point: Herzl's reluctance to espouse the cause of their new culture, he said, was due to his anxiety to placate the rabbis. Being unfamiliar with Eastern Europe, Herzl falsely believed that the rabbis' acquiescence to Zionism mattered. One rabbi at least, Moses Gaster, concurred with Weizmann. The cultural question would have to be faced.

Herzl was only half listening. He had just been snubbed by Lord Rothschild; he had frequently to rest at his hotel with fever. And he was awaiting news from a representative in Constantinople who was bribing his way towards securing him an audience with the Sultan. As a sop to his critics, Herzl agreed to the introduction of educational work into the Zionist programme.

Well-satisfied with the impact he and his friends made in London, Weizmann now surveyed the Zionist scene in Switzerland as a rising young leader. Sophia had spent the previous summer with his family in Pinsk, working as an intern at its Jewish hospital. There was expectation of a sale for him and Deichler with the Bayer pharmaceutical company in Elberfeld, where they had now been placed on a regular retainer. He plunged with renewed zest into his Zionist activities.

The students were by no means all Zionists. Many followed Lenin and Plekhanov, with their spectacular call for revolution in Russia, and the world. Others found politics in any shape tiresome. One day the chemist's eye caught one such girl student in the refectory, conversing in Russian with a friend. She was beautiful. His heart leapt. It was the nineteen year old Vera Khatzman, newly arrived from Rostov-on-Don. Weizmann discovered where she lived, and left little notes at her lodgings. Soon the deceptions began.

A year sped by and Weizmann could not face up to his emotional dilemma. He wrote home as though nothing was changed, and continued to visit Berne without informing Sophia that he had fallen passionately and irrevocably in love with another. His tracks were covered in part because he was already the centre of an adoring female circle helping him to organise a society of young Zionists in Geneva, called *Hashachar* ('Dawn'). They came freely to his lodgings to address envelopes, and sat at his feet when he lectured on Zionist ideology. But Vera Khatzman was rarely among them. She, the proud Russian miss, had attended a French school and spoke no German and little Yiddish. Her father had been forcibly recruited to serve twenty-five years in the Russian army (an inhuman abduction of young Jews that was abolished in 1874) and this had earned him right of residence outside the Pale of Settlement. Zionism held only the faintest of attractions for Vera. And she was inhibited from publicly associating with Chaim until their relationship was normalised. Rumour had reached Sophia in Berne, and the frowning Motzkins in Berlin.

The Zionist Congress was a great annual get-together where Weizmann would reunite with his Berlin comrades, and with acquaintances not readily encountered from the Russian cities. Ahad Ha'am refused to associate with Herzl's movement once he had observed the man in action, but in Ussishkin the younger Zionists felt the reassuring presence of a benevolent father-figure. In such an organisation the students had all the advantages: leisure to plan their strategy, ability to express ideas, the cohesion developing from their concentration in a few universities. They were a force. The idea of a special youth organization was soon in gestation. Weizmann took the initiative in planning it, assisted by willing hands of his *Hashachar* society in Geneva.

The most suitable moment to bring such an organisation into being would be at a conference immediately preceding the next Congress, in December, 1901. A meeting was therefore arranged to take place in Munich the Easter before, to draft a programme for submission to the conference later in the year. Weizmann looked to Motzkin to lead a strong group from Berlin. The latter had so far shone at every Congress, and was without doubt the statesman of the younger generation.

Motzkin refused Weizmann's invitation to come to Munich. He had a good personal reason – the wounded Sophia Getsova, who was unforgiving and inconsolable. Additionally, Motzkin knew that Herzl considered they were not yet strong enough for a separate organisation of youth, whose wild talk could prejudice his negotiations with the Sultan. Having been an official emissary to Palestine, Motzkin was less inclined than his younger friends to query Herzl's every move.

Weizmann went on with the Munich meeting undeterred, explaining to Herzl that they would be avoiding publicity anyway, for the Tzarist secret police kept close watch on Russian student activities. He conducted practically the entire agenda on his own, and inevitably was entrusted with the organisation of the full conference. He leapt at the responsibility.

He began sending out circulars to sustain enthusiasm, and planned a recruiting-drive in Russia for the summer. He was due home in any case, for the marriage of a younger sister and the daunting task of bringing the change in his affections to the notice of his family. In the meantime he would work on a programme for attracting the 'intelligentsia' to the movement, and for educational work among the masses.

Despite the dangers of splintering Zionism, a youth organisation had sound justification. A powerful antithesis to Zionism had risen with the formation, in the year of the First Zionist Congress, of the revolutionary Bund. This offered the attractions of a socialist philosophy, and solidarity with Russian workers of all creeds and races, without total surrender of the Jewish identity. Weizmann understood only too well the spell cast by the Bundists over the student generation. Some of his own friends, both from Berlin and Geneva, were changing sides. If Zionism was to make headway in Eastern Europe it needed to shed its middle-class cloak and take to the offensive. Though the Bund maintained secret headquarters in Vilna, many leading members were resident in Switzerland, where they trailed after Plekhanov and out-bid each other in their vilification of bourgeois Zionism.

But the conversion to the movement most dearly desired by Weizmann was Vera Khatzman's. She spent that Easter at Montreux, and he frequently stayed with her there, sometimes cycling the fifty miles along the lake from Geneva. In their separation he sent her letters and postcards daily. The cards might contain just one word of greeting, or love, while the letters had large doses of propaganda, and accounts of his triumphs in debates with the Bundists. She knew that he aspired to make his Youth Conference rival the Congress as a showpiece.

He had an opportunity to confront Ahad Ha'am and Ussishkin with his plans. They were in Paris to persuade Baron Edmond de Rothschild, already patron of several colonies in Palestine, to extend his shield also to those under the auspices of Odessa. (He would have nothing to do with Zionists, and sent the Russians packing.) Weizmann told them of his dream to make the students an involved body of practical workers, not bystanders providing Herzl with a passive audience. To their old-fashioned, dubious minds it had a somewhat arrogant ring, and Ahad Ha'am refused an invitation to deliver a paper at the conference. Philosophically, Weizmann's thoughts turned once again to Motzkin. The latter parried the request.

Herzl, aware that strong words had been spoken against himself at Munich, pressed anew for cancellation of the Youth Conference. This was asking too much of a man on the point of venturing forth to conquer Russia, and all Weizmann promised was to return via Vienna and discuss the matter with the leader personally.

His route took him through Nikolayev and Kherson, the home towns of his most faithful helpers in Geneva, Anne Koenigsberg and Catherine Dorfman. He spent some days in Odessa, and visited his old Berlin comrade Bernstein-Kohan on active Zionist service in Kishinev. Pinsk was fitted in between-times. It was by then high summer, and Rostov was intended as the terminal point of the tour. At home there, Vera was waiting to introduce her lover to her family. In the end he quailed from the prospect, pleading lack of time. She was finding him, in some respects at least, exasperatingly undecisive in their courtship.

Despite its much-vaunted devotion to the cause, Russian Zionism was in poor shape. Weizmann found a lack of vitality and a poverty of intellect everywhere. Odessa, that fountain-head of the cultural revolution, he scorned in a letter to Motzkin as a centre of disintegration, a 'paper-kingdom of circulars and non-paid-up-shares in the Jewish Colonial Trust', with the Zionist notables there 'ever watchful lest anyone invade their kingdom . . . They thought I had come to undermine their authority.'

He gave a similar description to Herzl when he arrived in Vienna – a sorry admission indeed from a man ever upholding the virtues of the East over the West. Evidently Herzl felt encouraged, and was impressed by Weizmann's energy. He studiously excluded present company from his dismissal of Ussishkin and his supporters as men without substance. He came to look more kindly at the Youth Conference, offering a little money for its expenses. Weizmann refused the money, but left Vienna with a new respect for the machinery of the movement, and greater regard for its disciplines.

The students allowed themselves six days of discussion before Herzl opened the Fifth Congress in Basle. To Weizmann's relief Motzkin made his appearance, giving their deliberations definite stature. But against this Nachman Syrkin, another Berlin contemporary, was leading a socialist-Zionist group that threatened secession.

Despite conflicts and misunderstandings enough to fill those six days, the conference managed at last to unite into what they called the 'Democratic Fraction', and enter the Congress proper as a voting bloc of thirty-seven delegates. For the first time Herzl faced an opposition determined on a share of the work. Cultural activities had long been the subject of tedious speeches, but this time the theme was shaped in commanding form: Zionism should take the initiative in a major undertaking – to establish a Jewish University. Weizmann and Martin Buber had been chosen to force this issue through the Congress, and their demand to have the practicalities of such a university investigated was given sanction.

The idea had been ventilated before, and been easily disposed of as a piece of innocuous symbolism. Zionism had no money for such grandiose projects, anyway. This underestimated the calibre of some of the young academics in the Democratic Fraction. They saw their university enterprise as realistic, in contrast with their leader's activities in the political field, which they deemed fantasist. Weizmann decided to make it his own.

He embraced his role of organiser with a zeal which the movement associated only with Herzl. In addition to Buber, he recruited other likely collaborators. One of these was Berthold Feiwel, a handsome young scholar from Brünn with an impressive literary record. Like Buber he had worked for a period on *Die Welt*, and was furthermore a member of the Greater Actions Committee. Feiwel was engaged with Davis Trietsch of Berlin in setting up a Zionist publishing house, *Jüdischer Verlag*. Weizmann, no writer himself, warmed to people able to relate their national ideal to literature. He recognised this endeavour as complementing the university project, and so adopted it as a Democratic Fraction activity.

Transforming his lodgings in the rue Lombard into the headquarters both of the Democratic Fraction and the Jewish University, he felt he was making Geneva the third city in Zionism, after Vienna and Odessa, and sallied forth to do battle with the Bundists wherever they congregated. One debate in Berne, against the brilliant Vladimir Medem, six years his junior, occupied three full evenings. It was presided over by the writer Ansky, author of *The Dybbuk*, who later recalled Weizmann's final words: 'At the moment we fight each other here in Switzerland, far from our homes. The time will come when we shall meet in more familiar surroundings, in Russia. We shall meet there on the real field of battle, and history will deliver its verdict.'

Herzl undertook to raise the subject of a Jewish University in Palestine with the Turkish authorities. Ussishkin too gave the project his blessing, though he was displeased at the creation of the Democratic Fraction. Weizmann reassured him. The Fraction was to be the task-force of practical Zionism, he promised, and would carry Russia's voice to the West. Their allegiance was to Odessa rather than Vienna. Evidently Weizmann too was learning to be a diplomat, for hadn't he spoken of Odessa with derision?

The more he thought about the university, the more he saw the value of keeping it as a separate Fraction preserve. He suspected that Herzl was not wholly serious about the plan, for the leader surely knew that Palestine, with its minute Jewish population, was hardly a suitable place just then for the university. In fact, the chemist had decided that it should be located in Europe, to serve Jews driven to the West because Russian universities would not accept them. The students were being dispersed in dozens of cities and pursued courses which took them away from Jewish life, thus depriving the people of their natural intelligentsia.

To get the Democratic Fraction moving they needed members, and this meant a manifesto. Motzkin reluctantly agreed to draw one up. Weizmann would help Buber and Feiwel to produce a pamphlet on the Jewish University and find the money to cover printer's bills. When the first titles were issued by Trietsch's *Verlag* the Fraction would promote sales. So there was work in plenty.

Weizmann travelled to Berlin to give Motzkin, ever tending towards repose, a jolt. But the latter now nursed a new grievance. This time it was because Weizmann, without authorisation, had been negotiating a common front with Syrkin's group, too left-wing and too close to the Bund. Weren't they primarily a bulwark against the Bund, Motzkin charged?

Weizmann was embarrassed, recognising that he had erred. He promised not to make policy decisions without prior consultation, and Motzkin returned to work on the manifesto. He consented to join forces with Weizmann and attend an All-Russian Zionist Conference in Minsk the following September. Together they would put the Fraction over, and with it the university project.

In contrast with Motzkin's attitude, Berthold Feiwel greeted Weizmann in Berlin with the warmth of true friendship. He had a job of sorts at the *Verlag*, but this was barely a livelihood, and Feiwel was on the look-out for something more regular. Why didn't he come to Switzerland and work for the university project? The money would be Weizmann's problem.

Feiwel arrived with Esther Schneersohn, who had earlier been part of Weizmann's Geneva entourage and now regarded Feiwel as her own. He was unwell, so the three of them went off to a pension in the mountains and worked contentedly – Weizmann separately at his chemistry lectures for the autumn semester, Feiwel on his editorial work for the *Verlag*, both together on the university pamphlet. Weizmann felt keenly the absence of Vera from this happy scene. She was in Rostov. He picked some flowers from the mountainside and sent them to her across Europe. This was July,

1902, and he implored her to shorten her vacation and join them – he would willingly cancel his own travel plans and forego the Minsk Conference if she came. But she wished him to attend, for then he would be in Russia and she wasn't giving him another chance to evade her family. Zionism was still a bore to her.

Seven processes, mainly dealing with naphtha derivatives and all of them having great industrial possibilities, were in the course of registration with the German patent authorities. As a team Weizmann and Deichler were a rare combination of pure scientist and applied scientist, and neither had any doubt that one day riches would come their way. But for the moment money was tight, and Weizmann was a regular visitor at the pawnbroker's, with nothing left over to indulge in Zionist activities at his own expense. The intention was for Feiwel to work in Zurich, Trietsch in Berlin and Buber in Vienna. He urgently needed a patron.

Samuel Shriro was a Lithuanian who had made a fortune developing the Baku oilfields. He had been a forty year old intruder at the Basle Youth Conference, where he was greatly impressed by the chemist's handling of the agenda. Weizmann now visited him in his holiday home and came away with a hundred roubles, enough to print the university pamphlet. Soon he was able to write gleefully to Catherine Dorfman: 'I found a Maecenas here in the mountains and stripped him of everything I could.' Indeed, Shriro contributed a further thousand roubles – about 2,500 Swiss francs. If only Weizmann would come to Baku and address a meeting there he could promise much more. And would he undertake some research for him, into the utilisation of oil-waste? It looked as though the coming tour of Russia would be a triumph. In a spirit of great confidence Weizmann invested in a typewriter.

Motzkin was still dragging his feet over the manifesto, and Weizmann bombarded him with requests to get the thing finished. He could not show himself in the Russian cities without something official about the Fraction. It was done in the end, and proved to be a challenge to Herzl in no uncertain terms. It referred to the 'personality cult' in Zionism, which had to be replaced by democratically controlled institutions within the movement, particularly the bank. It demanded an immediate start on land purchase in Palestine and its cultivation on collective lines.

To moving farewells from Feiwel and Esther, Weizmann set off for Russia. Pinsk was first on his list, and it came as a cold shower. The town was a tomb-like place in the eyes of its son now twenty-seven years of age. And the family problems! His younger brothers Moses and Samuel were having difficulties with their careers. Moses had started a course in agriculture and now wanted to revert to his old love of chemistry, and study abroad. Samuel was ready for engineering school, and had bought his uniform; but he had been refused. The family business was evidently not doing too badly, to afford such frustrations. Chaim invited the two brothers to accompany him to Minsk, where he was to join Motzkin and take the conference by storm.

It was a typically Russian affair. The platform sagged under the weight of its personalities, and the delegates under the weight of the speeches. Ahad Ha'am developed his theme of spiritual Zionism far beyond the patience of most delegates. Ussishkin did somewhat better, with his attacks upon Herzl and the claim for a Russian voice in the movement. The conference showed little inclination to listen to the Fraction leaders, and the university project was accorded only polite cheers. Weizmann extracted undertakings from the sixty Fraction sympathisers present to ginger up youth activities in their towns, and to form fund-raising groups for the university.

One feature of the conference not a bit to his liking was the public emergence there of a religious party in Zionism, the *Mizrachi*, formed by the rabbis to resist the new trend towards secular culture. They believed Zionism could not exist without the Messianic concept as taught in Orthodox Judaism; the others thought Zionism could not survive with it. As for Motzkin, Weizmann notified Vera that 'he goes around with a hang-dog look . . . I try and have little to do with him'.

To condemn the conference, as Weizmann did, as a protracted talking-shop was unjust. Russian Zionism could not express true dynamics when its meetings were permeated with government agents and there was no clear divide between legal and illegal activities. The authorities approved of Zionism insofar as it was an emigration movement, but regarded suspiciously such activities as educational work, which fostered internal separatism.

The two Fraction leaders now divided up the territory, Motzkin taking Moscow and St Petersburg. Doubtless Motzkin was assailed by the same feeling of hopelessness as Weizmann himself. Minsk could not but remind them of the stagnation of Russian Jewry, the absence of outstanding figures, the contrast between the reams of verbiage spoken here and Herzl's sheer poise in his confrontations with authority. Ussishkin was the voice of a brontosaurus, emanating grunts; Herzl was an eagle, soaring ever higher, alighting where he chose.

How had the leader spent the past year? His audience with the Sultan had been followed by more meetings in Constantinople. He could have his Charter – almost anywhere in the Ottoman Empire except Palestine. Openly haughty, inwardly tempted, he had turned the offer down. In the spring he completed a novel about the Palestine-to-be; he was to call it *Old-New Land*. He had then gone to London, to appear before the Royal Commission on Alien Immigration into Britain.

Herzl was in fact making dramatic strides, though his detractors, Weizmann among them, saw his efforts as Viennese light opera. On learning of his journey to London Chaim had written to Vera, seven years her fiancé's junior and still unconcerned with such matters: 'I suppose all the synagogue politicians imagine that with Edward the Seventh's illness Herzl has been invited to rule England for a while. And why not?'

Only the perspective of the Pale of Settlement, where Jews did not normally venture in the neighbourhood of officialdom, could have produced this jaundiced view. In fact events of immense significance to the future course of Zionism were now in train. The Aliens Commission had resulted from a clamour to arrest the arrival of foreigners (almost totally East European Jews) ostensibly packing London's Whitechapel with their sweatshops, their imported disease, and other terrors. The Anglo-Jewish establishment trembled at the prospect of a wave of antisemitism in their country. Lord Rothschild was on the Commission. He would of course ensure fair play for the Jews, but fair play could have a stern ring to refugees in search of a haven. Rothschild was the French Baron Edmond's cousin, and could not abide the name of Herzl.

Previously, he would not receive the Zionist. Now, with the intention of vetting his evidence, he entertained him and, amazingly for a financier, came under Herzl's spell. The latter declared his intention of founding a Jewish colony in a British possession. Rothschild replied: 'Take Uganda.'

The notion struck Herzl as extraordinary. No, he was thinking of Cyprus and the Sinai Peninsula. They were close enough to Palestine to convince his impatient followers that he really was in sight of their goal. Rothschild was interested. He would discuss the idea with Joseph Chamberlain, the Colonial Secretary. 'You are a great man,' he told Herzl, 'I really mean it, a great man!' Herzl's heart-beats were weaker, but he scented success.

Among the correspondence awaiting him on his return home was a letter from Weizmann. It told of the work he and Motzkin had attempted at Minsk, and about people likely to be of assistance in the university project.

Announcing an impressive itinerary through the Ukraine right to the Caspian Sea, Weizmann asked to address the forthcoming Zionist Conference in Vienna (they were now having full Congresses only every other year). He was anxious to introduce a sense of the East European reality to their discussions.

Understandably, the letter had less impact upon Herzl than another, from his representative in London, Leopold Greenberg. Interviews had been arranged for Herzl with Chamberlain and Lord Lansdowne, the Foreign Secretary. It could be the master-stroke. Herzl wrote in his diary: 'No Moses ever enters the Promised Land!'

Weizmann was making his goodbyes in Pinsk when a visitor was announced. It was William Evans-Gordon, whose 'British Brothers League' had engineered the anti-alien agitation in England. He had come to inspect the Pale of Settlement personally on behalf of the Aliens Commission. So mighty England was not above sending a representative to verify the wretched situation of the Jews in this land! Weizmann escorted the guest round Pinsk, and waded through the marshes with him to some nearby villages. Perhaps Herzl was, after all, correct in looking towards London. This Englishman might have his uses in the future. In fact the 'British Brother' became a Zionist – of the antisemitic kind, wishing the Jews 'back to their own country' for riddance. If only it were possible!

Now the gruelling journey across southern Russia: primitive trains, long halts at stations, an endless expanse of steppe, the huge canyons of the Caucasus before reaching Baku. But halfway across – Rostov, and Vera! She presented her fiancé, almost twenty-eight now and so thinned on top that he looked much older, to a household of five sisters and two brothers. It was presided over by a veritable Cossack for a father. The ex-soldier was a striking six and a half feet tall.

Vera felt at last that her engagement was official. It had been touch and go, what with their long separations, his association, almost conspiratorial, with those clever young women in the Democratic Fraction, his guilt over Sophia. And his tenderness towards her lived uneasily in his soul beside his larger ambitions. She now spoke frankly. She had no liking for her lover's *idée fixe*, a Zionist university. He would be neglecting his career, she told him, and would never earn enough for them to marry. He dismissed her fears. Science was precious to him. But he did admit to his ambition to being a leader in the Jewish world one day. They separated without fixing on a date for their marriage.

In Baku Samuel Shriro showed off his young friend as a chemist of great promise, and added another thousand roubles to his earlier contribution towards the university campaign's expenses. Further, he reported that friends had promised 2,000 roubles more. This was the highlight of Weizmann's tour, and he began working happily on his speech for the conference in Vienna.

Herzl was infuriatingly uninformative at that conference. He would not divulge what had transpired in London, and the delegates only knew that Lansdowne had refused him Cyprus but would entertain a settlement scheme in Sinai, around El Arish.

Of course, he saw everything else, such as the university, as harmless small-talk. Weizmann made an occasion of it nevertheless. Fortified by the facts he had amassed from his Russian experience, he made a heart-felt plea for more cooperation in realising the plan. An appropriate resolution was passed, but only after it had been re-drafted by Ussishkin to omit references to Geneva as the organisational centre, and to specify the location of the university in Palestine.

Weizmann drew little solace from this outcome. He was voted no money, proffered no encouragement. The mere mention of Palestine postponed its materialisation to a distant limbo. Well, he had every right now to keep the project as a Democratic Fraction endeavour. He had some imposing notepaper printed and began following up his contacts in Russia, where there were wealthy Jews enough to comprehend the university's importance. The following spring he was back there again, this time concentrating on Poland. He received more undertakings of support, and was now so confident as to plan something further: a monthly periodical. It would be called *Der Jude*, and would be a bridge between Zionists of East and West. In his enthusiasm he promised the editorship separately both to Feiwel and Buber.

Then the frustrations began. He was firing off a dozen letters a day; most of them went unreplied. Vague notification of Fraction activities reached him, but to all intents the group had gone to sleep. Feiwel's industrious research in Zurich unearthed penurious Russian students in almost every city of Europe. But Buber seemed lost in his own studies in Vienna, while Trietsch in Berlin had the *Verlag* as his alibi for not giving his all. From Motzkin of course there was only silence.

The Democratic Fraction was a fiasco, though Weizmann tried desperately to conceal the situation. The students were mercurial and irresponsible, and a year was a long time in their lives. They were an unsure foundation for a political organisation. But Weizmann needed an extraneous excuse for failure. It presented itself in Kishinev, at Easter, 1903.

Easter was ever the pogrom season in Russia, Holy Friday usually coinciding with the Jewish Passover. In Kishinev that year the terror was greater than for many decades. A well-contrived pogrom was instigated by a government-sponsored antisemitic newspaper, with the police helping the riots along. Fifty Jews were killed, hundreds of their houses were destroyed, their shops pillaged and some 2,000 families ruined. It was to instil a bitterness in Russian Jews against their native heath to be supplanted only by Germany a generation later.

Kishinev proved a catharsis. A Hebrew poet, Bialik, achieved fame for his threnody *Surely the People is Grass*, taking his text from Isaiah. In hundreds of towns in the Pale Jews and Jewesses, including the younger Weizmanns of Pinsk, took their protection into their own hands and began an illicit storage of arms.

The pogrom dried up Weizmann's source of funds, for everything was now directed to aid the victims, and the sums faithfully promised him on his two propaganda tours were diverted to relief work. He tried struggling on, but the university project died as a realistic endeavour, and with it the Democratic Fraction as a force. Feiwel, without regular income once again, returned disconsolately to Berlin.

Further bad news: the El Arish settlement scheme, which Herzl had hoped to produce in triumph at the Congress due that August, came to grief. The Russians, now in no mood to listen to pleas for patience, began hounding Herzl as a failed leader. His posturings with statesmen, they cried, were keeping Zionism from what it could usefully and legally do in developing the Jewish agricultural nucleus within Palestine itself. And in the publication of *Old-New Land* they found an excuse to unleash personal animosities to feed the conflict over policy.

The novel purported to describe a utopian Palestine twenty years hence: the Charter was won, and the gifts of European civilisation were turning the Land of Promise into the Promised Land. Ahad Ha'am, ever alert for the doom of political Zionism, was particularly vindictive in a long review. He argued that by positing a society that was a slavish copy of existing states, the author had revealed total ignorance of Jewish values. Change the names of the characters and transplant the locale to Africa, Ahad Ha'am wrote, and the novel would just as easily apply to a Negro nation. Deeply wounded, Herzl pressed Nordau to reply in *Die Welt*. Nordau responded with relish, and castigated Ahad Ha'am for his 'vile, treacherous attacks

. . . a chaos of confused terminology without an intelligent thought clearly and intelligently stated'. Ahad Ha'am 'belonged to the worst enemies of Zionism'.

Could they be at the beginning of a Zionist civil war? Weizmann evidently believed so. 'The struggle between East and West within Jewry has now worsened,' he wrote to Vera. '*Die Welt* has flung the apple of discord into our camp. I trust we shall finally succeed in letting the world know where hegemony in Jewry rightfully belongs – in the hands of the author of *Degeneration* [Nordau's controversial book] or with the young, spiritually free Eastern Jews.'

Well, if war it was indeed to be, he would not have his own little army outside the fray. He instigated a declaration in defence of Ahad Ha'am. It was signed by a large group of his friends, including Buber and Feiwel, and received publication wherever the anti-Herzlian temper prevailed. It produced the illusion of a living Democratic Fraction marching into prominence.

Weizmann followed this public declaration with a personal letter to Herzl that ran to sixteen typewritten pages and embodied all his frustrations as spokesman of a younger generation seeking to give service to their cause. The leader was chided for surrounding himself with the wrong people, devoting himself to the wrong priorities, assuaging the wrong Russian Jews, i.e., the new *Mizrachi* party. Doubtless the formulation was Feiwel's, who also signed the letter, though the substance was true Weizmann polemic, for it reflected his deep understanding of Russia.

Vividly, the document described a society shortly to disappear in upheaval. It supported a demand for Fraction participation in the inner councils of the movement, with powerful arguments for the retrieval of Russo-Jewish youth from the ranks of the revolutionaries.

The sons and daughters of the middle-class intelligentsia, rather than the proletariat, were being abducted wholesale, Weizmann wrote. 'Hundreds of thousands of very young boys and girls are held in Russian prisons, or are being spiritually and physically destroyed in Siberia.' The letter spoke of the thoroughness of police surveillance over Zionism, of the material poverty endured by a great proportion of Jews, the authoritarianism of their religion, and how cultural activities as advanced by the Fraction could alone provide the Jews of Russia with a 'loftier view of life'.

Herzl might have taken all this more tolerantly were it not clouded by Weizmann's unsolicited leap into the *Old-New Land* controversy. Now he replied with supercilious brevity, and though expressing regard for

Weizmann himself, he did not disguise a wish to see his unruly colleagues of the Fraction out of their ranks. Herzl was now taking up the Russians' challenge in a fashion characteristic of him. He showed his disdain towards them when, to their consternation and disbelief, he arrived in St Petersburg to treat with von Plehve and de Witte, the Tzar's Ministers of Interior and Finance. This was negotiating with the enemy ('the executioner of Kishinev', Plehve was called); worse, it was a foreign Jew interceding with tyranny as though the millions within Russia had not the capacity or leaders to represent their own interests. The Sixth Congress was a fortnight away.

Herzl was received with all the courtesies, particularly by Plehve, who had grown up among Jews and claimed to be their friend. Plehve strongly rebutted the charge that his staff were behind the Kishinev pogrom. If emigration were indeed the objective of the Zionist movement then he would readily give it full legality in Russia, except that they could not hold great conferences 'which are denied our own people too'. Fingering a large bound volume of confidential reports on Zionism, Plehve recalled that the Minsk Conference had been concerned largely with cultural nationalism, which ran counter to official policy of a homogeneous state. Why not help then in the emigration question, Herzl urged? But he failed to win an undertaking from Plehve to intervene in Constantinople on the Jews' behalf.

Witte, the Finance Minister, reproached Herzl with telling statistics of Jewish prominence in the revolutionary movement. In a population of 136 millions, he said, the seven million Jews provided half its ranks. Herzl repeated his plea: Zionism could be an ally in ridding Russia of them. It could be done by intercession with the Porte, and by legalising the Jewish Colonial Trust, so that Russian Zionists could conduct open fund-raising. In the event, Witte agreed to the establishment of a branch of the bank.

Not all of Russia's Jews classed Herzl's mission to St Petersburg as offering the authorities cheap expiation for the crime of Kishinev. In Vilna, on his way home, he was received with almost hysterical acclaim as their prince. The city had greatly expanded since the May Laws of 1882, for thousands of Jews had sought refuge there. They now comprised half the population, and eighty per cent of these were impoverished. But they brought a long succession of gifts to Herzl's hotel, packing the streets so that the police had to intervene. There were interminable speeches, and he was desperately fatigued. He was expecting a message from Greenberg in London. It had come. It said that the British government were agreeable to granting the Jews a region for colonisation in East Africa. At last, something tangible! Now for the Congress.

It opened on a restrained note. The Russians were without Ussishkin, who was in Palestine organising an opposition Zionist Congress, and their references to Kishinev, and Herzl's courtship of Plehve, and the Russian situation in general, were carefully guarded. Syrkin alone took his courage in his hands and castigated Herzl for dealing with the tyrant. Weizmann made a speech on a subject most of his hearers considered dead: Sinai and El Arish. Why hadn't they been told earlier about this project? Had all the possibilities really been exhausted? On the new East African proposal he had little to say.

Recalling the brave showing of the Democratic Fraction two years earlier, Weizmann had every reason for his own restraint. There was now no Fraction; the university scheme was dormant; the great rebellion against Herzl had been translated into mean debating points. He was momentarily at a loss.

The possible Jewish settlement in East Africa lay in the Ugandan region between the Mau escarpment and Mount Elgon, in what subsequently became Kenya. All that the Congress had to decide for the present was whether to despatch a preliminary fact-finding mission, or to reject the proposal out of hand with an appropriate message of thanks to the British government. 'It is not Zion and never can be Zion,' Herzl conceded. But given their wretched plight in Eastern Europe, and the fact that the Jews were emigrating anyway to regions other than Zion, this corner of Africa could serve to consolidate settlement in an autonomous, if not national, sense.

Weizmann saw the validity of the argument, but the knowledge that all the Herzl idolators accepted it whilst most protagonists of 'Lovers of Zion' opposed, convinced him otherwise. Herzl left advocacy of the plan to Nordau, who stifled his own doubts as to its wisdom and implored the Congress to regard Uganda not as a solution to the problem of Jewish homelessness, but as an 'overnight shelter'. On a roll-call vote 295 voted Yea, 178 Nay. And the schism between politicals and practicals widened into a chasm between two irreconcilable philosophies, producing a decade of turmoil and Zionist impotence.

The Congress dispersed in a mood of perplexity and recrimination, for the Nay-sayers determined to make a fight of it. They rallied enough support to prevent Zionist funds from being used for any investigation of East Africa. Weizmann recognised a new role for himself in the movement: to destroy 'Ugandism'. He seized it.

Vladimir Jabotinsky, 1918.

Sir Mark Sykes, a portrait by Pilichowski.

Weizmann with Emir Feisal, at the latter's camp in Waheida, 1918.

The Zionist Commission, 1918. Weizmann shown with, seated from left, Joseph Cowen, Sylvain Lévi, Leon Simon, David Eder. Standing, Israel Sieff, Aaron Aaronson.

Churchill, as Colonial Secretary, at the Cairo Conference of 1921. On his right, Herbert Samuel. In the second row, Gertrude Bell, second from left, and T. E. Lawrence, fourth from right.

Where to start? He had no hope of a place on the Smaller Actions Committee, for this was a barricade surrounding Herzl; and being Geneva-based he would not be elected as a Russian nominee to the Greater Actions Committee. Ussishkin, doubtless seeing himself at the head of the movement, had hinted from distant Palestine that he would lead a fierce onslaught against the Herzlian policy. But Weizmann was not so naive as to believe that the bluff Odessan could substitute for the charismatic Viennese. The policy had to be destroyed, but not the leader – not as yet.

Nursing their wounds, and worried for the future, some principal Russian delegates took themselves off to plan their next move. Weizmann produced his Fraction rump, and offered it as the practicals' European spear-head. They would inaugurate the long-promised periodical *Der Jude*, generate propaganda and rouse the younger generation, to restore the integrity of Zion to Zionism. A small sum of money was made available to get the work started.

At the London Congress, in 1900, Herzl had declaimed: 'England the great, the free, with her eyes fixed on the seven seas, will understand us!' Weizmann had not then been impressed. Now he saw Britain in a different light. Herzl had met a stone wall in Constantinople; he had received evasive replies from other governments for a shelter in Mozambique, even the Congo; his entreaties for the intercession of the German Emperor, and the Russian Ministers, had led nowhere. But from London he had brought two concrete proposals. Weizmann told himself that the Jewish future might well be bound up with Britain.

And his own future? Here too a decision had to be made. Carl Graebe was about to leave Geneva University, and this would mean the loss of his academic patron. Could the country that had made overtures to the Zionists provide opportunities for himself? Perhaps his own path to Palestine lay through an apprenticeship in the British Empire.

Thus for a man of ambition two good reasons existed for a trip to London. He could leap into prominence by taking a bastion of Herzlian political Zionism by storm, and he could sound out the possibilities of a university post there. About the latter reason he was coy, and as yet only Vera knew of it. As to the former, he needed some non-controversial errand to gain him the confidence of the people who mattered in the charmed circle of 'Anglo-Jews' who fostered the leader so effectively. So he refurbished the university idea, not officially dead, in a different form. He would organise it on a temporary basis, as an 'extension course', and invite some academic lights to lecture there. But to Catherine Dorfman he wrote of his intention 'to establish our headquarters in London', and he spoke airily of addressing a mass meeting.

He was serious about the temporary university. It could create an appetite for the real thing. Herzl used his journalist's reputation as a *laisser-passer*, so he would present himself in the wholly praiseworthy role of detached academic and student leader. But above all he was obsessed with Uganda. He would convert it into a weapon to break the stranglehold of the politicals on the movement.

He gave London one week. The people he knew best lived in the East End ('Whitechapel . . . What horrors! Stench, emaciated Jewish faces . . . Vilna's poverty in a London avenue,' he reported). But those he sought out were ensconced in more salubrious districts. He himself boarded halfway between, in Highbury, at two Swiss francs a day, breakfast included. He travelled up to Maida Vale to find Moses Gaster, the *Haham*, huddled over a table in a garden-booth, for the season was the Feast of Tabernacles, commemorating the Exodus. Gaster was a rabbi, to be sure; but a true soldier of Zion nevertheless.

As they talked Weizmann studied the rabbi closely. This man, to the displeasure of his well-to-do congregation, had been among the first to follow Herzl. Could he be the next leader of the movement? It was not improbable. Gaster believed in all that the practicals wanted: cultural work, a start in Palestine, less personal rule, the elimination of Vienna as Mount Sinai. He had turned violently against Herzl over Uganda, and was manifestly anxious to lead. Gaster was a man of influence, with access to the people who counted in London. Furthermore, he heard Weizmann out patiently on the subject of his career. He had paternal advice, mentioning names and promising to make enquiries. Gaster's closest ally in Zionism was the lawyer Herbert Bentwich, a founder of the English Zionist Federation. Bentwich, very professional, very correct, rather heavy, was a man to be reckoned with.

Probing further, and making detailed notes for the report he intended for Russia, Weizmann discerned that London's strongest pro-African was Israel Zangwill. ('Like Nordau, he is completely hypnotised by Herzl.') His reputation in the world of letters made him a Jewish figure comparable in position to Lord Rothschild's through his place in finance. Yet he did not appear to understand the mentality of the Jewish masses, in whom Palestine summoned an emotion no African call could produce. Weizmann decided that Zangwill was a photographer, rather than a psychologist, of the ghetto. But the man had stature, more so than Herzl's alter ego in

London, Leopold Greenberg, whom Weizmann suspected as the real author of Uganda.

Two other Zionists mattered in London: Leopold Kessler, the mining engineer who had led a fact-finding expedition to El Arish, and Joseph Cowen, prosperous gown merchant and cousin of Zangwill. Both would follow Herzl faithfully, but they were obviously greatly distressed at the divisions produced by the African scheme. Naturally, they all agreed to support Weizmann's 'university', Gaster agreeing to lecture there, Zangwill to serve on its committee.

Now for the Uganda project itself. Weizmann had not neglected to apprise William Evans-Gordon, the 'British Brother', of his presence. The two met at the Houses of Parliament and the Englishman brought his visitor to Sir Harry Johnston, who had been British Commissioner in Uganda. ('Diplomacy, just like Herzl's,' Weizmann boasted to Vera.) He quickly assimilated the facts. Johnston's verdict, and some Colonial Office reports, gave him the conclusion he was seeking: Uganda, even on its own merits, was unacceptable for Jewish colonisation. This was by virtue of the terrain's character, and because its native population was quite different from, say, the docile Australian aborigines. The East African tribes were pugnacious, and had been invigorated through contact with white settlers, and were fully capable of political maturity. The best land was occupied by British colonists. The proposition could prove a major Jewish disaster.

Already, Weizmann was framing a long letter to Ussishkin in his mind. It would demonstrate that he now knew more about the East African scheme than anyone, and had the measure of its supporters and antagonists in the capital where decisions were being made. He told himself that the march of events would not be dictated by the mass of 'aliens' in the East End: their life was wretched, their preoccupations great, and they were swayed by whoever spoke to them. Initiative was in the hands of the select group of Anglicised Jews for whom Zionism was extraneous to their needs, important to their self-esteem. He was convinced that if he settled in England he could form a bridge between them and the Ussishkin style of Zionism in Eastern Europe.

But would he settle there? So highly industrialised a society obviously had work for his branch of chemistry, and he could enter a manufacturing concern with ease. But he preferred to teach, and to enjoy the freedom and tranquillity of an academic atmosphere. Prospects were not unfavourable, with the likelihood of a post under Sir William Ramsay at London University. If not, he could perhaps join the son of the famous William

Perkin in Manchester, a centre of dye-stuffs research where his apprenticeship under Liebermann and Graebe would be its own passport. He still
had a few months in which to decide.

Ussishkin returned from Palestine breathing fire. Herzl had not only
produced a proposal that threatened to divert the movement from the
ancestral homeland; his intercession with Plehve in the guise of Russian
Jewry's guardian angel was a gesture of intolerable arrogance. Ussishkin
gathered his principal followers in Kharkov and drafted an ultimatum.
Herzl was to abandon East Africa, give the Greater Actions Committee
more say in their affairs, put a Russian representative on the governing
body of the Jewish Colonial Trust, and do nothing relating to Zionism in
Russia without prior consultation.

Weizmann was disturbed. He pressed for a copy of the ultimatum, but
Ussishkin would not divulge its contents before its presentation to Herzl.
Weizmann procured the information he sought nevertheless, through
Bernstein-Kohan. He could not see the impetuous Ussishkin as the victor
of such a confrontation. It could well result in his displacement as Russian
leader.

Roughly, it so transpired. Herzl received the bearers of the ultimatum
with wounding condescension, reducing the whole exercise to a farce. Far
from abandoning Palestine, as was suggested, he was still on the path to
the Charter, through the enlistment of powerful friends. He was about to
leave for Rome for an audience with the King of Italy and, it transpired,
with the Pope. Brushing the ultimatum aside, he levelled his own
accusations against the Russians. They were tormenting him at every turn,
he charged, and so undermined his work that East Africa too was now
endangered as a refuge for the persecuted. He pressed his advantage home,
knowing that the Russians had only reluctantly followed Ussishkin to the
brink. The emissaries were placed completely on the defensive, humbled
by the stature of this man, and his comportment as a prince ruling by
divine right.

Ussishkin's power as the Russian leader was exploded. He had to share
that tiny pedestal from which he surveyed the entire subcontinent with a
more moderate comrade – the Moscow oculist Yehiel Tschlenow, one of
the unhappy participants at Kharkov. Weizmann disguised his relief at
the outcome. He continued for some months to deceive himself into
believing he could work up a European opposition to Herzl. Then he
bowed to the reality.

Vera had unwillingly agreed to postpone their marriage until she obtained her medical qualification, but her fiancé was already losing sleep over the financial responsibilities that lay ahead. Before finally committing himself to England he tried for a post in Palestine, where a German charitable organisation, the *Hilfsverein der deutschen Juden*, was establishing a teachers' training college. It really was infuriating, the way such non-Zionist bodies could find money and personnel to do the work in Palestine the Zionists claimed was rightfully theirs!

Needless to say, he was well-equipped for the post, which was as chemistry tutor. But the *Hilfsverein* would not have him. Weizmann's reputation as a stormy petrel had stuck. It would have to be England after all.

Geneva was hued in glorious light that day in July, 1903, as he proceeded to Cook's to buy his ticket. Many of his old friends were on the point of marriage. Others had disappeared from the student scene. His *Hashachar* group had dwindled to a few stalwarts. Vera was again in Rostov. He was worried about his health, and the future was a question-mark.

With a wrench he surrendered the key to his lodgings in the rue Lombard, that power-house of dreams, and schemes, and sat with a group of friends at the Café du Nord for a final lakeside concert. They all signed a postcard for him to send off to Rostov. Then the news came through. Theodor Herzl was dead.

3

Soldiering in the Backwoods

THE ZIONIST ORGANISATION LIVED THROUGH THEODOR HERZL AND could easily have died with him, so slender still was its root in July, 1904. The lesser men he left behind watered the plant with their dissensions. Uganda gave them the controversy that assured its survival.

David Wolffsohn, a Cologne timber-merchant and Herzl's closest confidant and major domo, appealed to Max Nordau to take the organisation under his care. As the most significant public figure in the movement Nordau had, in his station of servant and guide, elevated Herzl to the plane where leadership is immune to strictures from the crowd. But while he readily lent Herzl his personality, he would not surrender it to the ideal. Nordau feared that the Jews, in enthroning him, would consume him.

This was not the reason he gave Weizmann when the latter discussed the future with him in Paris five days after Herzl's death. Instead, he chose the excuse of being married to a gentile, of not having Herzl's faith, or fire, nor his capacity for self-deception. 'Herzl could erect a facade without an edifice, believing that it would not occur to anyone to look behind it. This was because he had immense faith in his personality.' Nordau hinted that Weizmann himself could be a candidate, were it not for his youth.

Flattery needs at least a dressing of sincerity. Weizmann was, however, appalled by the cynical dismissal of Zionism as a facade. Nevertheless he included the reference to himself in an account of the discussion he sent to Menahem Ussishkin. The Russian leader's own aspirations to the crown were common knowledge.

Ussishkin's virtues were indisputable. He was crusading before Herzl experienced his revelation, and spoke for the largest Zionist constituency. He had a reverence for Jewish culture, and an ability to command. But Weizmann gave him no encouragement, recognising that the man had the strength without the skill. He was now calculating the future differently. It did not preclude ultimate leadership for himself, but this had to be preceded by financial independence. He would see Zionism only as his cause, not his career.

England was the key, and he was about to establish himself there. Consequently his earliest steps in London took him to the house in Maida Vale where Moses Gaster was waiting in the wings. The rabbi was not yet fifty, a man of fine presence, an orator and intellectual. He advertised himself as heir in his own way by attending Herzl's funeral in Vienna. He had no office of substance except his religious post as head of the Sephardi community; it gave him status in a country where the cloth carried automatic privileges.

Gaster was pugnacious, and now at war with Herzl's leading disciples in London – Israel Zangwill, Joseph Cowen, Leopold Greenberg. Weizmann saw the possibility of the rabbi's picking a quarrel with him too, but he merited deference. The camp of practical Zionism boasted no one to measure up to him, and it was ridiculous that he should be excluded from the leadership, in England at least. With his instinct for making useful friends, Weizmann told himself that he and this man needed each other.

London, he had discovered from his previous visit, throbbed powerfully as the city of cities. If only he could be sure of a university post here! Sir William Ramsay had hinted at a place at London University, but they were now in high summer, and a firm decision must await the new academic year. William Perkin, on the other hand, had extended an immediate invitation to Manchester. It seemed like banishment to the Arctic Circle.

Gaster advised him to accept Perkin's offer. Manchester's industries must open prospects of supplementary employment for a good chemist. He would give Weizmann an introduction to Charles Dreyfus, the leading Manchester Zionist and owner of a large dye-stuffs plant. Yes, Weizmann reluctantly agreed, it would have to be Manchester, at least for the present.

He postponed his journey north as long as he could, utilising the time to gauge the Ugandist mood in the capital in readiness for the winter campaign. Every morsel of information that could be used by the 'Nay-sayers' went back to Ussishkin: 'Cowen is an honest man but very weak . . . Greenberg conceals his cards and is as sly as a devil . . . They will try and attract Tschlenow to their side. His name was mentioned far too often, and they praised him far too much.'

Ever helpful, Evans-Gordon led him to the two British officials most concerned with the East African offer: Lord Henry Percy, Under-Secretary of State for Foreign Affairs, and Sir Clement Hill, Superintendant of African Protectorates. It was as Weizmann feared, or rather, hoped. British enthusiasm for a Jewish colony had distinctly cooled since the discovery that the Zionists were not united as to its benefits. With Chamberlain virtually out of politics, and British settlers in the region voicing their opposition, the project was in process of burial.

Weizmann believed he was the possessor of unique intelligence, and though keen for Ussishkin to know of his scoop, he carefully refrained from divulging its particulars. In fact Herzl had realised in the last months of his life that Uganda was a lost cause, and was holding out only in the hope of being compensated with a renewal of the El Arish scheme. Weizmann's achievement was limited to scoring a point or two against the politicals by usurping the role of Zionist diplomat. Herzl had made a mystery of such activities; it was now demonstrated that diplomacy was within the capability even of 'uncouth Russians'. And he made propaganda for true Zionism. He maintained to Percy that the Jews had no complaints against Turkish rule, and were making rapid strides in Palestine.

As a junior personality in Zionism, Weizmann was on his way to assume a university appointment where, in the estimation of the movement as a whole, he could with no great loss disappear without trace. His foray into the corridors of power was therefore an impertinent initiative, and particularly regarded so by Yehiel Tschlenow when he got wind of it in Moscow. But reprimands from that quarter troubled Weizmann little. His strategy for changing the outlook of Zionism depended on keeping in the good graces of Gaster and Ussishkin. What, by contrast, were the plans of those now in control?

By default, Herzl's mantle descended on the Cologne faithful, David Wolffsohn. The timber-merchant's strength lay in his hold over the purse-strings, as head of the Jewish Colonial Trust. He was a political in the fullest extension of the term: no wastage of resources on experiments in Palestine until the award of a Charter; the subordination to this end of all activities deemed 'cultural'; a fair and full debate on Uganda when the survey was done. He gathered a staff around him in Cologne – it included

Feiwel as *Die Welt* editor – but everything was to hang fire until the next Congress. That would be a year hence, or, if you happened to be a newcomer in Manchester, an eternity.

The Victoria University, as it was called, was concentrated in a gruff pile of lofty stairways and labyrinthine basements that stood like an ill-designed trade-mark for England's least attractive but most prosperous city. In one of these basements the Russian chemist bending over his flasks experienced an emptiness such as he had rarely known. The professor who had engaged him, without stipend for the present, had left on his summer holiday. The college was deserted. Weizmann was by no means ignorant of English, but the street signs, and the Lancashire accent, belonged not at all to the language he had so assiduously studied from books and newspapers. Oh, for the sweetness, cleanliness, of Geneva! In January, Perkin had promised him, he could begin a course of Saturday lectures; but for the present he earned nothing. His brother-in-law Chaim Lubzhinsky, now established in Warsaw, had agreed to fill the gap, and Gaster had intimated his readiness to help out with a loan from time to time. Before long the offer was taken up.

Since the eighteen-fifties, when Professor Perkin's father made his great discovery that colour no longer needed to be taken from plant-life, no talented organic chemist was idle for want of an objective. Weizmann's apprenticeship in research was similarly within the family of coal-tar derivatives, and his scientific maturity had coincided with a tremendous upsurge of demand by a public in the full flood of its Edwardian prosperity. Every speculation brought the probability of a new discovery, and every discovery a fresh refinement to daily life, so there was work enough to occupy Weizmann in those early Manchester months. But he was excessively vulnerable to loneliness, and Zionism began to exert its attractions sooner than he reckoned.

Before long he was wandering in the poor Jewish quarter on Cheetham Hill to the north of his college, its streets reverberating with the Yiddish of his youth. Paradoxically, they were sounds he did not readily welcome. He felt he was walking among the blind. Indeed he was, and their one-eyed king was Charles Dreyfus. It was Weizmann's rare fortune that he, of all people, should be the man who manufactured dye-stuffs in Manchester.

Dreyfus was the door through which Weizmann, gasping as it were for breath in his basement, escaped into the upper air occupied by the Manchester bourgeoisie. The Alsatian-born merchant was the model British citizen, active in communal charities and municipal affairs. His

innumerable offices included presidency of the East Manchester Conservatives and the Manchester Zionists. Welcoming Weizmann as a
colleague and fellow-European at his gracious residence remote from
Cheetham Hill, he offered him a part-time consultancy with his Clayton
Aniline Company at three pounds a week. And would Dr Weizmann
honour the Zionist association with an address?

Pondering deeply over the subject, Weizmann decided to make it
'Political Movements of the Jews in Russia'. It was his thirtieth birthday,
and his fourth month in Manchester. Entering the musty synagogue hall,
and facing the shabby audience, he might almost have been in Pinsk.
Dreyfus introduced him in a speech of clipped vowel-sounds that betrayed
the Teuton's English. Weizmann, recognising his hearers for what they
were – artisans without education, in England but not of it – chose his
pure Yiddish. Reading his notes as though delivering a university lecture,
he kept them for three hours.

'I had them as though under a spell,' he informed Vera. A mild
exaggeration perhaps, but within weeks he was asked to repeat his talk in
Liverpool, then Leeds and other towns. The early rumblings of the 1905
Russian revolution, presaged by strikes in St Petersburg and Warsaw and
the intervention of the Tzarist police, were just then being reported in the
Western Press.

Though theoretically the concern of the immigrant groups he now
encountered, Zionism in England barely touched the mass. The Manchester Zionist Association, like its sister-groups elsewhere, hunted without great expectation for new recruits. It recognised in this one a newcomer of a calibre rare in a provincial city. Without ado Weizmann was co-
opted onto their committee. Soon he was pressed to accept office, any
except the presidency, which was Dreyfus's by right and apparently in per-
petuity. For a man intent upon assaulting the leadership in London it was
as good a start as any. Of the quartet dominating the scene there, Zangwill,
Cowen, Greenberg and Herbert Bentwich, only the last-named was a
practical, and thus a likely ally in placing Gaster in command.

He had early confirmation that in England everything was possible, even
to a humble foreigner, when, in January, 1905, he found himself deep in
conversation with the Prime Minister. Dreyfus had introduced him.
Arthur Balfour was on a visit to his Manchester parliamentary constituency.
A discussion of Zionism ensued. Gratified by the encounter though
Weizmann was, he attached little significance to it. He was more concerned with converting Jews rather than gentiles to the cause.

He regarded Israel Zangwill with particular distrust, for since Uganda had exploded in their ranks the writer had extended the Zionist thesis to a quest for a Jewish homeland anywhere on the globe. He wanted their funds used for whatever colonisation project a government might choose to offer, and it could be in Siberia or Timbuctoo. Even Greenberg saw this as traducing the sacred purpose for which the Jewish Colonial Trust existed. Gaster on his part surveyed the scene impassively, contending that Zionism had now ceased as an organised movement and had to begin again with re-affirmation of the Basle Programme 'to create for the Jewish people a Home in Palestine secured by public law' at the coming Congress.

The Zionist electorate was being nursed into quivering life. London would without doubt go 'Ugandist', but Weizmann planted Ussishkin's flag all over the provinces. He travelled to Leeds and secured Berthold Feiwel's nomination in preference to Zangwill. Of course, the voting apparatus being the contraption that it was, Zangwill received the mandate of another group. But it was a rebuff nevertheless.

Haunted by the spirit of the fallen leader, once calumniated by many but now canonised by all, the Congress assembled in 1905 in the certainty that the East African project would be rejected. The Survey Commission had in any case reported unfavourably and the Executive needed only a rubber stamp. Passionately, Zangwill begged them to retain the good offices of Britain and other governments by avoiding a categoric affirmation of Palestine. Syrkin, of the Russian Left-wing, supported him, and Tschlenow was selected to demolish their case. Weizmann darted between the private meetings of the Russian and English delegations – he was a member of both – and when the vote went overwhelmingly against any dilution of the Basle Programme Syrkin marched his people out of the hall. Zangwill, taken by surprise, had no alternative but to follow them.

The demonstration cleared the air, and the new Executive, or Smaller Actions Committee, attempted a coalition of politicals and practicals. Wolffsohn was formally endorsed as President, and was joined by his ally Greenberg. Ussishkin and Bernstein-Kohan won places there too, but problems arose regarding their transfer to Germany, and an opportunity to establish peace in Zionism was thereby forfeited.

Gaster won nothing. He reproached the energetic Weizmann for not doing enough on his behalf, though in truth he could not occupy any post which involved sitting in the same room as his sworn enemy Greenberg. And the delegate from Manchester? He came at last onto the Greater Actions Committee. To many Zionists it would mean little, but he would utilise the position to the maximum – it had taken Weizmann seven years of soldiering in the backwoods to get there.

Although Zangwill formed a movement of his own, the Jewish Territorial Organisation, to give a faint stir of excitement to the correspondence columns of the *Jewish Chronicle*, Zionism in England remained in a trough. Far from being permitted to soldier on, Weizmann spent a year practically unemployed in Manchester. He was enjoying the city less and less, and the separation from Vera, who could still not get him to put a date to their marriage, was proving a strain. True, his scientific work continued to progress, and from being a Research Fellow he was appointed Demonstrator in Organic Chemistry and immediate assistant to Perkin. He loved working with students, but this was not the pace of promotion he had hoped for, and the necessity to catch up on his industrial research during vacations at Dreyfus's grubby factory fatigued him. His thoughts strayed nostalgically to the Geneva days. 'I used to be a public figure, now I'm a hardworking drudge,' he lamented to Vera as he brooded in his laboratory, with nowhere to go, on *Yom Kippur* Eve.

The winter of 1905 brought bad news. The struggle between government and workers in Russia was in full train. Hundreds of towns and villages were locked in violent strife, repression was fearful and the dead numbered in their thousands, some 900 Jews among them. This at last was the face of revolution. But the pogroms did not cease with the Tzar's announcement summoning the Imperial Duma, and clamour was raised world-wide against the brutality and cynicism of the régime. For the first time in Russia's history the Jews intervened in national politics, and twelve of them gained election to the First Duma. Weizmann's brother Moses and his sister Fruma were among those sent to prison for their part in a Jewish self-defence operation. How he hated the land of his birth!

This land, England, he thought of only as his personal Uganda, a temporary shelter. Though he followed every step of the drama in Russia, he had no great interest in British political affairs. Having lived in Germany and Switzerland, he was dubious of Britain's power to keep her industrial lead, and disturbed by her amateurishness, revealed in all aspects of life. The hungry faces of the workers he encountered during the long early morning tram-ride down to the factory frightened him. But soon the Russo-Jewish situation was to intrude upon the British scene too, particularly in Manchester. The government resigned at the end of 1905 and the Conservative leader's seat was in peril.

Balfour's name was anathema among many Jews. They had forgotten the generosity of the East African offer under his administration, they remembered the antisemitism of his Aliens Act. In carrying that measure through, the Prime Minister had made a speech which today would be considered unexceptionable, but it read then like an anti-Jewish tract. Now, with a general election, he had to try and survive in East Manchester against the Liberal tide. In the neighbouring constituency of North-West Manchester Winston Churchill was rampaging against the Tories. The two areas held enough Jewish voters to affect both results.

Weizmann, somewhat to his own surprise, discovered that he counted as a local Jewish leader with a following among the immigrants. How else to explain the scene: the aesthete of an ex-Prime Minister fighting as it were for his political life, in momentary respite from the sordid hustings, receiving this gauche figure, an alien of his Aliens Act, in his hotel suite for extended conference? Of course it was the work of Dreyfus, who was head of Balfour's election committee, and who had broken the ice for Weizmann the year before.

But what actually transpired at their meeting? Weizmann made no public reference to the discussion for fourteen years, when with Balfour seated at his side, he recalled the words that have entered Zionist folk-lore and are presumed to have converted the British statesman to the cause: 'We had Jerusalem when London was a marsh.' By then, propaganda was making its own demands for embellishment. Blanche Dugdale, in her biography of her uncle, quoted Balfour's version as he remembered it in 1929; after which it was Weizmann's turn again, in his Memoirs, *Trial and Error*, committed to paper in the forties.

Compared with the almost verbatim reports, febrile with excitement, he sent to Vera when he spoke with the less-important Percy and Hill at the Foreign Office, Weizmann's note to his fiancée on this occasion barely achieved the laconic. 'I had a meeting with Balfour today,' he wrote, 'and had a long and interesting talk with him about Zionism. He explained that he sees no political difficulties in the attainment of Palestine, only economic ones. We talked about Territorialism. I explained to him why this was not possible.'

Nevertheless Weizmann was hardly the man to miss an opportunity, and doubtless he had much to tell Balfour on the difference to a complete Jew between the Zion of his heritage and a quixotic Zion in Africa. We cannot say how much of this impressed his hearer. Nine years were to elapse before the two met again.

By contrast, Churchill was out uninhibitedly collecting glory among the

Jews next door. He had fought the Aliens Bill, and he had his own antidote to Dreyfus in the Liberal, though non-Zionist, Nathan Laski. He had addressed a public protest meeting in Manchester against Russian persecutions. Weizmann had served on the meeting's organising committee, and so had ensured that Gaster too would be there. It had been a scene of different hue, a situation to compel the young aristocrat's attention. For the scientist kept to his practice of speaking in Yiddish, and the despised patois was not often heard in the presence of a prominent British politician. Churchill now wanted the university lecturer's help. He met Weizmann again at a private dinner, and took pains to suggest that a Zionist delegation meet his Minister (Churchill was Lord Elgin's Under-Secretary at the Colonial Office). Nothing if not thorough, he then had his election agent contact Weizmann with the request that he influence the Jewish vote in his favour.

Weizmann was nonplussed. He, a recently-arrived foreign Jew, to help the descendant of the Duke of Marlborough to get into Parliament? He sought guidance from Wolffsohn, who passed the matter over to Greenberg, with what result is not known. In the event, Balfour lost his seat, while Churchill won a resounding victory in the Liberal landslide.

Meanwhile, Vera was undergoing a purgatory of her own: preparing for her medical finals. With her fiancé's departure from Geneva the city lost all charm for her. Her letters were edgy, while his breathed little of the tenderness that had enraptured her while in Rostov. She felt weak, she said; she had headaches. Why did she have to go through with it in Geneva? Surely she could join him in England and complete her degree there without losing her Swiss 'credits'.

However, she became a doctor at last. Now Vera refused to accept another moment's delay for the wedding. It was May, 1906, and six years since their first meeting. Love had blossomed and been subject to every test. All their Swiss friends were married, but her man kept her at bay, as though she were an uncomfortable item on the lengthy agenda of a Zionist meeting. He continued to dally, quoting the difficult formalities on the Continent, and problems with his parents as to where the ceremony would take place. Angry, and worried, she travelled home in June, to find that her father had died the day before her arrival. Her fiancé was still not sure in July; the impending termination of the academic year would keep him occupied in interviews with the parents of his students, and then there was the Annual Zionist Conference in Cologne to command his undivided attendance,

They squeezed a modest ceremony in at last, before the conference: bride and groom, Chaim's parents, his sister Miriam and brother Feivel, under the canopy of a small synagogue at Zoppot, near Danzig. No congregation, no members of Vera's family, no friends. All the prevarication had resulted in a last-minute rush. Miserably she accompanied him to Cologne, and then they took a holiday in Switzerland.

'One day soon,' he was fond of telling her, 'we shall get our cart out of the mud.' The Russian expression seemed to embody the promises he could never keep, and she did not take enthusiastically to his austere rooms in Manchester, where they were to set up home. But that autumn he was awarded his second doctorate, so a professorship could not be far away. His patents were earning him royalties, he had received money from Shriro of Baku for his research into oil-waste, and he intended asking Dreyfus for an increase. Soon, he assured Vera, they would move into a fine house.

A wedding present arrived from Gaster. He got her to pen a few words at the end of his 'thank you' letter, written in German. She wrote them in French. Vera had barely finished applying the feminine touch to the old bachelor quarters when she found her husband buried in discussion with Harry Sacher, a Londoner up from Oxford and working on the *Manchester Guardian*. She gathered that they were staging a *coup d'état* at the coming conference of the English Zionist Federation.

She had spent part of her honeymoon at one meeting in Cologne, and was beginning married life with another here. Vera resigned herself to the truth: Zionism was going to be her life. Perhaps she should discard French and begin to acquire Hebrew, as Chaim constantly implored. But she never did.

For all her aloofness, Vera emerged in time as a forceful adviser behind the scenes, and a public figure in her own right. The partnership was not without its hazards, for it had to survive frequent periods of separation: Chaim's was a roving eye, and there would be his lapses. But they came through their eventful life together a devoted couple. Their union was both of heart and intellect.

4

'A Gentleman from Manchester'

ACCORDING TO BERTHOLD FEIWEL, THE MACHINERY OF ZIONISM UNDER David Wolffsohn in Cologne was not merely creaking; it was grinding to a halt. Weizmann was therefore planning his preliminary moves with Harry Sacher in the deposition of the new leader: liquidating the junta controlling the English branch of the movement and replacing it with an Executive of 'practicals'. Zangwill was already out, and although he could always gain an audience for his Territorialist schemes, there was now little to fear from that quarter. The men who had to be defeated were Joseph Cowen and Leopold Greenberg, for Herbert Bentwich could be relied upon to bring the votes of his own following onto Weizmann's side.

Greenberg, fortuitously, was not in the mood for a fight. He was involved in negotiations that would end in winning him financial and editorial control of the influential *Jewish Chronicle*. He decided to quit the battle-ground, at least for a while, and Cowen was to keep a place warm for him in the Zionist Federation. Moses Gaster, whom Weizmann intended to produce as the saviour of the movement, remained coyly in the background.

The palace revolution was enacted in Birmingham in February, 1907. Weizmann the newcomer was ranged by Sacher and Bentwich, drawing upon their unimpeachable credentials of British birth. Cowen had the formidable Greenberg at his elbow. In a fighting speech, Weizmann contended that obsession with a Charter was drowning the movement in phraseology, and leaving them in a state of inaction. Let political work proceed by all means, he said, but it should not preclude practical activities in Palestine. Cowen repudiated the assertion that nothing was being done in Palestine. In any case, they should learn to walk before they could run, and he quoted as a warning the experience of the Rothschild colonies, where money had been no object, yet the villages stagnated through want of initiative.

But Weizmann had done his work well. The practicals were present in force and Gaster was easily elected President, with himself and Cowen as the Vice-Presidents. The conference terminated with declarations of goodwill all round. If the *Haham* could be made to suppress his awkward temperament, he would be accepted as Herzl's true successor.

So England at least was captured. But to complete his equation Weizmann needed a strong Russian element. There, everything the Jews had hoped for was in ruins. The Duma was peremptorily dissolved, and the revolution perished in a torrent of disillusionment and bitterness. As for Ussishkin, he was locked in rivalry with Tschlenow. Together they kept Russian Zionism polarised between Moscow and Odessa, with millions of disorganised square miles between them.

Furthermore, Gaster, though of use for a house-cleaning operation, developed into an impossible colleague in office. Wolffsohn, on the other hand, overcame the scorn of his enemies and was undoubtedly growing in stature. He so dominated their next Congress that he could afford a show of compromise, and conceded that it was time they made some concrete moves in Palestine. Weizmann observed that human beings, unlike the laws of molecular theory, were not immutable. Leo Motzkin roused his admiration for a speech on cultural needs in the authentic Democratic Fraction mould; Syrkin, having travelled from the Fraction through his socialist group to the secessionist Territorialists but was now back in official Zionism, sounded the warnings of the die-hard politicals.

Syrkin's was a lost cause. The mood was for practical work, and Wolffsohn disclosed that they were about to establish a bureau in Jaffa, with a branch of their bank, to coordinate their efforts there. Nahum Sokolow, whose Warsaw newspaper was banned in the Tzarist reaction so that he had fallen upon the Zionist headquarters for a livelihood, announced that they had taken the *Jüdischer Verlag* (another echo of Fraction days) under their wing and would be publishing works in Hebrew, their historic language re-born.

There now seemed no aspect of the old 'Lovers of Zion' programme that did not receive endorsement. Weizmann was on the edge of hit chair, savouring victory at last for his philosophy of Zionism. When

w.—5

called upon he turned his speech on the theme of 'synthesis', and advanced a plea for the strengthening of their all-round position 'in the country we regard as our home'. They should end their ideological rift by conducting political and practical activities simultaneously.

This was his first major address at their international forum. It was delivered with authority, and not only because he was at last a figure of some significance. He was due to leave for his first visit to Palestine. He had taken up a challenge by an old political, the industrialist Johann Kremenetzky, to stop preaching and begin performing. Kremenetzky, charging Weizmann to apply his specialist knowledge to produce a scheme for the establishment of agricultural industry in the Holy Land, was financing the visit.

The Russian group as a whole, stunted by the tragic events just enacted in their own country, acquitted themselves as poorly as Weizmann had feared. And far from being displaced, Wolffsohn emerged with almost the same personal authority as was enjoyed by Herzl.

But one Russian voice restored Weizmann's pride in his origins. For Shmarya Levin, again a product of his own Zionist nursery, gave the Congress some devastating intelligence on the state of Jewish education – not in the Diaspora, where they knew it to be bad, but in Palestine itself, among the children they saw as the nucleus of the future nation. Levin painted a picture of educational anarchy created by three Jewish institutions in pursuit of the children's souls. None was sympathetic to Zionism, all had resources to maintain schools in the country. Doubtless their intention was honourable, but their motivation was to do some empire-building for their own cultures. Thus the *Alliance Israélite Universelle* taught of French magnificence, and the *Hilfsverein der deutschen Juden* of German excellence. The Anglo-Jewish Association had only one school, in Jerusalem, but it might well have been in the English shires. What hopes for Zionism when such bodies ignored the Hebrew civilisation and raised the young as aliens in their own homeland?

Weizmann was profoundly impressed. This speech embodied the Zionist challenge as he understood it: the birth of a new nation, not the banal imitation of established ones. Now he was to see the process for himself.

For any Jew his first glimpse of the Holy Land cannot avoid being a highly-charged experience. To the Zionist of 1907, when arrival was preceded by all the dislocation and hubbub inevitable with steamers plying the Eastern Mediterranean trade, sensations could succeed each other to produce in the visitor an emotional storm. He would read significance into every snatch of conversation overheard: was this language really Hebrew? And why did this child speak in Arabic to his parents, who were replying in Ladino, the Judeo-Spanish of the Sephardim? His eyes would feast upon a tree, and be repelled by a beggar muttering in the Yiddish of Bucharest. Was this indeed a main road, and was that a Jewish farmer poking at his mule? And the heat, and the torpor, and the dried hills, and the pomposity of an official; and this valley described in the Book of Judges, and that township mentioned in Isaiah – he could not but mouth the verse now that he saw its context. To Weizmann in boyhood the Land of Israel had been less alien than the Russia on his door-step. He had lived with the thought until maturity, but the reality was as strange as it was familiar. He did not ask himself whether he was happy; he only knew that he did not feel sad.

In a country where immigration of Jews was severely restricted there was evidence enough of their presence. They formed some ten per cent of the total population of 800,000, and were largely town-dwellers untouched by the Zionist doctrine, which struck their religious sensitivities as un-Jewish. Such Jews formed the majority in Jerusalem, where they felt sanctified in an existence devoted to prayer, eventual burial in the holy soil being reward enough. Their poverty was their profession, for their economy rested upon the organised solicitation of alms from Jewish communities overseas.

Weizmann was little concerned with such people, evidence though they might be of the obstinate faith keeping the Jews in association with this land through 2,000 years of dispersion. Given a sound Jewish economic base, some would be absorbed in the re-born nation, the rest could be left secure in their piety. He was eager to investigate the condition of the agricultural colonies, those supported by Baron Edmond de Rothschild as well as the few under the aegis of the Odessa Committee or some other benefaction. How were their relations with their Arab neighbours? How tightly did the Turks exercise control?

He was a father now, Vera having made him deeply happy three months earlier in giving birth to their son, Benjamin. This land would not only be their future home but their children's heritage. Eagerly he sought out old friends. A bronzed Bernstein-Kohan received him in Tiberias, and accompanied him round the Galilee villages where he served as physician. He found Samuel Pevsner, with whom he used to attend Berlin student meetings, in Haifa. Now married to Ahad Ha'am's daughter, Pevsner directed the country's first Jewish industrial plant. It produced olive oil, and was thus of particular interest to Weizmann's present commission.

He endeavoured to sort out his impressions. Palestine had proved a rude awakening for some Zionist pioneers, whom he found haunting the Jaffa dockside in search of a berth to separate them from their disillusionment. But no such mood permeated the farm settlements. Despite the stifling embrace of Baron Edmond's philanthropy, he realised that the Parisian had achieved as an individual more than all the labours of Zionism collectively. The Baron had inculcated a love of the land in city-bred Jews and, as Weizmann later told a Manchester meeting, 'such people are laying the foundations of the future Jewish State'.

The basic weaknesses of these villages, he saw, lay in their dependence upon Arab labour. Only a handful of Jews actually tilled the land, and he felt that such a situation could only end in the Arabs' belief that they had a moral right to the soil they were cultivating.

Rothschild's holdings were mainly in the coastal plain. Up in Galilee, which he covered by horseback, Zionist pioneering as he understood it was truly in progress. Young newcomers from Eastern Europe, cheated of their emancipation in the 1905 revolution, were bringing a new ideology to the land. They felt they were undergoing a personal regeneration, through release not just from the ghetto but from the mentality of the ghetto. Having read Tolstoy, and been charmed by the socialism of the Bund, and inspired by the call to Zion, these young people, girls as well as boys, had determined on their path: to found villages on communal lines, to raise their children to speak Hebrew, and to see to their own protection rather than rely upon neighbouring Arab tribesmen.

Weizmann warmed to their dedication and intelligence in going into the fields to compete with Arab workers on their own terms. Who knows, but perhaps this feeling possessed him while observing one such labourer, a Pole, knee-deep in a furrow in the Jewish colony of Sejera. It was the twenty-one year old David Ben-Gurion, earning his daily bread.

His first tour of Palestine confirmed to Weizmann that the practicals were correct in planting a stake in the country rather than in pursuing that nebulous Charter. He was impressed by the Turks' respect for a legal contract. Land was available for purchase, though Zionist funds were insufficient for any except the smallest plots. And in his report to his sponsor Kremenetzky he spoke with qualified optimism about industry. A large factory would be premature, he said, but private capital could be safely invested in developing olive-oil production, and in experimenting with the manufacture of citric acid from lemons.

As Weizmann had surmised, the Turks were ready to accept a greater flow of Jewish newcomers. In fact, they were searching desperately for a way out of their choking indebtedness. They invited Wolffsohn to Constantinople with the offer of a bargain: the Zionists could settle 50,000 families over the next twenty-five years, at the price of £26 millions to the Turkish exchequer. What an overestimation of Zionist strength! Wolffsohn countered with the figure of £2 millions. The Turks bowed him and his derisory offer out.

So Wolffsohn too began to look like a leader running out of steam. In the absence of a policy he gave his restive following meticulous book-keeping. It was particularly galling that he kept a strong hand on the Jewish Colonial Trust. It frightened Weizmann that Wolffsohn would readily convey its capital to the Sultan at a stroke, but would only part with it in driblets for their own tasks. Controversy between 'politicals' and 'practicals' revived, with possession of the bank the real prize of office.

The excitement of his visit over, Weizmann felt trapped by his known identification with two quarrelsome men, Gaster and Ussishkin. How could he achieve the dominant role he hungered for while in their shadow? But how could he lose them? In England he had the reputation, since Gaster's election, of an intriguer. In Russia he was *persona non grata* to Tschlenow. He was without an ally on the Executive. Sokolow was his friend, but in the caste-structure of Zionism a salaried official barely counted.

His own income was now considerable, and money went to brothers and sisters, nephews and nieces, spread in universities throughout Europe. He played his part heroically in the provincial social life of Edwardian Manchester, escorting his wife to the garden parties the professors' ladies gave in their elaborate hats and in strict rotation, joining college outings to North Wales, or Buxton in the Peak district. Vera's frail beauty and Continental speech never failed to alert the courtesies of the middle-aged academics in their circle. He was proud of her, but he would not think of himself as anything but a sojourner in England.

Perkin, always the perfect gentleman, took every opportunity to assure Weizmann that the coveted professorship was in the offing. Weizmann would not consider going to Palestine until he achieved it. His ambition, fired by a striking record of successes in his chosen field of chemistry, all marked by publication in the scientific literature of the day, led him to speculate in physiological compounds, and he decided to spread his investigations to the field of proteins. Willingly, he began at the beginning, in Professor Auguste Fernbach's laboratory at the Pasteur Institute. For the next four years Weizmann was to spend the spring vacation in Paris. His work there would one day be crowned with historic results.

In the pharmacopoeia of Zionism, however, he could discover no magic potion to cure the movement of its paralysis. But in 1908 it was revitalised by an external circumstance: the Young Turk rebellion. Sultan Abdul Hamid hurriedly promised parliamentary freedom and the decentralisation of the Empire, to the peoples spread over his European, Asiatic and African dominions. Could this mean dawn for the Jews?

A platitude of the time promised that one day the Sultan's ragged tapestry of bankrupt possessions would disintegrate. For the Empire's European minorities this was a prayer; for some Arab groups it was a cause; for the Great Powers it was an anxiety; for the Zionists it was a hypothesis. Unsure whether they would fare better in the collapse of the Sublime Porte rather than in its continued existence, Wolffsohn sent a measured greeting to the Sultan on the 'reconstitution' of his Empire, then postponed his next Congress to await events.

Weizmann, however, rejected the demand for caution. The Young Turks, he claimed, brought Zionist objectives nearer. He visualised easier immigration, reformed land laws, the ending of bribery and censorship in government, an industrial age in the Levant. He heralded permission to establish a Zionist society in Salonica (where the Turkish revolution had been fostered into life by an army group in which crypto-Jews of the Donmeh sect were prominent) as presaging closure of the abyss that had divided Ashkenazi and Sephardi Jewry for centuries.

They were, he was convinced, on the march. But behind a general conducting their affairs from his timber-merchant's office in Cologne? No, that was not possible. Feiwel and Sokolow thought likewise; they definitely intended abandoning the leader to his apologetics and betake themselves to Berlin. With Weizmann and Ussishkin, they engineered a scheme.

They would isolate Wolffsohn and build up Berlin as the centre, with the botanist Otto Warburg, the solitary practical on the three-man Executive, as figure-head.

Ussishkin began the operation. With barely a hint of consultation in the direction of the President of the Zionist Organisation, he initiated a programme of sustained propaganda in Constantinople, now an 'open city'. Using his Russian money, he established pro-Zionist newspapers there. He placed his brother-in-law Victor Jacobson in command, with a flamboyant publicist, Vladimir Jabotinsky, as his deputy. Wolffsohn had no alternative but to acquiesce. Avoiding a fight, he made a contribution from central funds.

Weizmann's part in the conspiracy was hampered by continued disarray in the English Federation. It was Gaster against Greenberg and Cowen again, with the tedious Bentwich, clutching the rule-book, loudly proclaiming grievances of his own. But the chemist succeeded in consolidating a personal following. Sacher was its nucleus, and the young journalist enrolled allies of equal mind among his contemporaries, men untouched by the Herzlian legend and irreverent towards the archaic squabbles of their elders. Weizmann had long been nursing an Anglicised version of his Democratic Fraction for just such a time.

Forewarned of his Ides of March, Wolffsohn came to the Congress in December, 1909, with a plan of his own. He still had expectations of an arrangement with Turkey; he would therefore expose the opposition as an army in motley. First he made some appropriately flattering remarks about the new régime in Constantinople. Then he blandly stated that he was laying down his office.

Taken unawares, Weizmann found himself in the delicate situation of executioner, though without a victim. In the absence of a sulking Gaster, he had been elected chairman of the steering committee, a role that enabled him to stage-manage the agenda and influence nominations for office. He announced that, with Wolffsohn's abdication, the President of the movement would not be elected as hitherto, by acclaim of the whole Congress, but by the Greater Actions Committee – i.e., the body in which the Russians preponderated, making for a permanent 'practical' majority. The names he submitted for endorsement as their new Executive were Tschlenow and Ussishkin (the Siamese Twins, Wolffsohn termed them), as well as Sokolow and three delegates from Germany and Austria.

He was howled down from the body of the hall: the voice might be the voice of Manchester, but the hand the Congress recognised was the hand of Odessa. Predictably, Ussishkin's name roused a chorus of disapproval, and a cry went up calling for Wolffsohn. This put Weizmann at a loss. He could not get a vote either way, and the final session threatened to last all night. A steward brought the Congress to order with the chastening news that the electric light in the hall would last only a further half-hour.

But the demonstration told Wolffsohn he was safe. Assuming the mien of elder statesman, he made a gracious appeal for Weizmann's nominees to be given their head. Of course this was refused. It was now three thirty a.m., and delegates were trooping out to find their hotels in the dark. An election was now impossible, and Wolffsohn's victory was complete – he was left to carry on for another two years as before. 'It all seems like a bad dream,' Weizmann told Sokolow.

He had long relished the prospect of a confrontation with Wolffsohn, who roused in him feelings of ill-will that he barely troubled to conceal, so that tales travelled back to Cologne depicting the Manchester man as a sly intriguer hungering for attention, if not power. He perceived that he was now among the least popular men in Zionism. Even sympathisers of the practical stance were distressed at his rough handling of Wolffsohn, and Nordau, who had once titillated him with ideas of leadership, now castigated Weizmann as an adventurer. But, convinced that the Turkish revolution represented, for the Jews, a Charter without the document, he was unrepentant. Zionism had to win the right to be seen as an ideology of national liberation, not a super-charity conducted patronisingly by westernised leaders on behalf of the 'persecuted brethren of the East'.

He was only half a person when not working for his ideal, and his collision with Wolffsohn was warning enough of the wilderness close by. Wolffsohn had to go, English Zionism had to be brought to life, and he himself must secure his base. It took him a year of long journeys in the cold third-class compartments of Britain's dawdling trains to find the Zionists, let alone talk to them. Sunday was the only day for such campaigning, when 'picture palaces' could be hired and synagogue halls were available. Audiences were depressingly thin, Vera's protestations echoed in his ears, Greenberg gave him only meagre notice in the *Jewish Chronicle*, but at last he found himself *wanted*. Early in 1911 he patched up a truce with Cowen. They arranged for the Federation to meet in Manchester and Weizmann was again elected Vice-President, this time under the other's leadership. Gaster spoke of betrayal, and Weizmann ceased warming his hands and heart in the hospitality of Maida Vale.

A new friend in London replaced the rabbi. Ahad Ha'am, philosopher of cultural Zionism, had transferred there from Odessa – arriving in his other incarnation of tea merchant. Ahad Ha'am was employed in this capacity by a benefactor, Kalonymus Wissotzky, who spent the extensive profits of his Russian tea business on good causes, one of them a subsidy for the Odessa *Hashiloach*. The thinker had lost the editorship, Wissotzky had died, but Ahad Ha'am's association with the family survived. He was a trustee of an educational bequest willed by his wealthy friend, and served on a committee employing Wissotzky funds in an ambitious scheme to establish a Technical College in Haifa.

Recalling Weizmann's support in the celebrated controversy over *Old-New Land*, Ahad Ha'am welcomed the chemist as a brother. Soon his home in Belsize Park became an oasis for Zionists of the cultural-practical bent. For Weizmann it was a place to converse in their beloved Russian, for Sacher it was to hear Ahad Ha'am philosophise in his strained though correct English, and for Leon Simon, Sacher's dearest Oxford friend, Ahad Ha'am was Dr Johnson to his Boswell, all recorded in Hebrew. The newcomer still kept aloof from the movement, but as a Wissotzky trustee he was directly involved in a project of magnitude for the development of the Jewish presence in Palestine.

Thus the situation began working Weizmann's way. Wolffsohn might well discourage settlement activities pending legal safeguards from the Turks, yet Jews were arriving in Palestine nevertheless. He could dismiss the practicals as unworldly dreamers, but colonisation was becoming a reality, and villages were springing into bustling existence. Visitors returning from Palestine spoke lyrically of the gleaming northern suburb of Jaffa called Tel Aviv. One of them brought back vivid evidence from Galilee of what the pioneers were achieving in a settlement organised on communal lines, for which the term 'kibbutz' was not yet ready; he had made the first Zionist propaganda film.

Wolffsohn recognized that the tide had turned against him. In 1911 he really resigned the Presidency, though without surrendering control of the Jewish Colonial Trust. The head office was moved from Cologne to Berlin and Otto Warburg formed an Executive of practicals. Weizmann could not have hoped for a better result, though the victory would not be complete until the purse-strings were wrested from the old guard. Two of the new Executive had been his allies in the long years of strife: Shmarya Levin and Victor Jacobson. Another was Nahum Sokolow, who had cause for gratitude to Weizmann when times were bad. The failure of that old firebrand Ussishkin to achieve election caused him not a moment's loss of sleep.

And himself? Membership of the Smaller Actions Committee could have been Weizmann's for the asking. This would have demanded full-time salaried service and transfer to Berlin. This was not the moment for such a choice, because of his wish to go to Palestine in the status of an emigrating university professor. Furthermore, his chemical work had reached a crucial stage.

England was then racing neck and neck with Germany for a process to manufacture synthetic rubber. Perkin was leader of the English research team, with Weizmann as his assistant. In the team also was Auguste Fernbach, of the Pasteur Institute, who had been enrolled on Weizmann's recommendation because of his achievements in bacteriology. The work involved three distinct processes, in one of which Weizmann, working with Fernbach, had discovered a mixture of bacteria which could ferment the starch in potatoes by a novel method, and lead to an improved route to acetone and the higher alcohols. At this stage of the proceedings Fernbach negotiated a separate contract with the sponsors of the research, in which Weizmann was nominated as a twenty-five per cent partner and beneficiary.

Suspecting Weizmann of working behind his back, Perkin became difficult. He initiated a consistent disparagement of the chemist he had but recently spoken of in terms of glowing praise. The relationship of intimate collaboration was substituted by one of jealous rivalry. Weizmann's promotion to a professorship could have no more powerful advocate than Perkin, but neither could it have a more formidable barrier.

Naturally, he began to fear the worst. The closed society of Manchester University was proving irksome, and desperately he looked for his promotion elsewhere. It suddenly dawned on him that all his ambitions could fall into place with a post at the Haifa college, in which one friend, Ahad Ha'am, had the voice of a trustee, and another, Shmarya Levin, carried an official Zionist vote. In June, 1912, Perkin delivered a much publicised paper in London which eulogised the role of Fernbach and others, but ignored Weizmann completely. The paper made exaggerated claims for the perfection of the synthetic rubber process, and Weizmann spoke critically of it. Perkin, incensed, dismissed him from the research team.

Weizmann persisted on a line of enquiry of his own into acetone production. His desire for a post at Haifa became obsessive, and an open secret in the faculty common rooms, with Perkin publicly hastening him on his way 'to Jerusalem'. Ahad Ha'am cautioned him not to build on it, as the new Institute's finances might not stretch to a chemistry department requiring a professor of Weizmann's calibre.

As time progressed his provincial laboratory turned into a prison, and every week of waiting became a torture when Perkin won appointment to a Chair at Oxford. Manchester was now rightfully his, and immediately; Haifa could take years and still be uncertain in the end. Weizmann smoked heavily, and his health (he suffered from neurasthenia) deteriorated. Colleagues assured him his succession to Perkin was a mere formality, despite the hostility. He knew otherwise, for Perkin also had a brother-in-law in the department.

In the meantime Zionism was attracting attention in the higher political world. Transfer of its headquarters to Berlin did not go unremarked. The Germanic *Hilfsverein,* a partner with the Wissotzky Trust in the Haifa project, was increasing its schools in Palestine and its zeal reached the public prints. During a two-day debate in the Turkish Parliament strong words were spoken against the Zionist Organisation, which evidently disposed of so much influence as to be a powerful vehicle of German policy in the Near East. Ears pricked up in the Quai d'Orsay.

France was having difficulty holding her own against Germany in Africa, and was placing herself on guard in the Levant. Why then should she not make friendly sounds in the direction of the Zionists? It was, after all, French flair that had created the *Alliance Israélite Universelle,* so eagerly planting the Gallic *esprit* all round the Mediterranean, and it was French finance, in the form of Baron Edmond de Rothschild, that had settled a thousand Jewish families on Palestinian soil.

The new Zionist Executive, unskilled in the ways of 'diplomacy' and lacking Herzl's blinkered dedication to a grand design, became a political body despite itself. It responded by sending messengers to argue the case for a homeland in all the capitals of Europe. If nothing else, Russia could be relied upon to provide their argument. The trend towards constitutional rule there had ended disastrously for the entire population, but nowhere did the reaction parallel the Jews' tragedy. Every aspiring Russian politician had to bow to the anti-semitic mood; every large city had its experience of murderous demonstrations.

Soon Russian justice, and Russian obscurantism, would create an appropriate symbol: the trial of Mendel Beilis for ritual murder. No better advertisement for Zionism existed than this two year long process, for it had the effect of placing not a solitary Jewish unfortunate, but the whole of Christendom, in the dock. Weizmann observed this Russia for the last time in 1911, on a visit to his dying father. Once more he was shamed by the extremes of Jewish life: the demoralising poverty of the mass, the ostentatious wealth and superficiality of the few. He castigated Jewish society in Warsaw as being engaged in a *danse macabre*.

Italy snatched Tripolitania from the Turks, and the Balkan peoples saw their opportunity to evict their masters and create a checker-board of new independent states. Zionism was now ostensibly the last national movement committed to the status quo in the Ottoman Empire. It took pains to proclaim that it was not seeking a Jewish State. When Herzl wrote his pamphlet, its spokesmen averred, he had no real understanding of what the Jews intended by Zionism.

The notion particularly impressed Baron Edmond in Paris. He was an animal *sui generis*, and in helping his people he could not avoid working also for the greater glory of *la Patrie*. He now began to interest himself in Palestine not merely as a haven, but as a homeland. If it was indeed true that the Zionist headquarters, located in Berlin, had the mentality of Berlin, then it was his duty to use his resources to divert the movement in another direction. Hitherto, Paris had slept as a centre of Zionism. Now Paris awoke. The Baron let it be known that he proposed making extensive purchases of land. And, doubtless with an eye on Berlin's initiative in building a technical college in Haifa, he was reminded of the old Zionist plan to establish a university in Jerusalem. If they intended going ahead, he said, he would be prepared to participate.

Such intelligence could not have come more propitiously for Chaim Weizmann. He had just experienced a succession of disasters. His scheme to build a chemistry department for himself at Haifa had collapsed. Perkin's Chair at Manchester went, predictably, to the brother-in-law. He had failed moreover to gain election as Fellow of the Royal Society, the accolade of scientific distinction in Britain. Furthermore, both Vera and little Benjamin were unwell. She had, in 1912, taken her English medical finals and would be spending the winter with their son recovering in the South of France. As 1913 dawned, Weizmann in his loneliness fell into his old depression. Little release was to be found in Zionist activities, for the English branch of the movement, despite all his efforts, remained a lame duck.

True, Harry Sacher and Leon Simon proved faithful and energetic disciples. They jointly edited a Zionist periodical and could be relied upon to give Weizmann more generous coverage for his speeches than Greenberg granted them in the *Jewish Chronicle*. But they were headstrong, and contributed their own mite to Britain's imperial ambitions by fostering her cause as Palestine's protector in the event of Turkey's collapse. This he considered foolish. Why should the Zionists encourage any Power's expansion in the Near East? They were not doing so badly under Palestine's present masters. Why alienate the Turks for an eventuality that might never arise?

Thus the Baron's conversion to the idea of a Jewish University in Jerusalem came to rescue Weizmann, now forty, at a critical period in his life. Here was his old project, on which he had laboured alone, given the most exalted endorsement. The Zionist Executive must commit itself to it. The Jewish presence in Palestine had so strengthened during the previous decade that a university would not now be beyond its capacities. This time the plan would not die in the womb.

It was a field in which he had no rivals, and he was, of course, authorised to take up again the work he had made his own in Geneva. For collaborators there stepped forward his colleagues from that zestful youth, Feiwel and Motzkin. No problem of a chemistry department here: it would be written into the scheme, and would mean goodbye to Manchester at last. He now found compensation where but lately everything was gloom. He was promoted Reader in Biochemistry, 'almost a professorship', he termed it.

Without a second's delay, Weizmann began laying the groundwork: committees of support to be established, academics enrolled for their knowledge of curricula and budgets, further potential benefactors wooed. His pace disconcerted even the trusted few around him. Ahad Ha'am, fearing perhaps that a university would detract glory from the Haifa scheme, warned him of the inadvisability of choosing a site in Jerusalem, as this could introduce political hazards. Others felt the plan would displease the German government, which had itself emitted interest in sponsoring a university in Palestine. Sacher and Simon came to the view that the needs of land-purchase, which must take primacy, would be sacrificed by the diversion of money and effort.

If these were the misgivings of friends, what of the more formidable opposition of his long-time adversaries? The politicals of yore – they had lost their cause but not their identity – described the plan for a university as a waste of money, and alleged that it was not demanded by the Jews of Palestine, nor the Zionist movement, but by 'a gentleman from Manchester'. Nordau treated the whole idea with disdain. Other objections were voiced by the socialist pioneers in the agricultural settlements. They associated universities with the topsy-turvy Jewish standards of the Diaspora; what Palestine needed most was a Jewish peasantry.

The Zionist Executive in Berlin took fright at these objections. Weizmann had been assured that the Congress of September, 1913, would be mainly devoted to the university, but now the agenda was revised to give one day to its discussion, and then the university was relegated to a single session at the end of the Congress proceedings.

He pressed forward nevertheless, his fighting spirit roused. He knew the Baron was impervious to critics, though encouraged if he saw others besides himself making a financial effort. Weizmann sought Ussishkin's help in raising Russian funds – a reasonable expectation this, as Ussishkin took the credit for fathering the project. But Ussishkin produced a trail of difficulties. The university, if ever it were to materialise, would be Weizmann's creation alone.

Five days of the Congress had to go by before Weizmann was given his opportunity to speak on the subject. It was to be the last international gathering of Jews prior to the war. Unity still eluded the movement. It came as a shock to them all that Max Nordau was not to be present. He sent a telegram condemning the new leadership for abandoning Herzl's path, and it was striking to observe how his defection placed into relief the absence of great Jewish names in the movement's affairs. A century of emancipation in Europe, a great Jewish community born across the Atlantic, Jews distinguished in the arts, sciences and politics, had given many nations talents of the first order, but had deprived their own people of its natural élite. Despite its years of endeavour, Zionism had not persuaded the Jewish intelligentsia that the Jewish soul was worthy of preservation. Nordau's place would one day be filled by Louis Brandeis, but the eminent American jurist had not as yet been seen at a European forum.

Recognising that his motion to establish the university would have a difficult passage, Weizmann produced a Herzl letter to himself from 1902, indicating the late leader's support of the concept. He recapitulated the reasons for its abandonment at that time: Kishinev, and a lack of awareness of the cultural question. In a gesture towards the political complications, he spoke of the university as a vehicle for advancing relations between Jews, Turks and Arabs. But especially, he saw it as the nursery of the living Jewish national language and the focus of Jewish activities in the literary, artistic and scientific spheres.

His reference to their language was studiously chosen. Hebrew was now developing into a controversial issue – the test by which Zionists and non-Zionists alike were judging the intensity of purpose behind the work in Palestine. The 1913 Congress witnessed, for the first time, a substantial representation from Palestine itself, to heckle speaker after speaker each time words were uttered in German, or English, or Yiddish. Most Zionists were still unacquainted with spoken Hebrew, Ussishkin alone insisting upon using the ancestral tongue.

If anyone could have wished the language question away, it was Weizmann. A storm was threatening to demolish the delicate edifice of support he was erecting for the university. The trouble had its origins in the Haifa Technical College, now approaching completion. Coming as it did under the aegis of the *Hilfsverein*, the majority on the Institute's executive committee were Germans; they could not conceive of satisfactory science tuition in any but their own language. Beside Ahad Ha'am, the Zionist nominees on the committee were Levin, dearly loved by Weizmann, and Tschlenow, who had resigned his Moscow oculist practice to join the Executive in Berlin.

Since Levin's impassioned words in 1907 it had become an article of Zionist faith that a Jewish school in Palestine teach in the Hebrew language, now advancing in majesty as a corner-stone of the revival. A clash of interests therefore ensued, bringing repercussions in Palestine. Demonstrations took place at the existing *Hilfsverein* schools (they all employed some Hebrew, as it happened), windows were smashed, the Turkish police intervened. As militancy grew, the *Hilfsverein* threatened to close down its operations in Palestine. The Zionist Executive was dismayed at the prospect, but felt it had no alternative but to support the Palestinians.

Weizmann, a Hebraist himself, considered the conflict artificial. But he naturally upheld the primacy of Hebrew for the Jews in the Holy Land. The three Zionists resigned from the Institute committee, and Weizmann, who was Ahad Ha'am's deputy, loyally refrained from moving into one of the vacant seats.

Soon the whole of Germany was to know that a group of its citizens were being frustrated in their patriotic role of exporting *Kultur* to the Orient. This prompted the French to discover the virtues of Hebrew, giving Edmond de Rothschild heart to speak up in its favour. So did Nordau, expatriate Hungarian though he was, and denigrator of the cultural aspects of Zionism though he had been. The controversy was ranging ever wider, and the *Frankfurter Zeitung* published an article on Zionist 'terror and intimidation'. Its author was the leading *Hilfsverein* official. This organisation was as good as its word, and began closing its schools. The Zionist Executive, penurious as ever, responded by hurriedly opening schools of its own, imploring its constituent bodies to find the money to pay for them.

Weizmann saw the materialisation of his own dream imperilled. If the movement had now to concentrate its energies on a general schooling system, what support could he expect for his Jerusalem university? Further, he had won the goodwill of some German scientists and public figures, notably Paul Ehrlich, whose Nobel prize for immunology had brought world fame to his Frankfurt Institute. Ehrlich, an intimate of the Rothschild family, was held in such esteem by the Baron that his attitude could make or break the entire project. Ehrlich was of the assimilated Jewish type, than whom no fiercer German patriots existed. Zionism had become anathema to such people.

Holding his breath, Weizmann worked his way through the laboured protocol demanded in securing his first interview with the Baron. This he at last achieved in January 1914. The personality of the old wizard (he was almost seventy, but would live another twenty years) intrigued and captivated him. Eighteen years had passed since Edmond's abrupt dismissal of Herzl, and in the interval he had sunk colossal sums in Palestine, making his decisions as though Zionism had never been born. His conversation was a capricious monologue of half-completed sentences in which he frequently contradicted himself, but nothing he said lacked insight. To the Jews of France, the Rothschild name had brought something less than security, for the antisemitic hatred directed towards Rothschild power did not spare the lowliest Jewish beggar. Edmond was vulnerable, a mixture of guilt and goodness, and beneath the aristocratic exterior lay the universal perplexity of the Jew pondering his identity. The simplest proposition put before him had to be analysed for its remotest implications, then passed to his advisers for further consideration.

Weizmann knew he had scored a success. The Baron recognised that

Zionism was a fact. He re-affirmed his endorsement of the project, but thought a complete university was premature. He would subscribe to a research institute in Palestine, on the lines of the Pasteur, and he made it clear that only a scheme supported by Ehrlich would gain his support.

Weizmann begged those closest to Ehrlich to protect the scientist, lest 'he catch a cold from the anti-Zionist wind now blowing in Germany'. He also did his duty for the new Hebrew schools but went about the search for money without enthusiasm, sensing that every pound collected for them would be a pound less for the university.

While he had been exhilarated by his interview with Baron Edmond, his colleagues, hearing of the research institute idea, now regarded their Maecenas as a liability. They expressed disappointment also in the sum he was expected to subscribe. Idle chatter, never corroborated by Weizmann, had made this fifty million francs (some two million pounds at that time) but the Baron now let it be known that he was good for not more than 200,000 francs annually, with a contribution towards building costs. Also, the Baron made a fetish of avoiding publicity for his benefactions, and would not allow his name to be used in the university propaganda campaign. So, Weizmann's cold comforters emphasised, their most powerful weapon had to be surrendered.

These points were marshalled with no mean effect by Vladimir Jabotinsky, once the Zionists' Press expert in Constantinople and now back in Odessa. He had been selected by Ussishkin to organise the university campaign in Russia, but instead of raising funds he had taken it upon himself to indulge in polemic with Weizmann. He was against concluding a formal arrangement with Rothschild on the latter's terms. Weizmann was wrong, he said, to consent to an establishment 'where scientists could work and strive to gain the Nobel prize'. They needed a university in the accepted sense, tailored to the needs of young students.

True or false, the arguments were chorussed by Ussishkin and Tschlenow – Wolffsohn too. None of them cared for Weizmann's handling of the negotiations; they all wanted to play for time. He refused to retreat. It angered him that they could be so cavalier towards the most important associate their movement had ever recruited.

He was convinced that the Baron would eventually accustom himself to the concept of a full university, and so he prepared his documents accordingly. All seemed in order for the crucial meeting in Paris, where a 'treaty' of collaboration was to be signed between the House of Rothschild and the Zionist Organisation for the establishment of a Jewish Research

w.—6

Institute as prelude to a University. The meeting was arranged for August
12, 1914.

Summer days arrived. The storm in Weizmann's heart subsided. The
climate of his temperament drove him alternately from black despair,
when he could feel misunderstood and victimised, to a confident serenity
and quick, sure decisions. Manchester suddenly seemed congenial without
Perkin, and he and Vera were moving into a station of privileged affluence,
with servants occupying the top storey of their spacious Brunswick Road
residence. They had 'pulled the cart out' at last, Vera was happily at work,
and if Benjamin was proving a somewhat demanding seven year old the
doting father observed little but perfection in the boy. The news from the
Continent was bad, but this was England, in repose, in the tea-time of her
authority.

Weizmann had been so absorbed as barely to notice the gathering of the
clouds. But in July, in writing to Tschlenow of his plans, he remarked:
'What will happen to all our work if war really does break out? God
knows, I can't even imagine such a catastrophe.' He then took his wife
and son off to Switzerland.

His arrangements for that summer also included biochemical research
under the supervision of Ehrlich at the Frankfurt Institute. There was
much to look forward to, and his thoughts indulged in his dream of soon
reaching Palestine, where he would be the first Jewish Professor of
Chemistry and (why not?) His Britannic Majesty's Consul. He was a
British subject now, a word in the right quarter by the amazing Moses
Gaster having expedited his naturalisation.

The dreaded catastrophe interrupted the dream as Weizmann was seated
in his hotel carefully putting his papers in order for the Paris meeting
with Edmond de Rothschild. Soon he was back in Manchester, for the
new chapter in the world's history.

5

The Secret of Bacillus B.Y.

WITH ITS FIRST SHELL-BURST, THE WAR PUT AN END TO THE OLD ZIONIST movement as Theodor Herzl had constituted it. That machine depended upon coordinating the will of men who were primarily Jews. Now they were primarily Englishmen, Russians, Germans, Americans, and they would be swayed not as single people, but as citizens divided by countries seeking to conquer each other, or to cherish their safety in neutrality. The Zionist Executive in Berlin endeavoured to preserve what had been laboriously created, and keep the parts in working order at some place detached from the fray where contact with the components could remain alive. Chaim Weizmann dismissed the scheme as unreal.

In its early weeks the war demanded patriotic hysteria, and sanctification by the Almighty, on both sides. The young bodies rotting beside their bayonets along the Marne released a multitude of saints beckoning from the heavens for more willing martyrs. Tannenberg's slaughter might be described as due retribution, or the miracle that saved Paris; Germany's entry into Belgium could be righteous or atrocious. It depended upon one's passport.

Events spoke to Weizmann as an Englishman. *Germania delenda est,* and every vestige of the Zionist doctrine contaminated by the thinking of Berlin had to be destroyed too. In that reeling initiation of 1914, with the French government in flight and Poland pincered in the armies of Hindenburg, his reaction was Kiplingesque. He could not reconcile Britain's alliance with Russia to his mood, but for him the war was a happening that outstripped time: 'I see this as a struggle between Siegfried and Moses, and I believe in the indestructability of Moses, who withstood more terrible things than seventeen inch guns. The wisdom and justice of the

Bible will once again be honoured, and perhaps the people who gave the Bible to the world too.'

He was addressing these remarks to Israel Zangwill, of all people, proffering the Anglo-Jewish leadership to a man he had but lately abominated; to such a degree was he ready to erase the old rivalries. Sharing the general illusion that this would be a brief war, Weizmann wanted the Jews to be represented at the peace by men of substance and authority, not the shadows of men who had cringed to statesmen in the past. Zangwill from England, Edmond de Rothschild from France, Luigi Luzzatti, former Italian Prime Minister, Henry Morgenthau, the American Ambassador in Constantinople – he saw these as winning justice for the Jews, and it would help rather than hinder that none of them was committed to the old-style Zionism.

'I have no doubt,' Weizmann informed Zangwill, 'that Palestine will fall within the influence of England. Palestine is the natural continuation of Egypt and the barrier separating the Suez Canal from Constantinople, the Black Sea, and any eventuality that may come from that direction.' So he was in quest of a new liberation movement, with the pick of the Jewish race behind it, to give their cause the advocacy that would win the Jewish homeland.

No European tragedy could be complete without its Jewish irony. It was just a few months since the trial of Mendel Beilis in Kiev had given pitiful notoriety to the debasement of Weizmann's people in Russia, and now 300,000 Jews were at arms under Archduke Nicholas, defending the system of the Tzars. No English or French Jew wished his country to lose, but who among them hoped that Russia would win?

Millions of their co-religionists happily immune on the other side of the Atlantic did not share this dilemma: Russia was *the* enemy. A Hebrew prayer in American accents went out for German victory on the Eastern Front; if France and England went down thereby, so be it. Among those joining in that prayer was Shmarya Levin, closest to Weizmann on the Berlin Zionist Executive, and now an Austrian citizen, marooned in America awaiting his restoration to the seat of authority.

Yehiel Tschlenow was on his way home to Russia, Nahum Sokolow would soon be following. Victor Jacobson languished in an apparent backwater in Constantinople and, joined by Leo Motzkin, would be setting up the Zionist clearing-house in Copenhagen. News filtered through to Weizmann that they should all meet on neutral territory to study the situation. He could think of nothing less desirable than Zionist busybodies searching for something useful to do in the blaze of war. Such a meeting would renew suspicion of their being a German puppet body. He would have no truck with anything Russian either. Salvation for the Jews, he was sure, would come only from England, with the assistance of America.

Zangwill disdained the olive branch. Who was this Weizmann anyway, to plan so grandiosely for the future of the entire Jewish people when he did not treat even on behalf of the irrelevant Zionist movement! The rebuff was wounding, but the new academic year had begun and the chemist addressed himself to his microscope, with his wife tending the ailments of working-class mothers in a municipal ante-natal clinic. The home fires too had to be kept burning.

Letters arrived from Levin, inviting him to come over to America and help educate its great Jewish proletariat. The might of the New World was on all lips in those days, and the prospect interested him. Then, to repay Germany for the years of courtship, and Russia for the years of hostility, Turkey came into the war. The Suez Canal was threatened, and the hour struck for Chaim Weizmann.

The Allies had over two million soldiers bogged down and starved of ammunition on the Western Front, and bitterly the British Prime Minister, Herbert Asquith, reproached the Turks for their treachery. Having lost their European empire, he declared, they would now forfeit their Asiatic possessions. For Europeans as a whole it was a statement of no great weight, and they barely heard it. But the Jews did. Among those Asiatic possessions stood the Land of Promise. Weizmann's thoughts were racing: if the Turks lost it, who would have it?

Britain had found herself a new ally, he decided. But how to forge the alliance? The Zionist Federation, in default of any other, was the agency in Britain of the Zionist cause. It was led, if leadership it could be termed, by Zangwill's kinsman Joseph Cowen, closely shadowed by Leopold Greenberg. Weizmann was technically a Vice-President, but not of their circle. War, however, prompts men to their own initiatives, and imperceptibly he began taking over the reins, handicapped though he was by his provincial isolation.

Weizmann's Zionist friends in Manchester were without influence, or standing. Two wealthy young brothers-in-law, Israel Sieff and Simon Marks, had become devotees, but they were inexperienced unknowns. Harry Sacher would soon be joining them from London, to resume his former place at the *Manchester Guardian*, but as yet his value was as link with Leon Simon to the Anglicised leaders of the Jewish community in London. In the university Weizmann's seniority carried weight, and the academic world stood, in war-time, adjacent to power. For the moment, however, Weizmann's only resource was his determination. But fortune took a hand, in a most unlikely quarter, just a few days after Turkey's entry into the war. The ladies' committee of his wife's clinic were giving a tea-party.

Among the males who were suffered at that tea-party was Weizmann. Another was an elderly widower, who transpired to be C. P. Scott, the owner-editor of the *Manchester Guardian*. It was a historic encounter. Scott, once a Liberal Member of Parliament, had the ear and received confidences from the Chancellor of the Exchequer, Lloyd George. The great editor (Scott accepted the adjective without modesty, deeming it his right) confessed to Weizmann that he knew nothing of Zionism, a strange admission for a man who for four years had been Sacher's employer, and whose paper had once given Weizmann a free-lance assignment to cover the Congress. Stranger still, Weizmann knew nothing of Scott, and did not connect the name with the famous newspaper.

A talk in the editorial office ensued. Weizmann formulated his ambition: to bring Britain and Zionism together, so that the Jews might develop Palestine as a bulwark protecting the Suez Canal from the north. Scott was diffident. The notion of an extension of British territorial power as a result of the war offended his Liberal instincts. Nevertheless he offered to introduce his visitor to Lloyd George, and perhaps bring him also into communication with the Prime Minister.

It occurred to neither man that the Chancellor of the Exchequer could already be acquainted with Zionism. Yet the politician's Welsh nonconformist breeding brought him closer to ancient Palestine than to Roman Britain, and biblical prophecy rang as realism in his ears. Moreover, when Greenberg was preparing Herzl's submission for the Ugandan project, he was drawn by chance to Lloyd George, then in solicitor's practice, who devised a draft charter. But most recently and positively, the subject of Palestine had been revived by Herbert Samuel, his colleague in the Cabinet, and a professing Jew at that.

Lloyd George informed Scott that he would gladly receive Weizmann, and he would invite Samuel to join the meeting. Weizmann's reaction was 'Alas!' His dealings with the Anglo-Jewish gentry were not happy. And though recognising the value of winning such people over, he coupled them with the German assimilationists as instinctive opponents of the national cause. He knew nothing of Samuel, but expected only frustration from that quarter. What a miscalculation! Weizmann had overlooked the circumstances of Samuel's intervention in his personal life four years earlier, when he desired prompt naturalisation as a British subject. The link between the two had been Moses Gaster, and in fact that most improbable rabbi and Zionist leader *manqué* had long given his distinguished friend regular instruction in the movement's affairs, matters which touched Samuel profoundly. He was versed in the conflicts between politicals and practicals, and had followed the vicissitudes of the university project and the language struggle. Unlike his Jewish familiars, among them his cousin the junior Minister in the government Edwin Montagu, Samuel remained a relaxed combination of Englishman and Jew, and saw no threat to his standing as a British citizen from Zionism. Turkey's plunge on the side of the Central Powers had drawn him to a conclusion identical with Weizmann's, except that he would work at the centre of power for a Zionism consummation, while the chemist could only work at its perimeter.

Travelling even faster than Weizmann, doubtless because he was alive to a complication, France, with which the other was as yet unconcerned, Samuel had already outlined to Lloyd George, and the Foreign Secretary Edward Grey, an arrangement for the division of 'Greater Syria'. Their ally across the Channel could have the north. It would be a fair trade, and Palestine would develop as a Jewish State under British aegis. Thus all would benefit, and in England the foul word annexation need never be uttered.

Weizmann had the plan from the lips of Samuel himself, and it seemed that Messianic times had arrived. The Cabinet Minister said: 'Together we shall rebuild the Temple as a symbol of Jewish unity.' The chemist would soon be engaged in negotiation with many men, some senior in office and with greater responsibilities than Samuel, but this was the compact investing Weizmann with the leadership of the national movement.

In its pristine simplicity, the plan rode over a hundred obstacles. Palestine had first to be occupied, but the catastrophic losses then being sustained on the major battleground, where the Anglo-French armies were time and again out-manoeuvred, did not augur for an early British offensive on the Nile. And would not a Zionist commitment to Britain generate a violent Turkish reaction against the existing Palestine Jewish population? Would the Arabs, already the object of attention as a potential ally, accept a Jewish State in their midst? Would the American government look idly on? Certainly the Jews of the United States evinced little desire to see the Union Jack aloft over Jerusalem.

Furthermore, Samuel's proposal seemed totally irrational to the British Prime Minister, as well as to most of his Cabinet colleagues; it gathered few plaudits from the recognised spokesmen of Anglo-Jewry; the portion allocated to France fell well short of the ambitions that Power nurtured in a region she had long considered her special interest; and when heard in Berlin it would certainly be received with derision, by Jews of every stamp no less than the Germans as a whole, as an immoral pretension impossible of realisation. Germany could justifiably point to its liberal occupation of Poland after Tannenberg for assurance that the millions of Jews released from the Tzarist yoke would flock in gratitude to its support.

This mountain of objections soon became apparent to Weizmann, and he kept his cards close to his chest. He became a target of suspicion nevertheless. Levin, the Austrian, read Weizmann's intentions into his letters, and disclosed them to the American Zionists. Soon reproaches reached him from New York that he was fastening the movement to the coat-tails of imperialism. And Gaster, as the genie who had produced Samuel, demanded to be consulted at every step. So did Cowen. Weizmann adopted an air of innocence towards these questioning bed-fellows.

More disquieting, those two apostles of Zionist neutralism, Sokolow and Tschlenow (the two 'Ows', Sacher labelled them) were on their way to London. This could have one purpose only: to frustrate any Zionist démarche that would disturb relations with Constantinople. Weizmann handled them with a show of deference, and in a report of his discussions implied that he had done no more since the outbreak of war than work for a united Jewish front and take soundings among public figures as to their attitude to a revived Jewish homeland. Not a word of his scheme for British suzerainty.

He readily allowed the 'Ows' full rein with the leaders of Anglo-Jewry, convinced that many empty weeks would pass while he continued with the central task. Apart from Samuel, only one Jewish name struck him as important – Rothschild. Ideas ventilated among members of the august family, both in London and Paris, were bound to circulate in the splendid drawing-rooms where the fate of nations was being decided. Of course, they did not all think alike; some Rothschilds glowered at him from the camp of Zionism's sworn enemies.

By early 1915 Weizmann had thoroughly taken the temperature in

England. Clearly, sympathy for the Jewish cause was substantial, but it did not extend to enthusiasm for an exclusively Anglo-Zionist arrangement in Palestine. Sensitive to foreign opinion and dubious of Arab reaction, the British favoured an international régime for the Holy Land. He believed this merely to reflect the inhibitions of a Liberal administration, but a meeting with Arthur Balfour taught him that the Conservatives would go no further.

The term internationalisation had an ominous ring in Weizmann's ears. Who would form the elements of such a régime? Russia, persecutor of the Jews? France, who colonised by imposing her own culture upon subject races? Palestine would become the plaything of Great Power rivalries. No, England alone should be the protector of Palestine, for England exerted a light hand upon her colonies, and implicit in her control was their elevation to self-government. Weizmann put his faith in Scott and Samuel to change the mood. Between them they could make Lloyd George, the government strong man, an advocate of the Zionist-British partnership. Scott was by now personally convinced, and this was half the battle.

It was not easy to hold all the cards in one hand and his microscope in the other. Weizmann was conducting a subtle tactical game, but now other self-appointed spokesmen were arising and, like himself, breaking the thread of Zionist authority leading to Tschlenow and Sokolow. To the British he spoke of this country's control of Palestine as a universal Jewish wish, but if he stated this out loud he would be repudiated by the facts, with world opinion still drawing a picture of England climbing into Palestine on the Zionist back.

Luckily for Weizmann, he held a secret that was essential for Britain if it was to keep its army and navy in a firing position. He called it Bacillus B.Y. He had begun the search for it with Auguste Fernbach in Paris, but discovered it by an independent fermentation process in Manchester. Bacillus B.Y. was the path to acetone. It was in desperately short supply for the explosives Britain would need if she were held to a long war.

The world was becoming heavily populated with potential Zionist leaders, some emerging from within Palestine itself, where the Jewish community was a mixture of nationalities whose strongest interest in the war was to remain outside it. The Zionist Organisation there had a German at its head who was discretion itself, but the Turks suspected all nationalist movements and this was no time to take on trust the word of European pioneers who had doubtless arrived illegally in the first place. As the Turks advanced through the Sinai peninsula to take up positions before the Suez Canal, enemy (mainly Russian) aliens who refused to adopt Turkish nationality were either expelled from the country or sent north. Women and children were not deported, and most remained in Palestine, their deprivations alleviated by relief sent from America.

Communal organisation, never strong, was left in tatters as the population dwindled. Some young men, among them David Ben-Gurion and his Russian comrades, protested their loyalty but were removed nevertheless. They found their way to America, where they conducted Zionist propaganda among the Yiddish-speaking proletariat as though the war was only a temporary aberration. Joseph Trumpeldor, a one-armed veteran of the Russo-Japanese War with the status, unique for a Jew, of reserve officer, arrived in Alexandria determined to fight for the Allied cause. Chasing up the most promising elements of the raggle-taggle making up the Palestinian refugees in Egypt, he formed them into a unit for collective enrolment in the British Army.

Two other Russians had the same idea, though on a grander scale. Pinchas Rutenberg had fled St Petersburg with the collapse of the 1905 revolution, in which he had been prominent. He visualised the Jews of the world, particularly in neutral America, as raising a large force to help conquer Palestine and receive just reward: a say in the future of the Holy Land at the Peace Conference. Vladimir Jabotinsky, the journalist whose surface brilliance easily won admirers, joined him. Jabotinsky's activities for Weizmann's university project had ceased with the war, and he had left Odessa with newspaper assignments among Russia's allies. He and Rutenberg took soundings in France, though without hopeful result.

These were Russian Jews after Weizmann's own heart, and he saw great merit in their project, despite its ring of unfeasibility. But he judged the open proclamation of a military alliance with the Entente to be imprudent. It would bring the weight of American Jewry down against them. There was little prospect of an early conquest of Palestine. So why, he demanded, rouse the Turks with empty thunder?

The two Russians were unmoved. They had as much right as Weizmann to decide what could be helpful to their people and what would not. Rutenberg took his mission to America but was promptly silenced by the pacifist Zionist mood. Jabotinsky linked up with Trumpeldor in Alexandria. They went forward with their plan to put the Jews in khaki, and the Zionist notables could take it or leave it.

Armed with a list of 600 volunteers, they brought a proposition to General Maxwell, commanding the British Forces in Egypt: collective enlistment against an undertaking to deploy them under their own flag for the assault upon Palestine.

What assault upon Palestine, the general asked? No such operation was pending, and he had no authority to distribute flags of all nations on request. He would welcome them as locally enrolled support troops of muleteers, to serve where he, not they, determined, and they could be called the Zion Mule Corps. Jabotinsky, in pursuit of greater glories, declined. Trumpeldor took the 600 into training.

The bombardment of the Dardenelles had begun, and with it the bid to break the Central Powers at their weakest link. Weizmann waited in expectation. With the Straits successfully breached, the British would be the unquestioned masters of the Middle East, and France would take what was given her: Syria proper. Or so it seemed. It was February, 1915.

That month a representative of Nobel's (the explosives company then had a plant in Scotland) visited the Manchester chemist to observe a demonstration of his fermentation process. Fernbach had obtained acetone and butyl alcohol from potatoes; but slowly, and in minute quantity. Weizmann claimed that he could distil these substances from maize, and on a mass scale. Experimentation continued for a week. Butyl alcohol was not for the moment in demand. What mattered was to produce sufficient acetone, formerly available by wood distillation, to feed the guns with smokeless explosive, thus concealing their positions. The man from Nobel's was satisfied, and notified the Admiralty.

The shocks of war were turning Whitehall into a nest of deceit. The government contended that all was in order, with Lord Kitchener apparently doing no wrong as military overlord. But a sense of defeatism brooded over the British Cabinet. The Central Powers were unmatched in fire-power, and the munitions shortage was tormenting Lloyd George. England and Russia could not put enough men in the field when, instead of the required twelve million shells a month, only a quarter of this figure were being produced.

In May, Asquith was compelled to form a coalition. Lloyd George finally left the Exchequer to become Minister of Munitions, Balfour emerged from the wilderness as First Lord of the Admiralty, and Samuel, to Weizmann's chagrin, was relegated to Postmaster-General, a non-Cabinet post. A hundred thousand Allied troops, among them 600 Zionists with their humble mules, were clinging precariously to Gallipoli, for the great Dardenelles adventure was turning into a mis-timed horror.

A microcosm of hope in the general gloom: Bacillus B.Y. The Admiralty put Weizmann's fermentation to large-scale application. Provisionally, he declined payment of the usual fees. He would supervise the manufacture of acetone as a national service, he said, in the expectation of suitable compensation if the process were adopted by the government after the war. Now he was summoned to the Minister of Munitions.

Lloyd George disclosed the entire muddled picture of Britain's explosives position. France, in contrast, was making immense progress in her war industries. Weizmann undertook to visit France and establish contact with chemists there, and proceed also to Switzerland, where he knew the best specialists. A few days later he was instructed to make an immediate move to London and take charge of the technical work. Unlike the Admiralty, Munitions placed him under a year's contract on a salary basis.

It all happened so quickly, he was in a daze. The Admiralty work involved the erection of special plant, but Munitions commandeered existing distilleries in the breweries – it was a characteristic Lloyd George touch, for the Welsh nonconformist complained that it was easier to defeat the Germans than the drunkenness among the armaments workers. Weizmann and Vera found a temporary home near his laboratory at the Lister Institute in Chelsea. They took in a lodger: Jabotinsky, fresh from Alexandria.

To Whitehall civil servants the foreign chemist loomed as an enigmatic figure, jealously protecting his work from prying eyes as though a conspiracy were afoot to steal his secrets. His political activities struck a sinister note to men who vaguely coupled Zionism with social revolution, the camp in which they placed Russian Jews in general. They were troubled by Weizmann's access to men in authority, for whenever he felt a grievance it travelled from the *Manchester Guardian* editor direct to Lloyd George, who backed him to the hilt.

Weizmann was now developing precious uses also for his butyl alcohol, a by-product of the acetone process that had been regarded as waste by other chemists, including his old academic chief William Perkin. In fact, its derivatives ultimately supplanted the original acetone process in value, particularly in such infant industries as aviation and automobile manufacture. Scott required no instruction in Whitehall's supercilious ways. He advised Weizmann to lose no time in applying for his due recompense, lest muddle and prejudice ultimately cheat him of it. The government was trusting his judgment to make decisions critical for the progress of the war, yet he was regarded as an outsider, denied a seat on those committees where problems of supply were freely discussed, and where men shone for their abilities and reaped glory for their achievements.

Thus his removal to London came not a day too soon, and for the cultivation of his political no less than his scientific stature. Those who purported to speak for Jewry were gathering their forces to circumvent his Zionist campaign. Talk of a national entity for their people in the Holy Land terrified them. Jewish aspirations in Palestine, these local notables averred, would be satisfied by a relaxation of immigration restrictions and a measure of communal autonomy. Weizmann refused to be intimidated. What impudence, that people completely detached from the philosophy of Jewish nationhood should take it upon themselves to surrender a birthright! He would fight in the places of authority where he was known, and respected. Tschlenow returned home after a few months, feeling there was little to detain him in London, but Sokolow, gentle though he might be, left no one in doubt as to where he thought leadership resided.

The only position Weizmann dared usurp without too much offence was the Presidency of the English Zionist Federation. With Cowen in the seat it had little significance, but Weizmann could transform it into the pivot of Zionist action.

He was by no means certain, as the Dardanelles became a débacle and the strains of war took their price in men's tolerance, and the government still fought shy of endorsing Zionist aspirations, that he could bring off a master-stroke on behalf of his people. In a fit of depression he wrote to Dorothy de Rothschild, the beautiful and accomplished daughter-in-law of Baron Edmond: 'The upheaval in the world has aroused everybody except the Jews. It has not brought a single man who could be capable of guiding the people to a great destiny.' But Dorothy encouraged him. She was fighting for Zionism in her family and fostering Weizmann's name in all quarters.

Soon Trumpeldor found his way to England with 120 of his demobilised muleteers. To add to Weizmann's problems, Jabotinsky now appropriated them as the samples in his briefcase of a great legion of volunteers. He pounded the pavements of Whitehall and dogged Zionist meetings with his strategy of national Jewish participation in the conquest of Palestine. Jabotinsky let it be known that Weizmann supported him.

The times were hardly propitious for such a scheme. The government was now deeply involved with the Arabs in the expectation of an insurrection against Constantinople, and was simultaneously negotiating a secret treaty with the French for the disposition of the spoils to come. Thus on all counts a Jewish army would raise unwelcome complications. The Jews of Britain particularly took fright. They had no desire to see their community in a separate formation. The Zionists among them recoiled from a vision of Anglo-Jewish battalions locked in combat with battalions of Turkish Jews, with civilians suffering massacre on the tragic Armenian precedent. The non-Zionists regarded the king's uniform as sealing their acceptance as true Englishmen, not dividing them off as an ally of hypothetical nationality. Weizmann found he could not raise the subject even to his most intimate colleagues, Ahad Ha'am, Sacher and Simon, without stirring up a storm. Gently, he dissociated himself from Jabotinsky's cause.

Early in 1916 England introduced conscription, a humiliating admission in a country where citizenship and patriotism were vaunted as synonymous. But in the East End of London, and in Cheetham Hill, the citizenship of the Jews was in many cases Russian, rendering them untouchable by the conscription law. These aliens cursed Jabotinsky as a trouble-maker; he merely redoubled his efforts. In the end the War Office began to weaken. Perhaps this confident Russian *could* deliver the goods – he inferred he had thousands waiting to enrol, in America besides Britain.

All over the United Kingdom great steel containers were bubbling with Weizmann's acetone. Problems arose in abundance in those dark, satanic mills, requiring the scientist's frequent absence from his laboratory and the Zionist scene in London. Manufacture was introduced in India, with prospects also in France and Canada. But Weizmann's relations with the official in charge of explosives at the Munitions department, Lord Moulton, were frigid.

One day Moulton received visitors: none other than Fernbach accompanied by his lawyers. The process was in fact his, asserted the Frenchman, developed at the Pasteur Institute. Weizmann roundly dismissed the charge, repudiating Fernbach's potato starch method as a failure, as indeed had been proved. Potatoes yielded acetone only in driblets, but in one plant alone, at Poole, Weizmann had achieved fermentation of 90,000 gallons of liquid, and he challenged any process in the world to equal it.

Fernbach retreated, though without conceding victory to his rival. Now Weizmann's anxieties for his post-war recompense could not be suppressed and, supported by Scott, he took the matter up with renewed force. Weizmann claimed a lump sum that he calculated would give him lifetime independence – the long cherished aim of his scientific career.

The government's attitude did not extend to such munificence. Somewhat tardily, he was made a cash award of £10,000. It was paid after the war, and judiciously invested in his young Manchester friends' thriving commercial enterprise, Marks and Spencer.

Butyl alcohol yielded a rare acetate, calculated before Weizmann isolated it at about £19,000 per ton, and now freely available at £70 per ton. Weizmann's reputation as a benefactor of industry spread through the world. Eventually, his maize process was discontinued in England and manufacture taken to the source of the crop across the Atlantic. It was bad news for Fernbach, who suffered defeat when two court actions, in England and the U.S.A., upheld the validity of his rival's patents.

And Weizmann's political formula for the redemption of Zion? That wonder was yet to come, but already the Jews could observe how a war-time laboratory was bringing their people to a peace-time goal. Within twenty years of Theodor Herzl's first Zionist Congress at Basle, the national movement was approaching a victory.

6

Forging the Compact

IN THE SPRING OF 1916 HERBERT SAMUEL, TROUBLED BY THE GULF separating the Zionist aspiration from what he knew of Britain's own plans for the Turkish Empire, brought his mentor Gaster together with Sir Mark Sykes, the government's principal advisor on the Near East. Sykes ('a bundle of prejudices, intuitions, half-sciences', Lawrence of Arabia styled him) seemed approving of all he heard of the Jewish national movement, as though learning of it for the first time. He did not reveal a great deal from his side, only enough to indicate that Britain and France were in a state of advanced negotiation regarding the future of the entire region.

Sykes had seen Samuel's memorandum on Palestine, now much-revised to fall somewhat short of the Jewish statehood of its author's earlier lyricism, and deduced from it that Zionism could be the secret weapon to win for Britain something coveted by France: control of Palestine. The romantic in Sykes surrendered to the Tory realist of the old Imperial school.

The war had not demolished the nineteenth century European assumption that wide areas of the globe could be held and developed without impairing the interests of native populations – indeed, local benefits would ensue, doubtless to be received with gratitude. It was thus no contradiction to discuss self-determination for subject peoples in the same breath as spheres of interest, the cynicism being visible only to the neutral observer or a rival aspirant. And opposition from the peoples destined to be the object of these blessings hardly arose for consideration.

Sykes's French opposite number, François Georges-Picot, was his Gallic equivalent. They promoted their respective causes with precision and zeal, concluding with the secret Sykes-Picot Treaty. This promised the two

James de Rothschild in dubious pose with some recruits for the Jewish Legion, 1918.

Weizmann with Arlosoroff (right) at a meeting of Transjordan sheikhs, Jerusalem, 1933. Among those standing are Isaac Ben-Zvi, who was to succeed Weizmann as President of Israel, and Moshe Shertok (Sharett), a future Prime Minister.

Balfour formally opening the Hebrew University, Mount Scopus, Jerusalem, 1925.

Powers indefinite freehold over an area bounded by the Mediterranean, the Red Sea, the Arabian Sea and the Persian Gulf. It was signed at a time when the British High Commissioner in Egypt, General McMahon, was dangling support for Arab independence to the Shereef of Mecca (Hussein, 'Descendant of the Prophet') in return for the latter's defection from the Turkish cause, and while Syrian patriots in Beirut and Damascus, who had been encouraged by the French, were being consigned by their Ottoman masters to the gallows.

Unlike Picot, Sykes had to reconcile his intentions for Britain with his sympathies for Arabism and Zionism. He was a friend of Armenian independence too, but realisation of this ideal would concern Russia rather than her Western allies. London was thus becoming entangled in a web of contradictory commitments in the Near East while Paris kept its eyes firmly on one objective only: the protection and extension of what it saw as French national interests.

Palestine as an entity stood precariously in the jig-saw of dispositions adumbrated both in the McMahon-Hussein agreement and the Sykes-Picot Treaty. It could easily disappear altogether. The pledge to Hussein was riddled with ambiguity and made no mention of Palestine at all. Not so the Anglo-French arrangement. It specified that the rectangle extending from the Dead Sea and Sea of Galilee to the coast, in fact the whole of central Palestine, form either an Anglo-Franco-Russian international regime or an Anglo-French condominium. Portions to the north and south, besides a generous enclave around Haifa Bay, would become totally British, or totally French, or go to Arab states under the protection of one or the other (see map p. 265). Little wonder, then, that Samuel, now back in the Cabinet as Home Secretary, thought it was time Sykes heard of Zionist aspirations from the movement's leaders themselves.

Though, of course, ignorant of the diplomatic goings-on in all their ramifications, Weizmann suspected, from the middle of 1916, that his concept of an Anglo-Zionist alliance in Palestine might easily fall casualty to the cause of Entente harmony. Indeed, the Sykes-Picot formula was no secret to Dorothy de Rothschild's husband James, who had doubtless learned of it, through his father the Baron, from the Quai d'Orsay. Zionism found no champions in the French Foreign Ministry after the outbreak of war, and Britain's flirtation with the Jews was labelled a chicanery.

As for the Arabs, Weizmann gave them only the barest thought. The Zionists had no Arab policy, and apparently needed none. The Jews could

W.—7

realise their ambitions in Palestine under the protection, for mutual advantage, of the British; and the Arabs would stand in a similar relation to the Jews, i.e., be 'protected'. True, the Zionists had in the past nodded acknowledgement to an existing Arab population in Palestine, but the idea that this people could be an obstacle rarely entered debate. Weizmann spoke in 1913 of the need to dispel Arab fears, arguing that the country had room for both peoples. 'We must explain to them,' he declared, 'that we wish to work together with them, and that it will be to their advantage if a great Jewish community arises in Palestine.'

He evidently understood Zionist colonisation to follow the pattern universally set in history, for no 'explanation' to the Arabs had as yet been proffered. The Jews' experience in Eastern Europe did not exclude harmony among different national groups living side-by-side. It had happened in seventeenth century Poland, where Jewish affairs were conducted by their own 'Council of the Four Lands', a system of autonomy still being advocated by many Jews in the Russian Empire of the First World War.

Stalemate on the Western Front, and the uneasy calm on the Near-Eastern battle-line south of Gaza and Beersheba, gave to the military aspects of the war the stupor of eternity. But the Entente Powers won a brilliant victory in seducing Arab allegiance from Constantinople's Holy War by means of the McMahon-Hussein agreement. The desert campaign on the Turkish flank under T. E. Lawrence and Hussein's son Feisal may not have constituted a great martial contribution, but it broke the Moslem world's identification with the Central Powers. Now the French could concentrate on their survival in Metropolitan France in the assurance of tranquillity among the Arab tribes of her North African possessions.

England thus had grounds in plenty for her reluctance to make a gesture that could be interpreted as an espousal of Zionism. The potential Jewish Lawrence, Jabotinsky, was still the travelling salesman of an army that didn't exist. A flickering Jewish resistance emerged in Palestine itself, in the form of a pro-British spy-ring led by an agronomist, Aaron Aaronson, but it attracted the displeasure of the Jews within the country, and would one day be betrayed by them. Aaronson received little encouragement from the British themselves. Zionism remained officially, theoretically, and factually, neutral. Weizmann in his way, and the unpopular Jabotinsky in his, were alone prepared to commit themselves. Sykes observed them both with silent approval.

With Sokolow beside him, Weizmann felt inhibited from promoting his plan in discussions, too nebulous to describe as negotiations, with the

British. As a pair they were in a vacuum, Berlin being enemy territory, Paris a Zionist desert, and Moscow a remote imponderable. Into the bargain, the two colleagues were not themselves of one mind, for Sokolow remained cold towards the fiercely British sentiments that anchored his comrade.

American Jewry remained a somnolent giant, and American Zionism an incapacitated dwarf whose eminent leader, Louis Brandeis, was a thrice-divided soul. Personally pro-Ally, he was tied to an outwardly neutralist but innately pro-German following, and as a Supreme Court Justice in the confidence of President Wilson he kept himself aloof from the fray.

To Samuel's embarrassment as Home Secretary and unofficial Jewish spokesman in the Cabinet, the alien immigrants ('slackers and shirkers', in the words of their own *Jewish Chronicle*) refrained in the main from taking the king's shilling, but continued to spend the war sewing the uniforms in which British conscripts were to die. Samuel was under pressure in the House of Commons, and threatened to deport them. Weizmann saw the danger of the controversy turning into a major scandal, and he appealed to Samuel to persevere with voluntary enlistment, with the reward of automatic naturalisation for the recruits.

Still they responded in pathetically small numbers. Here was Weizmann seeking to persuade the government of the Jews' faith in a destiny linked with Britain, yet there in the East End they were exploiting their Russian nationality (which they purported to abominate) to keep themselves out of the lines! This gave the anti-Zionist Jews unexpected ammunition in fighting the man who worked for Zionist and British interests as though they were one and the same.

He could not be frank with his colleague Sokolow; he could not openly support Jabotinsky; his so-called 'united Jewish mood' affronted the facts. How, then, could a government, itself tied down with commitments to others, regard him seriously? This situation may have continued indefinitely, were it not for Lloyd George's advent, as 1916 ended, as Prime Minister and supreme war-lord of England. To him, the Jews were a boon to this country, and the one he most admired was the scientist who had kept his promise about acetone.

While Minister of Munitions Lloyd George, despite constant prompting by C. P. Scott, remained deaf to pleas that Weizmann ('the most essential man in your department,' Scott said, 'and working practically for nothing') receive his acetone award. But as Prime Minister he repaid Weizmann a thousandfold, by keeping the subject of Palestine alive on the Cabinet agenda. Pessimistic about achieving a decisive victory against the Germans in France, Lloyd George was pinning his hopes on breaking the impasse with a push against the Turks in the desert.

Impatient with Sokolow, who drafted every document with an ear to objections by Brandeis and Tschlenow, dismissive of Cowen for his lame Presidency of the English Zionist Federation, dogged by the resentful Gaster, Weizmann decided this was the hour to assume the leadership in name as he had in fact. The President of the Federation in a Britain with its army in Palestine could, with little obstruction, exercise also the authority of world leader. Cowen was informed, and early in 1917 the transition was tactfully accomplished.

But one step forward was followed by two steps back, for Samuel, faithful to Asquith, left the government when Lloyd George manoeuvred himself into the Premiership. His place was taken by his cousin Edwin Montagu, a man whose hatred of Zionism, and resentment of his Jewish blood, was almost pathological.

Meanwhile Weizmann walked, as he confessed, 'on eggs'. He still had to look to Manchester for real, if over-zealous, encouragement. There, Israel Sieff and Simon Marks, now united by family ties with Sacher, formed a 'British Palestine Committee' which their happy economic position enabled them to conduct as a personal venture out of their own pockets. They brought in Herbert Sidebotham, Sacher's senior colleague on the *Guardian*, and began openly to campaign, in a new organ edited by Sacher, to 'reset the ancient glories of the Jewish nation in the freedom of a new British Dominion in Palestine'. Noble sentiments, but to Weizmann and Mark Sykes alike a blatant provocation of the French.

Sykes saw that he could no longer deny the Zionists a peep behind the curtain. He met them in February, 1917, at Gaster's Maida Vale home, with the rabbi in the Chair. Not unreasonably, Gaster thought of the meeting as implying his, rather than Weizmann's, leadership of the movement. Into his drawing-room stepped Samuel, Sokolow, Cowen, Bentwich and Sacher, Lord Rothschild (zoologist son of the deceased banker) with James de Rothschild, and Weizmann. Army headquarters in Cairo were working out an early attack upon Gaza and a drive through Palestine.

The Zionists gave the English official their proposal. It was as agreed between Weizmann and Samuel at their very first talk: a Jewish nation to be established in Palestine under exclusive British suzerainty. Sykes enumerated the difficulties: objections by the nascent Arab movement, Russia's aspirations, and French insistence on annexing at least a part of the region. Italy too now expected her price. But possibly the Zionists could ask for a British protectorate south of the line extending from Acre to the Sea of Galilee. This was the condominium rectangle of the Sykes-Picot Treaty. His hearers were appalled.

James asked point blank if an agreement had already been made with the French, rendering further discussion superfluous. Sykes hedged, and invited Samuel to speak on this, but the ex-Cabinet Minister, ever correct, refused to be drawn. However, the group discerned enough to suspect the worst, and the meeting dispersed with the Jews bleakly gazing into the distance as though the express train with their special compartment had just disappeared out of sight. Sykes gently intimated that the Zionists had better begin working on the French. It was of course the most desirable procedure – for him. The French might swallow the pill of a British Palestine if it were sweetened by Zionist advocacy. Sokolow was selected to take the matter up with Picot.

Sacher returned to Manchester convinced that Sykes's ostensible friendship was a threat to the very basis of Zionism. His new periodical had already spelt out his own views on the area of the notional British Dominion. He had included Damascus and the whole Golan plateau, with the Hedjaz railway down to Akaba as frontier, and taking in the Negev to Rafah.

Weizmann had looked angrily on this amateur map-making as wild and injudicious, but he too had his suspicions of Sykes. These were confirmed in March, 1917, on the conquest of Baghdad. Sykes composed a proclamation to the city giving encouragement to the Arabs but containing not a mention of the Jews – and this in a capital where they constituted a third of the 200,000 population, the largest Jewish community in Arabia. Sykes was due out to Egypt as political officer with the advancing British armies, and Weizmann intimated to Scott, for the benefit of Lloyd George, that he might accompany Sykes and himself negotiate with the Arabs as Palestine was occupied. He was indeed despatched on a journey by the Premier, but it was not the errand he had in mind.

Europe was dragging a weary course through its third year of war, and bread riots in Petrograd sounded the knell for Tzarism. While revolutionary Russia's continued participation in the war hung in the balance, Lloyd George nevertheless dreamed of a great popular movement in that country driving the Germans back, and Weizmann too clutched at straws, hoping for the weight of a free Jewish multitude in Russia to bring much-needed reinforcement to the Zionist cause. In the early weeks of the

Revolution it seemed he could be right, even though Tschlenow tartly advised him in a letter that it was foolhardy to build on a British victory in the struggle. If only American Jewry could be made to respond; if only Brandeis would emerge from his Washington isolation and declare his position – just one powerful speech would convince Whitehall that the Jews merited recognition as a trustworthy ally!

Brandeis dared not speak. Insofar as the mass of American Jews read the situation, the Anglo-Russian alliance was rooted in a barbaric partnership between the savage oppressor of the Irish and an Asiatic despotism. American Jews had telegraphed to Herbert Samuel in October, 1916, protesting at his threat to deport aliens in Britain failing to enlist.

Weizmann was stepping carefully with the Americans in the knowledge that his name as yet evoked little enthusiasm across the Atlantic. The Germans had an agent among the Jews there, a Zionist and art-dealer, Isaac Straus, whom Weizmann scornfully dubbed 'the man who stole the Monna Lisa'. Maybe, but he was so acceptable that he even sat, for a time, on the Zionist Committee in New York. The French likewise stationed a Jewish representative in America, but their man, a Sorbonne academic, was less cleverly chosen.

Not unwisely, Britain placed little store on such activities, perhaps because of what they had learned from Alexander Aaronson, brother of the leader of the perilous espionage network behind the Turkish lines; he had conducted a brief intelligence operation in New York. But early in April the situation changed dramatically for American Jewry. Events brought their country into the war as an 'associate', if not an ally, of the Entente Powers. Soon the dough-boys would have to brave those remorseless submarines in a harrowing crossing of the Atlantic. The American Zionists, who had but recently castigated Jabotinsky's efforts to form a Jewish Legion as 'an absurdity as well as a disloyal act', now had to think afresh. Nevertheless they saw little cause for gloom when the British assault upon Gaza stumbled to a halt, for President Wilson had excluded Turkey from his declaration of war.

America was, however, an awakening giant, presenting exciting possibilities for the advancement of Weizmann's dream of a Jewish future in a British Palestine. He begged Sacher to undertake a mission there. The journalist was willing, but before arrangements could be made it was learned that a more exalted emissary would shortly be on his way: Arthur Balfour, Lloyd George's newly-appointed Foreign Secretary and a man Weizmann had long been cultivating for just such an eventuality.

An appeal went to Brandeis urging him to assure Balfour that American Jewry had no dearer wish than to see Britain firmly ensconced in Palestine. This could turn the scales, for the Foreign Secretary's sympathy with Zionism, and personal esteem for Weizmann, would not extend to braving out alone the displeasure of the French. Moreover, Sokolow's departure for Paris, recommended by Sykes, was making his colleague uneasy. Suppose Sokolow were to succumb to the persuasiveness of his hosts? He might even return with a French declaration favouring Zionist aims. That, after all, was the object of Sokolow's errand, but it was the last thing Weizmann desired at this stage. French endorsement would be welcome only after the British had shown their hand, and made an effective advance into Palestine, and fixed the country's northern frontiers not at Acre but at the Lebanese foothills.

Soon after America intervened in the war, Scott informed Weizmann that a French editor had divulged to him particulars of an Anglo-French pact to establish an international regime in a truncated Palestine. So treachery was not too harsh a word to apply to Sykes! Their friend at court had spoken of negotiations, and French susceptibilities, not of a treaty signed and sealed. Imperiously, Weizmann ordered Sokolow to return to London. The latter, wounded, replied with dignity that his work was unfinished, that he was optimistic for the outcome, and that furthermore he was proceeding, at Sykes' request, to Rome. Barely containing himself, Weizmann went to Samuel with a warning that the Zionists would not allow themselves to be sacrificed. 'This is dividing the skin of the bear before it is killed!' he protested.

Samuel shamefacedly agreed, but excused himself for not having spoken earlier: he could not divulge a Cabinet secret. Nevertheless, he admitted that the agreement was not satisfactory to Britain, and Weizmann would be justified in building up Jewish opposition to the arrangement.

In Balfour's absence, the Acting Foreign Secretary, Lord Robert Cecil, was similarly a recipient of Weizmann's ire. The Jews would never agree to a division of Palestine that would destroy thirty years of colonisation work in the north, he was warned. A Jewish irredentist movement would be born; Britain would not be able to hold the Haifa naval base she desired if this were located within an unfriendly international regime; the entire scheme offended the new anti-annexationist principles upon which America had entered the war. Furthermore, the cynicism of the arrangement could speed Russia's drift out of the Entente.

The Zionist leader informed Cecil that he was ready to travel to Palestine (and Sykes was now more than eager to have him there to help assuage Arab resentment) but only if it were clearly understood that his objective was a Jewish Palestine under British aegis. This was all very well, Cecil countered, but wasn't it time that the other induced the Jews of the world to voice such a desire themselves? He had touched Weizmann's Achilles heel.

Balfour was soon to have confirmation of this, from his own discussions with Brandeis. The Justice saw little hope of endorsement of an Anglo-Zionist combination by President Wilson, who had no wish to alienate the Turks. He therefore refused to encourage his chief to make any public statement on Zionist aims, and, of course, said little that was helpful on his own behalf. The Foreign Secretary returned home pessimistic about acceptance of a British regime in Palestine from that quarter, except on the unlikely basis of an Anglo-American condominium.

Nevertheless by the middle of 1917 Weizmann's tenacious hammering of his case, the eloquence with which he put his arguments, his stature as a Jewish star in the ascendant, even his aristocratic dismissal of opposition, Jewish and gentile, were bringing their consummation. The Prime Minister himself lectured Sykes before the latter travelled to the Near East. No commitments were to be made to the Arabs, Lloyd George ordered, as regards Palestine, and nothing done to hamper the Zionist movement's development under British auspices. Within days, editorials appeared in British newspapers welcoming the impending establishment of the Jewish State.

This was not what Weizmann had demanded, or even desired. He convened a special conference of the Zionist Federation to proclaim that he sought, in the first place, the international recognition of British suzerainty. And this would be the frame in which a Jewish homeland could ultimately be established: step by step, and only after the importation of people, their skills and their capital.

The speech raised official Zionist policy at last out of its morass of hints and whisperings and delicate private soundings. It was Weizmann serving notice on Brandeis, on Tschlenow, and on Sokolow, that they were now joined irrevocably not just to the Allies' side in the war, but to a single Power on that side. And it was advertisement to the government that he was playing his part, so they must hurry and play theirs. Only a man who regarded himself as the spokesman of the Jewish national will throughout the world could have made such a speech at such a time. Others, perhaps more qualified than he, could have assumed the role, but they shrunk from it. Sokolow at last returned to London, harbinger of generous sentiments from the French and Italian governments, and from the Pope. But Britain was in the act of conquering Palestine, and her voice would therefore be the paramount one.

Sir Mark Sykes, Catholic politician-diplomat and empire-builder, now sent an urgent request to Weizmann not to delay joining him at General Allenby's headquarters in the field. If this were not possible, he wanted Aaron Aaronson, Britain's former intelligence agent. As well despatch a time-bomb: Aaronson was hated as an enemy by the Jews in Palestine, while he in turn despised the London Zionists for what was to him cowardice in not acknowledging his recent endeavours against the Turks. Moreover, having been the first to raise the flag of Jewish resistance in Palestine, he felt he was entitled to the leadership of the movement. Weizmann decided that he knew better than Sykes what was good both for England and the Zionists, and Aaronson remained in England. He himself, at the behest of the Foreign Office, went off – to Gibraltar.

An unexpected element had entered the situation; one of those diversions that gave to the First World War its complexion of a macabre tournament designed and conducted by fantasists. Henry Morgenthau, the erstwhile American Ambassador in Constantinople, believed he could extricate Turkey from the Central Powers and sign a separate peace. The move was the reverse of welcome to the British, then planning to outflank the Turco-German forces at Beersheba. But the French, who unlike their ally were blanketed with devastation on their own soil, saw the undoubted attraction of the scheme. They could be reconciled to leaving an exhausted and pliable Turkey in command of her Asiatic possessions if this brought British troops back from the Nile to reinforce the Western Front. Lloyd George was not prepared to pay the price. Nevertheless, President Wilson had given Morgenthau his blessing and the Americans had to be humoured.

Weizmann considered Morgenthau's intervention wholly dangerous. He had long before revised his judgment of this American as a possible world Jewish leader, and now regarded him only as an insensitive millionaire out to purchase fame with his bank-balance. Weizmann at last comprehended the reluctance of Brandeis to support an Anglo-Zionist regime in Palestine, since the Justice had been colluding with Morgenthau to give the peace-seeking venture a mask of Jewish-American philanthropy. It was in this context that Weizmann's name first cropped up, for the bid to bring Turkey gracefully out of the war had been announced as a mission to investigate reports of atrocities against the Palestine-Jewish population.

To lend authenticity to this purpose, Morgenthau had chosen known American Zionists as his aides. One of them, the young attorney Felix Frankfurter, was a Brandeis confidant attached to the War Department in Washington. The presence of a British Zionist would complete the masquerade.

Atrocity-mongering is of course a common propaganda weapon in war, and the Turks had been evacuating foreigners, that is, Jews, from the south of Palestine in preparation for the impending battle. This was summarily undertaken without prior warning, and was accompanied by some harshness. But there was no brutality, and the Turks' spoliation had been restricted to stealing the Jews' livestock.

Playing gambit for gambit, the British sanctioned Weizmann's appointment as their emissary. Privately, he was instructed to engage Morgenthau at Gibraltar and dissuade him from proceeding further. Yet he was disinclined to accept, both because he suspected a concealed British motive in selecting him, and because his differences with the anti-Zionist Jews in London were by no means settled. Balfour had asked for a formula relating to Jewish aspirations in Palestine, and this was no time for him to be absent from the scene.

He put his doubts to C. P. Scott. 'Why doesn't Lloyd George delegate the task to Sykes?' he asked. Sykes was on more serious business, apparently, and Weizmann indicated the futility of the entire venture by hinting that his colleague Sacher might go and talk to Morgenthau. No, Weizmann had to be the man.

Accompanied by a secret service agent, he made what appeared to be a suitable cloak and dagger journey through neutral Spain. In regarding himself as a peculiar choice for a bizarre mission Weizmann was doing the government less than justice. Balfour aspired not merely to scotch the Morgenthau plan but to achieve its opposite: bring America into the Near Eastern war, and he had observed in Washington how Jews like Brandeis and Morgenthau wandered at will through the portals of power. Who better then to put out feelers among this Hebrew nexus than his favourite Zionist? No doubt the Jews had an exclusive, mysterious way of talking to each other (Balfour was educated in anti-semitism) and Weizmann's forceful advocacy could well impress his co-religionists at Gibraltar. A word in their ears would surely find its way back to the American President.

The meeting with Morgenthau took place in a secluded casemate of the Rock early in July. In a letter to Vera, Weizmann described the American as 'exactly the same type as Wolffsohn, but more modest and less clever'. Later he revised his view of Morgenthau's modesty: 'He has great ambition, not commensurate with his abilities and knowledge.' Nevertheless the scheme was not divorced from realism. Turkey was bankrupt, unable to wage war except as Germany's kitchen-hand. Anti-German sentiment had risen with the surrender of Baghdad, and Enver Pasha, the war leader,was in open conflict with Talaat, the Prime Minister. Reporting this intelligence to the Foreign Office, Weizmann emphasised that he had instructed Morgenthau not to involve the Zionist Organisation in his efforts, for the three subject peoples, Jews, Arabs and Armenians, refused to live any longer under Ottoman tutelage.

Weizmann performed his function as the faithful servant of an England at last entangled with his own cause. A British declaration in support of the movement was now a certainty, so he was eloquent about American participation in the Near Eastern theatre. He took it upon himself to promise that, if the Americans reached the point of making war against Turkey, a Jewish force could be created for service there. This was carrying the banner for Jabotinsky, and contrary to the expressed policy of the movement, in England or anywhere.

Morgenthau indeed had second thoughts about his peace soundings, probably due more to the changed circumstances since he first mooted the idea than to Weizmann's eloquence. Failure of the Russians to break through in the Caucasus, and of the British to breach the Palestine front, were giving the Turks fresh heart. He decided not to proceed. Weizmann pursued his canvassing of American participation through Frankfurter, who struck him as a 'clever young man, and apparently a good Zionist'. The latter wrote to him from Washington that the idea of declaring war on Turkey was not rejected out of hand in America, and he could think of no better candidate than the chemist himself for such a mission on behalf of Britain. If this be so, Weizmann conjectured, an immediate Zionist pronouncement by the Cabinet could help him achieve an historic diplomatic stroke for the Allied cause. A question poses itself: Did he engineer Frankfurter's letter in the first place? It was not beyond him, for he began at once planning such a trip, and received money from Baron Edmond de Rothschild to finance it.

New developments drove the idea into Weizmann's storehouse of unrealised dreams. For he had returned to London to a revolt by the Zionist Federation over his encouragement of Jabotinsky's Jewish army campaign. Trumpeldor had betaken himself to Russia to organise a Jewish invasion of the Ottoman Empire from the north. Jabotinsky, battling alone, was successfully steering a path through all the objections of the War Office only to confront his stiffest obstruction from the Jews. The storm had been simmering for two years. Weizmann was warned, most vociferously by the trio closest to him, Ahad Ha'am, Simon and Sacher, that he was taking the movement along a direction they could not accept: Jews were ready to fight as citizens, not as a nation. It was an argument that sat better with their opponents, whose spokesman in the government, the Secretary of State for India Edwin Montagu, was determined to kill any declaration of support for a Jewish National Home with his last breath. Jews of Russian nationality were already being packed home by a government unwilling to tolerate their apathy towards the war one more day.

Weizmann was disgusted. True, he had wavered. Earlier, when he observed the horror with which so many Zionists regarded Jabotinsky's project, he had kept his silence, hoping that the problem would go away as the aliens melted into British formations. But it had not, for they had not. It was now September, 1917. The War Office was bewildered. Jabotinsky had convinced them that the prospect of joining a legion to march through Palestine would bring recruits in great number, and yet other Zionists would not have it at any cost. Suddenly, to add to the gentile confusion, some Jewish patricians of imposing nomenclature, including a Cabinet Minister, said: 'Very well, if you will, but keep the term "Jew" out of the Legion's designation. We're as British as you are!'

Weizmann had asked for the British announcement of Zionist support that month, to be issued as an historic gift to Jewry for their New Year. Now he felt the paralysing hand of the Diaspora mentality restraining his every move. It had been a difficult, unsatisfactory year, in which, among other trials, his maize fermentation had to be transferred to Canada and a period of great tension had ensued while he experimented with horse chestnuts (those 'conkers' of English schoolboys' favourite autumn game, now adapted to a sterner purpose). Also, he was having eye trouble, and this perplexed the doctors and depressed him. In a fit of anger, he resigned from the Presidency of the Zionist Federation.

But the wheel had turned too far. Weizmann was the man most essential to Zionism's purpose in its moment of destiny. Circumstances, and personality complications, were disqualifying every rival for the leadership. Sokolow, too serene, as cautious as he was contemplative, belied his position as a world figure in times of crisis. Tschlenow was now reined, not liberated, by the mood of revolutionary Russia, and though he would shortly come back to London, he would arrive as a visitor from a toppled world. Brandeis was unlikely to step down from his place in the Supreme Court to lead the quarrelsome Jews. Gaster's vanity prevented his association with any team. Henceforth the demand for British support of political Zionism could not be divorced from the creation of a Jewish army to help conquer Palestine. But Weizmann alone among the principal figures concerned saw them as the same cause.

He lectured his detractors: 'For three years we have been working for a people without a name, a people not yet ready to wage the tremendous struggle necessary to establish a Jewish society. The war came too early for us.' Nevertheless they begged him to remain. It was of course what he wanted.

The government finally agreed to enrol volunteers in battalions of an existing regiment, thus burying the provocative adjective 'Jewish' in a numeral. Jabotinsky took his recruits into the Thirty-Eighth Royal Fusiliers, and Weizmann denounced Montagu to Philip Kerr, Lloyd George's foreign affairs adviser, as a 'great Hindu nationalist who thought it his duty to combat Jewish nationalism . . . When such gentlemen come out in the open they are always defeated, so they work in the dark and we are powerless . . . Their only claim to Judaism is that they are working for its disappearance.'

With the exception of Montagu and Lord Curzon, every member of Lloyd George's Coalition favoured a statement to the effect that 'His Majesty's Government accept the principle that Palestine should be reconstituted as the national home of the Jewish people.' But in view of the opposition, Balfour told Weizmann, he was cabling President Wilson direct for his views. The Zionist simultaneously contacted Brandeis.

The situation was unchanged as far as Washington was concerned. The President considered the times to be inauspicious for a public announcement from the White House, and Brandeis himself continued to equivocate. The formula now seemed too forthright also to the British. September was almost gone, and Weizmann, who now enlisted Lord Rothschild in his pressure on the government, managed to capture Lloyd George for a few minutes' conversation, to be told that the issue would be on the agenda of the next Cabinet meeting, October 4. Weizmann relentlessly maintained the pace, firing off letters to Balfour and Philip Kerr, to warn them against being deceived or intimidated 'by the talk of a few Jewish financiers who happen to have lived in Great Britain for three or four generations'.

Montagu was present at the October 4 meeting, and again succeeded, with a plea that combined his political objections as the representative of the people of partly-Moslem India with his personal objections as an Englishman of the Mosaic faith (in fact he had little religious faith), in preventing a decision. It was indeed his last anti-Zionist gasp, for he was about to leave for the distant territory in whose name he affected such eloquence.

The original draft for a declaration had now been analysed and amended by a dozen Jewish worthies, including Brandeis. Some were violently anti-Zionist, and the consortium of brain and temperament could never result in a statement agreeable to all of them. Weizmann hovered around Downing Street for the Cabinet meeting of October 25, expecting to be called. It would have been an historically unique event, but the item had to give way to more urgent military affairs. Disconsolately, Weizmann retired to his laboratory, to find that the London Fire Brigade had just left, and that it was half-destroyed. He was now a mass of nerves.

With Montagu's departure, Curzon remained the lone Cabinet voice opposed to any encouragement being given to the Jews for a national future in Palestine, as an injustice to the Arabs. His colleagues, however, resisted on the grounds that they did not entertain the creation of a Jewish State, which Weizmann himself saw as a development so far in the future as to be purely academic. He had been persuasive to the Foreign Office that the mass of Jewry, which implied mainly those in America and Russia, were Zionist to a man. He had caused resolutions to be passed by any identifiable Zionist group in England, and he produced these whenever prominent Jewish individuals in England raised their dissident voices. He ensured that every scrap of evidence indicating German movement towards a Zionist declaration was given to his friends in Whitehall.

The logic of his campaign, surely his alone in the spectrum of world-wide Jewish sentiment, was that a British pronouncement could achieve a double purpose for his adopted country: bring American-Jewish influence to bear on a Washington declaration of war against Turkey; and keep a crumbling Russia, where the Jews were a factor both in the Kerensky party and the newly-formed Soviets of the Bolsheviks, within the Entente.

On October 31 Weizmann prevailed. The Cabinet agreed the wording of a statement, the celebrated Balfour Declaration. It succeeded neither in bringing American troops to the Near Eastern theatre, nor in keeping

Russia in the war. It did, however, serve the imperial design of Herbert Samuel and Mark Sykes in granting a certificate of good intent to Britain's sole occupation of Palestine. It gave the Jews a secular twentieth century legality for the Return to the Holy Land, when hitherto that legality rested only on an ancient presence, a majestic literature and a mystical idea.

7

Valley of Dry Bones

AFTER A NINE-DAY VOYAGE THE CANBERRA DOCKED AT ALEXANDRIA AT last, and Chaim Weizmann, fortified with letters of authority from Lloyd George and Arthur Balfour, disembarked from the military transport at the head of a Zionist Commission. It was late March, 1918, and he would be in Palestine for the Passover. What more appropriate season than the Festival of Deliverance for this first official Jewish delegation to enter the Holy Land!

He had come to cement the partnership forged with England for their joint endeavour, a Jewish National Home under the protection of the British Crown; to be achieved, apparently, with the acquiescence of the Arab peoples, who were themselves anticipating a new era of freedom in the dismemberment of the Ottoman Empire.

Turkey was far from defeat, and Palestine's conquest still a long way off. The army was held to a line above Jaffa that stretched towards Jericho and the Dead Sea. It was a small corps, and General Allenby, commanding the Egyptian Expeditionary Force, knew only too well that this theatre was peripheral to the main struggle. The outcome would be decided on the battlefields of France, which were draining the strength and absorbing the concentrated emotions of the nations in a holocaust that had lately claimed the life of the general's only son.

Weizmann had been reluctant to arrive earlier, ignoring the appeals of Sir Mark Sykes to do so. The Egyptian atmosphere was highly charged. Major controversies were breeding minor conspiracies here, concerning strategy, and the ultimate destiny of the region, and the role of the French as a sensitive junior ally in the Near Eastern war. The Palestine refugees were lying in wait for him, as though he possessed the funds to com-

With pioneer settlers in the Jezreel Valley. Beside Weizmann is Levi Eshkol, Prime Minister of Israel during the war of 1967.

Yitzak Sadeh, founder of the Palmach, the Jews' permanent defence force, with Moshe Dayan (left) and Yigal Allon in 1938.

Ramsay MacDonald, British Prime Minister
1924 and 1929–35.

Haj Amin el Husseini, Mufti of Jerusalem.

Blanche ('Baffy') Dugdale.

With Albert Einstein.

pensate them for houses commandeered and farms lost, and could write out permits for their return home.

On the other hand he feared a danger in arriving late. A Jewish presence was vital with every foot of land yielded, to demonstrate that the Jews, a different people now that they had Britain's promise, radiated purpose and capability as a nation on the point of self-determination.

The forty-three year old chemist had left London the most renowned, if not the most influential, Jewish personality of the day. The king had received him at Buckingham Palace – Sykes had sponsored the little ceremony, then regretted it. That erratic man sought at the last moment to have the audience cancelled, but Weizmann would not agreee. He knew the limitations of the feeble organisation he could truly describe as his movement, so every gesture helped. Now he had made his impact and earned his status in the world: the Jews always honoured most those of their sons who won their fame among the gentiles.

His perseverance of three years, the strain of argument with friend and foe, had made him into steel, though tempered always with humour and glossed with high irony. He could plead but never beg, he could express a pathos that nullified despair, and he turned self-pride into an attribute. Some found his manner overbearing; to others it conveyed an aristocracy of personality, humbling the aristocracy of blood. He spoke for the Jews as one risen out of their tragic and anomalous station in history, and though he loved his people in the abstract sense, he was discomforted by their character, and detached from their painful, sterile self-absorption. A mystique attached to his war work for Britain. This won him respect in official circles as a sage, familiar to them from the Bible; but he also inspired suspicion, for to the upper-class British mind modern science stood close to alchemy, as Zionism did to Bolshevism. Indeed, even Weizmann's face bore an uncanny resemblance to Lenin's.

His Zionist Commission was a group of estimable men, but hardly as Weizmann himself would have chosen it. He had thought of a delegation of exalted names and great talents, by implication an extra-territorial administration, to herald the new era of Jewish participation in world affairs: Brandeis or Frankfurter perhaps from America; and from Russia the most representative Jews, now ostensibly released from the crushing neurosis of Tzarism.

The Americans remained caged by their government's non-belligerency towards Constantinople, or so they maintained. They would send relief, and a medical unit. They could accept no political role. Weizmann had yet

w.—8

to learn the degree to which an American Zionist was first an American, second a Jew, and a Zionist only when that treasured ethos, Americanism, sanctioned it.

His first choice for Russia, Tschlenow, had died in London shortly after his arrival late in 1917. Telegrams pressed Moscow for further nominees, and two names returned with unfailing regularity: Leo Motzkin and Menahem Ussishkin. The former waited in Copenhagen with bags packed, only to be rejected by Weizmann. Ussishkin, in Odessa, was marooned by the revolutionary tide swirling over the Ukraine. Throughout the war his views had not wavered: Zionism must be pro-Turk, anti-Ally; it must denounce any Jewish army invading Palestine, whether it be Jabotinsky's enrolled in England or Trumpeldor's in Russia. But he was now a converted soul.

Ussishkin was acceptable – had to be, in fact, because Weizmann realised he could not be ignored. The old campaigner earnestly believed he was due to join a government of which Weizmann was the Prime Minister. However, it took a further year to bring him out of Russia, in time for no more than the delivery of a Hebrew oration before the victorious Powers assembled in Paris.

Weizmann was discouraging of any candidate from France. Zionism merely whimpered there, and like their American confrères, the Jews there saw the cause through the eyes of their government. He was reckoning without Baron Edmond. The latter forced on him Sylvain Lévi, a professor of Sanskrit and official of that most assiduous of French empire-building organisations, the *Alliance Israélite*. Lévi took no pains to conceal his role as a servant of the Quai d'Orsay, but Balfour, alive as ever to the susceptibilities of Britain's questioning ally, did not find this unwelcome. The Foreign Secretary asked Weizmann additionally to enrol an Italian, doubtless visualising one Mediterranean representative neutralising the other. A gentleman of the Rome Jewish nobility was produced, but he arrived in Palestine only at the end of Weizmann's stay.

There also disembarked at Alexandria Joseph Cowen, once an adversary but now revealing unsuspected virtues as Weizmann's loyal second-in-command, and Leon Simon, on three months' leave from his Civil Service post. Cowen had persuaded his brother-in-law, the psychiatrist David Eder, to join in his medical capacity, and this added a man hitherto cold towards Zionism (his wife was an aunt by marriage of the Bolshevik Maxim Litvinov). Israel Sieff came along as the Commission's Secretary, and was worked the hardest of them all.

These formed the Commission proper. Accompanying them were men of ambivalent status who at times caused heart-searching, and the occasional scene. One of them was Aaron Aaronson, recently returned from America. Immediately upon issuance of the government's Zionist declaration, the Foreign Office arranged with Weizmann that the former espionage agent undertake a mission among the Jews of the United States. He had been instructed to make no speeches and give no interviews, a prohibition he resented.

What, then, had been the purpose of Aaronson's mission? America was already in the European war, so his task manifestly was to persuade his friends in the direction Weizmann himself had begun in Gibraltar: induce them to work for American participation on the Palestine front. This conformed to Weizmann's undertaking of a *quid pro quo* for the Anglo-Zionist alliance. It was a double miscalculation. American Jews had little influence in those days on their government's policy. They followed it, but could not lead it. And the defeat of Turkey ranked not at all among Washington's priorities. Aaronson's sojourn in the United States was short-lived.

Another uncertain passenger on the *Canberra*, the Baron's son James, was of the Commission only when it pleased him. He had transferred from the French army to the British, his Zionist ardour could fluctuate, and he sometimes remained apart. On one occasion he was reprimanded by Weizmann, an incident which struck Sylvain Lévi as *lèse-majesté*. His name was his authorisation, and he lent some of its glory to the Commission as a whole. In Palestine he would be acclaimed as the Crown Prince of Israel, the son of the country's greatest benefactor. Enrolment of Palestine Jews in the British army was still awaiting sanction, and one day he would conduct the recruiting campaign.

James de Rothschild was officially A.D.C. to Major William Ormsby-Gore, the Zionist Commission's political liaison officer and an old hand from the Arab Bureau, the intelligence branch of the Foreign Office in Cairo. Like his superior Sykes, Ormsby-Gore placed great trust in Aaronson. He considered himself a Zionist, and was familiar with the tangling skeins of Britain's negotiations with Arabs, Jews and French. Weizmann was glad to have him aboard. In truth Ormsby-Gore's brief was as much to restrain the Zionist Commission's intentions as to facilitate them. He was not long in doing so. He resisted Weizmann's determination to time his entrance into Jaffa with the Passover, on the grounds that a demonstration could ensue to give offence to the Arabs.

Weizmann was wounded, but he had grown reconciled to disappointments, beginning with the Balfour Declaration itself. The pronouncement
he had extracted from the British government on November 2, 1917, did
not of itself accord recognition to his personal role in the negotiations. It
was addressed to Lord Rothschild, James's kinsman, who occupied no
significant office in public life, and was to reveal little attachment to the
Zionist cause subsequent to 1917. Balfour's letter to Rothschild deliberately eschewed the character of a great document of policy, and of
course carried no hint of Britain's own purpose in Palestine:

> I have much pleasure in conveying to you, on behalf of His Majesty's
> Government, the following declaration of sympathy with Jewish Zionist
> aspirations which has been submitted to, and approved by, the Cabinet:
> 'His Majesty's Government view with favour the establishment in
> Palestine of a national home for the Jewish people, and will use their
> best endeavours to facilitate the achievement of this object, it being
> clearly understood that nothing shall be done which may prejudice the
> civil and religious rights of existing non-Jewish communities in Palestine,
> or the rights and political status enjoyed by Jews in any other country.'
> I should be grateful if you would bring this declaration to the knowledge
> of the Zionist Federation.

No statement could have spoken more warily, or less directly, to the
man who had been offering himself as Britain's bridge to Zion. Both
Balfour and Lloyd George subsequently declared that it did not preclude
the creation of a Jewish State, but at that time Britain had neither the
right, nor the ability, nor the desire, nor the courage, to award the country
to the Jews. The terms 'Palestine' and 'Jewish national home' were, like
Italy before her unification, geographical abstractions. The obliqueness
with which the Zionist Federation is mentioned speaks volumes for official
hesitation to regard that organisation as fully representative of the Jews;
its very endorsement by Clemenceau's government, and its acquiescence,
after some initial shock, by King Hussein of the Hedjaz, renders its
draftsmanship – the combined effort of Lord Milner and Leopold Amery –
both a triumph and a tragedy.

Weizmann consoled himself in the knowledge that, even were Palestine
then Britain's to give away, the Jews could not have taken it in their
keeping. Zionism had not the people nor the means. One day, he anticipated, vast numbers of immigrants would be coming, but only after years

of preparation. The first step was for Britain to install herself legally and effectively in the country. A Power that had granted self-government to large parts of its colonial empire would surely not deny the Jews theirs, provided they availed themselves of the historic opportunities now before them.

Despite the studied nuances of the Balfour Declaration, the Jews took from it all that they hoped, the Arabs all that they feared. Few American Jews were prompted into paroxysms of enthusiasm, and those who read it to signify the ultimate creation of a Jewish government were spared by Washington's stand from any obligation to facilitate such an eventuality. Weizmann, like Jabotinsky, had conjured up the vision of Jewish soldiers in their hosts sailing the Atlantic to participate in the conquest of Palestine – almost an American military campaign in itself. But Washington forbade its citizens to volunteer for service in that theatre, and the expectation remained unfulfilled.

Those arriving at the British recruiting office in New York were foreign nationals, mainly Russian and Palestinian refugees. They included the young socialists David Ben-Gurion and Isaac Ben-Zvi (the one would be an Israeli Prime Minister, the other an Israeli President, in the years to come), who switched allegiance immediately on publication of the British statement. Hitherto they had calculated on a Turkish victory. Now they appealed to their comrades to join them and fight for Britain, but their activities produced volunteers little in excess of battalion strength. As the Thirty-Ninth Royal Fusiliers, they reached the Near Eastern theatre just in time to kick their heels resentfully in the rearguard, for by then the war in the East had become a race to Damascus.

Thus the stature of the Zionist Commission disembarking at Alexandria was finely balanced. Without Weizmann it could almost be discounted; with him it embodied the will, if ever so vaguely, of a Jewish world of as yet unreleased and unknown strength. But pretensions of grandeur were out of place.

Dislocation, a halt to trade, the closure of most institutions – Turkish, Arab and Jewish – had done more to turn Palestine into a beleagured land than the ravages of war. The farming colonies were filled with vigorous, happy children to bring joy to the heart, but Jaffa was a half-empty town, Jerusalem an overcrowded and starving one. The front line ran destructively through the Jewish colony of Petach Tikva. Weizmann's sister Gita, whose ambition since childhood was to be a musician, had remained at her piano in Jaffa throughout; and she bravely belittled her hardships when, reunited with her brother in Cairo, she recounted her experiences. And

Fruma, their dentist sister, what of her? Gita believed she was in Haifa awaiting the arrival of her husband from Poland. In fact Fruma had been permitted, with the collapse of Russia, to return home. The story was not uncommon. Weizmann's own family was a microcosm of Palestine Jewry, perplexed, short of food, constantly on the move. The war hovered in southern Palestine as an uncertain crusade, Allenby acting with great caution as he sent back detachment after detachment to feed the Moloch in Europe.

If the Balfour Declaration was not a complete secret in Palestine, this was scarcely the fault of the general. Weizmann regarded as unpardonable Allenby's failure to make a public announcement of it, but the other quoted the Hague Convention on the laws and usages of war to him. An advancing army was obliged to maintain the civil *status quo*.

Weizmann considered the implications: all the officials of the old regime retained, to conduct the country as corruptly as their previous masters would have wished, and without a single Jew in a public post. But Allenby would of course have publicised the Declaration, and introduced administrative changes, had London instructed him to do so. Evidently no such order had arrived. In occupied Eastern Europe, on the other hand, propaganda leaflets with the text of the Declaration had been dropped from aircraft by the thousand.

Allenby had further reason for his reticence, for Jamal Pasha, the Turkish commander who conducted his war as though he was also the master of Constantinople, was offering substantial bait to Feisal in order to win him back, and the Arabs were mercurial to a man. Allenby urged Weizmann to visit Feisal in his desert headquarters; he would quickly realise how England's hands were tied. Weizmann agreed to do so, but why not also give encouragement to the local Jews? True, they were only a depleted minority, cowed and hostile, but surely worthy of attention as a potential source of support! Particularly in Jerusalem, where they formed the majority.

Jerusalem! After the reports he had received Weizmann dreaded going near the place. It made a sorry spectacle of quarrelsome sects in a state of near-demoralisation. Famine had brought prostitution and petty crime in its trail. Throughout the war a handful of Zionist officials struggled to impose some order, and the equitable distribution of relief funds. Allenby did not trust such functionaries. Mainly German nationals, they had been travelling to Damascus and Constantinople almost at will until he took the city.

So the Zionist Commission found itself bogged down in patchwork welfare. Urgent telegrams reached Sokolow and Brandeis from Weizmann demanding money, as well as teachers, doctors, engineers – in fact technicians of all kinds. Cowen sought to restore order to the affairs of their bank, the Anglo-Palestine Company, and promised loans to the farmers, submerged in three years of debt. Simon and Eder stationed themselves in Jerusalem, to worry about schools, and bakeries, and sewerage, and the problem of 3,000 Jewish orphans, many of them fathered by soldiers of a variety of nationalities. All spirit seemed to have deserted the land. The replies from New York and London spoke of unavoidable delays in the despatch of aid: the Zionist Commission must shift as best it could.

The Holy City, when Weizman arrived there, seemed to have changed little since Mark Twain had grieved over it fifty years earlier as 'the stateliest name in history losing all its grandeur, to become a pauper village'. Here was a place where religion, which meant as little to Weizmann as it had to Herzl (though both rendered it lip-service), commanded every activity, both sacred and profane. He found it difficult to be polite to the rabbis here, for they affronted his sense of logic, and confirmed his old feeling, from the days of Pinsk, that they were the enemies of progress, a force of darkness in the Jewish soul.

It horrified the Zionist leader to discover that he could barely find a Jew qualified to type a letter, or perform a little necessary plumbing, or supervise a modest kindergarten. He determined that, if nothing else, he would perform an act of rehabilitation, or rather purification, in Jerusalem.

He must impress upon the world that the movement he represented intended breathing life into these dry bones. He knew of only one way to challenge the stagnation around him with a gesture, and infuse idealism into the city with the power of words. Out of this soil Jews had risen to bequeath a civilisation to the world. It must do so again. And he informed Allenby that he intended, at once, to dedicate the site and lay the foundations of the Hebrew University.

Allenby proved most reluctant to sanction the minimal ceremonial necessary. Enemy patrols were venturing within fifteen miles of Jerusalem. But Weizmann insisted. It grieved him that among the hospices, churches, monasteries and colleges ornamenting the landscape – French, Italian, Russian and German, and of course the Mosque of Omar resplendent on Mount Moriah – nowhere could he descry a Jewish edifice to equal them; for, as the Prophet lamented, *Mine own vineyards have I not kept.* High over the Mount of Olives stood the area purchased by the Jews for the university: Mount Scopus, where Titus had camped, to begin his long siege of the city in A.D. 70. For the present, Scopus stood bare against the sunlight, the cobalt of Moab in the distance, the slate-like Dead Sea below.

The rabbinical authorities cursed the Zionists for their sacrilege in planning a secular institution here, but were over-ruled. The military required proof that this was indeed legally-acquired Jewish land. It was produced. At last a great assemblage climbed to the hill-top: Weizmann beside Allenby; Arab, Christian and Jewish dignitaries; a guard of honour led by Jabotinsky, from the Jewish battalions; French and Italian liaison officers; and everyone who could be spared from G.H.Q., beside a ragged swarm of beggars of all races.

A hush as the foundation stones were laid, twelve representing the tribes of Israel, and a thirteenth placed by the leading Moslem notable, the Mufti of Jerusalem. A message of goodwill, the only one to arrive in time, came from Balfour. It was July 24, 1918.

For Weizmann the day was linked with another, in Vienna. Was it as long as fifteen years ago that he had received an impatient hearing from Theodor Herzl regarding this vision, to which he had clung tenaciously through every twist of fate? Vera's absence alone marred the moment. It was the longest separation since their marriage, and he yearned for her.

His was the only speech. 'It seems at first sight paradoxical,' he said, 'that in a land with so sparse a population, in a land crying out for such simple things as ploughs, roads and harbours, we should begin by creating a centre of spiritual and intellectual development. But it is no paradox for those who know the soul of the Jew. It is true that great social and political problems still face us and will demand their solution from us. We Jews know that when the mind is given fullest play, when we have a centre for the development of Jewish consciousness, then coincidentally we shall attain the fulfilment of our material needs.

'The university will be the focus of the rehabilitation of our Jewish consciousness, now so tenuous because it has become world-diffused. Under the atmospheric pressure of this Mount, our Jewish consciousness can become diffused without becoming feeble, and our Jewish youth will be reinvigorated from Jewish sources.' He reiterated an undertaking made to the Zionist Congress five years earlier, when he moved the resolution to found the university: 'Intended primarily for Jews, it will of course give an affectionate welcome to the members of every race and creed. *For my house will be called a house of prayer for all the nations.* Here the wandering soul of Israel shall reach its haven.'

Mount Scopus would have seven more lean years, for as yet the only money to initiate the university was in the form of a promissory note from Baron Edmond. Weizmann would have to go out and collect the rest himself, in journeys taking him across the world. And when the beautiful structure, clad in the pale gold of Jerusalem stone, finally appeared on the sky-line, Lord Balfour himself came to Palestine to open it.

If the university ceremony symbolised one aspect of the reincarnation of the Jewish people as a nation, it was a metaphor for a society at peace. But the world was at war, and a symbol of nationality imposed itself more appropriate to the times. Hundreds of young people, observing the Fusiliers of the Thirty-Ninth Battalion encamped in the plains, and the Thirty-Eighth marching through the streets of Jaffa on its return from the front, clamoured for the right to enlist. To their delight many of the 'Americans' in khaki were Hebrew-speakers, now reunited with their families among the local population.

What was Allenby to do? He was a cold man, and had adjusted his sights so as to close his campaign in victory on his existing strength. He shared the English fixation of discerning the spirit of Bolshevism in every Jew of Russian origin, and he would prefer 'those chaps' to hang around with their lemonade carts outside the barrack gates rather than meet them as soldiers inside.

The Zionist Commission would not press the point, at any rate not officially. Privately, Weizmann encouraged the volunteers' spokesmen to have their people ready, and he kept in close touch with Jabotinsky. But he was not at all anxious to revive the controversies of the previous year in London.

Allenby relented. Jabotinsky, a lieutenant now but with a general's dream of commanding an army of 100,000, shared with James de Rothschild the work of recruitment, and before long even youngsters from the Orthodox Jerusalem families had their side-curls cut and flocked to the colours. They were to become the Fortieth Battalion of the Royal Fusiliers. It was another indication of the force the Jews intended putting into the phrase 'National Home'. Many girls volunteered too, but were not accepted.

And had Allenby thought of his recruits as socialists rather than Bolshevists his instinct would not have been wildly wrong. Their tent-lines echoed with sounds rarely heard in the armies of those days: political talk, with Corporal Ben-Gurion and Private Ben-Zvi energetically spreading the ideology of the Left among the newcomers. They were losing no time in planning the future organisation of a Zionist Labour Party.

Early in June, still six weeks before the ceremony on Mount Scopus, Weizmann, travelling by truck and camel, negotiated the desert ridge beyond Akaba. Sixty miles lay between him and Emir Feisal's encampment at Waheida, below Ma'an. To his left lay the Wadi Araba, the great rift leading to the Dead Sea; on the right the Hedjaz railway, which Zionist map-makers, anticipating somewhat, were writing into the eastern boundary of a Jewish State. Ormsby-Gore was to have accompanied the Zionist leader, but contracted fever on the old passenger boat carrying them round the Sinai Peninsula through a steaming Red Sea. Colonel Joyce, Lawrence's easy-going Irish comrade and quartermaster of the Arab revolt, was doing double duty as Weizmann's companion as well as his guide.

As they approached Waheida, Weizmann observed a German plane through his field-glasses. It put out a white flag and landed. Feisal was receiving Jamal's emissary, to hear what prize would be his for calling off the desert campaign and joining, as every good Moslem must, the *Jihad*, holy war, against the infidel. Feisal needed no instruction in Christian perfidy: it was all written out in the Sykes-Picot Treaty. But the agreement had come to Weizmann too as a rude surprise. The Jew and the Arab might perhaps destroy it between them.

Feisal struck Weizmann as an intelligent and honest man, 'handsome as a picture'. The Arab chief seemed to him not greatly interested in Palestine, but intent upon stationing himself in Damascus and claiming Syria before it fell into the hands of the detested French. Such an arrangement of Arab fortunes would suit Weizmann perfectly, and he laid a proposition before the other – a proposition he had already taken pains to rehearse in a letter to Balfour sent off just before this journey to Waheida.

Jewish assistance, he told Feisal, was available in the form of finance and organisational experience to help the Arab create a strong and prosperous kingdom. It was preferable that such aid be accepted from the Jews than from any other source, for, Weizmann pointed out, his people did not aspire to be a power in the area, and could not threaten legitimate Arab rights.

His discussions with local leaders, both in Cairo and Jerusalem, had taught Weizmann that protestations of goodwill toward the spirit of Arab nationalism were insufficient to overcome their hostility to his cause. He needed a substantial ally from their ranks. And if he could come to terms with Feisal it would help the British too, to save their sunken reputation in the Arab world. Commonly regarded as London's agent, Weizmann felt that a blow struck for Zionism would be endorsement also of Britain's role in Palestine. It would ease the difficulties of both in this region.

Whatever the Emir's grievances against England, or his aspirations regarding Palestine, he failed to express them to Weizmann. And while he would not commit himself to a specific arrangement with Zionism, he left the Jew with the belief, shared by Joyce, that the Arab leader was friendly towards the movement. Weizmann felt greatly encouraged when he returned to Cairo and reported to Sir Reginald Wingate the High Commissioner, Colonel Clayton of the Arab Bureau, and Lawrence.* In August it was suggested to him that he seek a further meeting with Feisal, but he was now the reverse of enthusiastic. He was irked by his lack of funds and the absence of trained personnel, and therefore decided that he had achieved all he could in Palestine.

Simon and Lévi had returned home, the former to his desk at the London Post Office, the latter bearing tales to Baron Edmond of Weizmann's plans to hand Palestine on a platter to the British. Weizmann felt reluctant about departing before a man strong enough to stand up to the military administration came to replace him. His successor needed to be a major figure. He must simultaneously handle with resolution the clamorous demands of the Jewish groups and employ the correct ingredients of sweetness and determination in talking to the Arabs. In default, Zionism was in danger of being thrown back to its starting-line of Turkish times.

His impatience with Sokolow and Brandeis had turned into anger. In reply to his repeated requests for money and personnel they fed him excuses, and messages of encouragement. Sokolow sent news from London of little social triumphs that he was invited to interpret as victories for Zionist propaganda among the great. It was now clear that the Americans would not post anyone of substance to Palestine to assume responsibility for the political work.

Yet already, Americans of another kind were meddling in the troubled situation – in the form of a Red Cross unit apparently restricted to non-controversial deeds of welfare. In fact it had been financed by anti-Zionist Jews and was nosing into political issues in such a way as to attract the disfavour even of the British. Weizmann was moved to plan an immediate

* Lawrence is erroneously described by Weizmann in his Memoirs as being present at the Waheida meeting.

journey to the United States, to shock Brandeis and his colleagues into comprehension of the magnitude of the task and the incipient dangers facing their movement. He detected the hand of Henry Morgenthau in this Red Cross team, and twenty years of Zionist activity had taught him to suspect the intentions of any organisation camouflaged in a veil of innocent philanthropy.

Brandeis had no wish to see Weizmann in America, and urged him to continue his admirable work in Palestine. Now Ormsby-Gore too was perturbed, and he and Weizmann arranged that the mission to America be undertaken, once again, by Aaronson. The Zionist 'secret service man' was promptly despatched, and was not surprised to discover Lévi on the same transatlantic liner, deep in conversation with the French Commissioner for military affairs in Washington, André Tardieu. Lévi's errand was to weaken the Zionist stake in Palestine by forming a Commission of 'neutral' Jews and to keep the door ajar for French influence.

Nervy and exhausted, Weizmann refused to remain one further day in Palestine after September. Handing over to the dedicated but uninspiring David Eder, he reached London just as the German Army at long last cracked, with Allenby now beyond Damascus. On October 30, 1918 the Sultan of Turkey capitulated. Britain, it seemed, had in her dominion a land-mass extending from the Fertile Crescent to the Persian Gulf, to keep or give away as she pleased. And France, for whom the infamous Sykes-Picot Treaty was anything but dead (it had not been repudiated by Britain either, for that matter) began at once to Gallicise Syria – starting with Upper Galilee. Allenby had proceeded in his advance with some despatch, but not fast enough to shake off François Georges-Picot.

Weizmann was received by his friends, and many erstwhile enemies, as would Ancient Rome a victorious captain returned from the wars. But he warned them that congratulations were less in order than a thorough re-examination of all the Zionist catch-phrases of the past. The Balfour Declaration was an opportunity to show that the Jews had the will, the talent and the means to achieve solid results; it was not an award for good conduct, or past services.

Two years earlier, in 1916, he and Vera had acquired a home in Addison Road, Kensington. It was immediately before their second son Michael was born. (Weizmann, ever cavalier with dates, places the birth a year later in his Memoirs.) The ceremony of circumcision, with Moses Gaster as godfather, took on the form of their public début in London Jewish society. Now their home in Kensington became the No. 10 Downing

Street of the Jews, for the chemist was indeed their Prime Minister in Exile.

The role was promoted with extraordinary devotion by his young friends Marks and Sieff. Privileged by great wealth, though still 'provincials' in the sense understood by English manners, they placed themselves completely at their leader's command. This gave Weizmann an advantage denied to Sokolow, who was Polish rather than Russian (a difference speaking volumes to students of the Jewish mentality), and a man of contemplation where the other was a man of action. Sokolow intimated rather than emphasised his seniority over Weizmann, but it was not lost on the movement that, idealist though he might be, his status was that of a professional servant of the cause. One day the painful question of precedence would have to be faced.

As far as the British were concerned there could be no doubt. An authoritative Jewish voice was more necessary than ever now to a government facing the new situation of an America demanding its say in world affairs. Shortly after his return to England Weizmann was advised by Leopold Amery, of the Cabinet Secretariat, of renewed moves to bring Palestine into the trusteeship of the United States. The course was favoured by those, like Balfour, who wished to remove a contentious issue from Franco-British relations. Amery looked to Weizmann for help in locking Palestine into the Empire, for the sake of territorial contiguity between Egypt and India.

Weizmann required no persuasion on this score. Now that he was clear of the local situation he felt little inhibition in stating his own expectations, particularly to an imperialist of Amery's stamp. Britain's requirement would be fulfilled, he said, if she ruled over an undivided Jewish Palestine. It should stretch from Dan to Beersheba and from the Mediterranean to the Hedjaz railway, embracing also the rich soils of the Golan, with a frontier on the Litani river north of Tyre.

They were a long way from this. But Weizmann, apprehensive at the obstinacy of French ambitions and the possible amputation of Galilee, pressed for an interview with Lloyd George. The Prime Minister invited him to luncheon on November 11. Weizmann proceeded to Downing Street to find the streets suddenly alive with cheering children, and men and women pouring from their offices, with flags appearing from nowhere. The war had ended. It seemed an inappropriate occasion to discuss high strategy, and when Weizmann was announced he found the Welsh wizard engrossed in the Psalms.

The victorious Powers were about to come together in Paris to hear out the claims of sundry petitioners, to disguise their rival ambitions in pious pronouncements, and to make the world safe for democracy. Perhaps Balfour, gentle disbeliever that he was, best understood the grand hypocrisy of it all. While in Palestine Weizmann had addressed much advice to him, on the need to scrap Sykes-Picot, on the jostling of competing representatives of the British flag in Cairo, on the rights of the Jews as they came under military occupation.

Weizmann considered that now that he was home he was entitled to a long discussion with the Foreign Secretary, who surely would himself wish for a personal report. The meeting, when it materialised, lasted barely twenty-five minutes. And, Weizmann complained to C. P. Scott afterwards, Balfour seemed half asleep.

Palestine too was partly asleep. Soon it would awaken, to Balfour's discovery that his famous Declaration had disturbed a volcano.

8

Dreams and Realities

To THE DISCOMFITURE OF BRITAIN AND THE DISMAY OF FRANCE IN THEIR
guilty contemplation of the Ottoman conundrum, Prince Feisal arrived in
person to claim his rights as an ally and representative of an oppressed
nation. Through Lawrence, he sent a message to the Eastern Committee
of the British Cabinet that he trusted the Zionists before anyone else to
help his people.

Evidently Weizmann's plea for an understanding between Jew and Arab,
reminiscent of Herzl's negotiations with the Turks when he too proffered
money and skills he did not command, had made an enduring impression
upon Feisal. With the encouragement of Balfour, he met the prince again
at the Carlton Hotel in London in December, 1918. Lawrence acted as
interpreter, and they reached agreement on further cooperation, to confirm
to the Jew that the man coming from the heart of Arabia did not envisage
Palestine within his heritage.

The Balfour Declaration is recognised, the right to large-scale immigration admitted; both parties would be concerned in defining the boundaries
between Palestine and Feisal's own Arab state. Nowhere in the nine
articles of the agreement, however, does Feisal concede Palestine's control
to the Jews. But it was nevertheless a promising first step for the new era
in the Middle East. Perhaps another Zionist leader would have regarded
the agreement as inadequate, but no other Zionist understood so clearly
the sickly Jewish condition in Palestine, nor the formidable Arab hostility
still to be overcome. Feisal had invited Jewish partnership in the development of the entire region. Did that not open a door to a likely constitutional
intimacy in the future?

Three weeks passed. This was time enough to strengthen Feisal's misgivings regarding the aspirations of France, and the emptiness of British assurances. He therefore added a reservation to his agreement with Weizmann: he would not be bound by its terms if his own people were not established in accordance with his claims.

Given that they were then only at the preliminaries of the post-war settlement, it seemed a reasonable qualification to the Zionist delegation when, in common with such other petitioners as Koreans, Irish-Americans and Armenians, it descended upon Paris for a hearing before the Council of Ten. But Lloyd George was evidently not standing his ground against Clemenceau, and the Tiger was soon acting as though Syria was an undisputed portion of the French Republic.

With the swaying of his fortunes, Feisal's attitude towards the Zionists vacillated. He told a *Le Matin* reporter that he was against a Jewish Commonwealth – the term favoured by the Zionists to express their interpretation of the Balfour undertaking for a 'national home'. He later made a generous retraction, describing Weizmann as 'a great helper of our cause', and hoping that 'the Arabs may soon be in a position to make the Jews some return for their kindness'. This was in a letter to Felix Frankfurter who, with Herbert Samuel, was advising the Zionists in their representations to the Powers. 'I look forward to the future in which we will help you and you will help us,' Feisal wrote.

All seemed well again. But 1919 was a sorry, disappointing year for the Emir. He gave another interview, this time to the *Jewish Chronicle*, in which he declared that the Arabs, far from accepting a national home that would ultimately become a Jewish State, were determined to fight to the last against the separation of Palestine from their patrimony. A few months later in Damascus he was proclaimed King of Palestine and Syria, whereupon the French drove him from the city and Lloyd George hurriedly made a throne available for him in Baghdad.

Much of this lay in the future, where the Zionists too would be suffering their reversals. Now they were poised to have their say before the Council of Ten. They were summoned late in February, 1919.

For the Jews it was a moment they would have wished to treasure in their history: their people heard, for the first time, by an assemblage of world leaders about to re-arrange the globe. Unhappily, they stumbled a little on this encounter with their destiny. For in the so-called Zionist delegation stood Sylvain Lévi, under instructions from his master Baron Edmond de Rothschild – himself no mean vacillator.

Uneasy though he was about accepting Lévi, Weizmann could have swallowed the indignity had an American or two accompanied him to the Council. The reluctance of Zionists from across the Atlantic to stand in solidarity with the European movement was a constant vexation to him. The Americans were at that moment in Paris in considerable force, under the leadership of Rabbi Stephen Wise, the nominee of Brandeis. Like the Justice, Wise was a Democrat close to President Wilson, and a major Jewish voice who rarely needed an invitation to make a speech.

It was a most curious situation. So many Jewish groups stationed themselves in Paris for the Peace Conference that they perforce formed a 'Committee of Jewish Delegations', and in this the Americans predominated in influence and number. They laboured zealously for the accord of minority rights, with the end of discrimination and pogrom, for the Jews of Poland, Hungary and Rumania. But when it came to advocacy of Zionism before the 'top table' they were overpowered by modesty. Even Frankfurter, great drafter of documents, failed to find his tongue.

It was therefore a less than representative delegation that Sokolow introduced. This, he stated, was the day for which his people had been waiting eighteen centuries: 'We claim our historic right over Palestine, the Land of Israel, the soil on which we erected a civilisation that has had so great an influence upon humanity.'

Disconcertingly, just as Sokolow's peroration began, Clemenceau left the chamber. He surrendered the Chair to Stephen Pichon, his Foreign Minister, who was accompanied by Lévi's ally Tardieu. Balfour and Milner remained to speak for Britain, Sonnino for Italy, Lansing and White for the U.S.A., Makino for Japan – tired, elderly men; they had heard pleas from many groups, and it was not going to be easy to hold their attention. Mercifully, the Zionists had already submitted a statement of their hopes that Palestine's sovereignty be vested in the projected League of Nations, with its government entrusted to Great Britain as Mandatory Power.

In his turn Weizmann spoke confidently of the country's possibilities as home and shelter for Jews without a future in their native lands. Immigration would be regulated by the Zionist Organisation with the assistance of the Jews of the world, he emphasised, and would ultimately reach the figure of four to five million inhabitants. He based this population density on a comparison with the Lebanon. There, 160 persons inhabited the square kilometre; in Palestine the corresponding figure was under fifteen.

Ussishkin next, vigorous as ever despite his six weeks' journey from Odessa. It was now late afternoon, and the Council evinced restlessness. But Ussishkin was calmly intent upon making his contribution to history.

What he said was of little import; that he said it in the language of the Bible evidenced the existence of Jews for whom their nationality was a truth transcending the laws and decisions of men.

It was a truth that Lévi, descended, he announced, from men emancipated by the laws of the French Revolution, felt a passionate duty to repudiate. Of course, the Zionists had performed wonders in their agricultural colonies in Palestine, and the revival of spoken Hebrew was to be applauded. But it would be wrong for the Jews of the world, enjoying rights in their lands of residence, to enjoy also special rights in Palestine. Double nationality would be created, to demand a dual loyalty. Lévi opposed the transfer of millions of their people to Palestine. The land was already fully inhabited, and could not be made to yield nourishment on European standards. Furthermore, such Jews who might respond to the call to immigrate would be Eastern Europeans, and he hinted that their mentality was perverted by their sorry condition over the centuries.

Mentality perverted? Lévi was intimating that the Russian Jews were advocates and organisers of the Bolshevik Revolution. And in moving to Palestine they would be carrying their poison with them. The argument could serve any case. Weizmann was himself not beyond using it, to strengthen his plea for bringing Jews to Palestine rather than have them seek new homes in the capitalist West.

But at this juncture he was nonplussed. He had no wish to take issue with Lévi and treat the Supreme Council to a Jewish debate. He had been inclined to respect Lévi as a sincere and civilised opponent of Zionism, but he was outraged to find him pleading with such partisan force before the most powerful tribunal in existence. He could not even discern the Baron in this echo of the master's voice.

The Jews, disconsolate, were preparing to withdraw, when Lansing spoke up: 'Could Dr Weizmann explain the meaning of the words "national home"? Do they imply an autonomous government?'

Weizmann seized his opportunity. 'No, we do not demand a strictly Jewish government, but conditions enabling us to send 70,000 to 80,000 immigrants annually, and gradually to develop in Palestine a Jewish life as Hebraic as life in England is English. Only when this nationality forms the majority of the population shall the movement come to claim the government of this country.'

He was allowed to elaborate further, and showed that it was precisely the Russian Jews, spoken of with such trepidation by Lévi, who were the founders of the agricultural colonies that were the pride of Palestine. Even under the Turkish regime their energy and resourcefulness had succeeded in changing desert into fertile lands.

The situation was redeemed. Balfour sent his secretary out to congratulate Weizmann, and Sonnino added his good wishes. But Weizmann angrily waved Lévi's proffered hand away as they dispersed. The following day Tardieu issued a statement to the effect that France would not oppose English trusteeship over Palestine. So the plan hatched by Samuel and Weizmann four years earlier to keep the French out of the Holy Land had succeeded.

Of course, a peace treaty with Turkey was still a long way from signature, and there could be no immediate rush to transform the country into a land 'as Hebraic as England is English'. As Weizmann had feared, no commanding figure came forward to replace him as head of the Zionist Commission, although some Americans eventually presented themselves. Jabotinsky, still in uniform, was nominated their political officer, and he saw his function mainly as keeping the regiments of 'Judeans' together. He realised even more clearly than Weizmann that, whatever might be prescribed for Palestine on the international level, the Arab movement was more than just a fact. It was a threat.

Resentment was mutual. Many Arabs in government service feared they would lose the posts they had clung to through four years of war, while it seemed to the Jews that their inferior status was unchanged by the substitution of British for Turkish rule. A petty incident quickly aroused tempers in the poorer quarters of the labyrinthine towns, and every report written by Jabotinsky, who was no mean poet, had to be in the language of melodrama. He had not the temperament to work harmoniously with his Jewish colleagues or to put a case diplomatically to his military superiors.

Jabotinsky's motive in fighting for the retention of the Judeans was to secure their recognition as a permanent security force. The British found the idea totally unwelcome, as did the soldiers themselves. Those not domiciled in Palestine yearned for repatriation and release, and to their champion's consternation a brigade of almost 5,000 men dwindled in a matter of months to some hundreds. Weizmann received complaints that Jabotinsky's swagger was causing the Zionist Commission nothing but trouble, while the Army found him insubordinate and pretentious.

Lieutenant Jug o'whisky, to use the sobriquet employed in the officers' mess, loudly interpreted the Balfour Declaration as a charter for the eventual Judaisation of Palestine. The idea was implicit of course in all Zionist policy, but its constant proclamation could only alienate Whitehall

and exasperate G.H.Q. Cairo. Weizmann felt he had no alternative but to
dismiss this stormy petrel from the Commission. It was not long also before
the military compulsorily demobilised him from the service. But he would
not be silenced. He remained in Jerusalem as a private citizen and organised
a clandestine self-defence corps there.

Immigrants were already finding their way to Palestine, among them
young Russians availing themselves of escape routes traced out of the
anarchy prevalent in a sub-continent in revolution. Joseph Trumpeldor,
who had dreamed of descending into Palestine with a Jewish army from
the north, arrived alone. Justice Brandeis came for his first visit in June,
1919, to be greeted as the embodiment of all the New World's wisdom,
benevolence and authority. So august an American had never before allied
himself to so controversial a Jewish cause as Zionism.

Weizmann carefully scrutinised this man when he subsequently arrived
in London. They could achieve so much together. Would the American
enter their inner councils as a leader, perhaps *the* leader? But, as Brandeis
developed his ideas for future action, Weizmann discovered that Zionists
through conversion and Zionists by birth were separated by a gulf almost
impossible to bridge.

Brandeis saw little purpose in the continuation of the organisation on an
international basis. He thought that political activities should now be left
to the Jews, strengthened by the new annual immigration, actually living
in Palestine. Let their co-religionists outside undertake the economic
development of the country, through financial investment and technical
assistance, in the way that America was attacking the problem of the sparse
regions on her own soil. The era of Zionist philosophers and politicians
was now over; the era of Zionist hydraulic engineers had begun.

Weizmann was astonished. Did Brandeis really consider the slender
Palestine community, in many respects an archaic survival from an earlier
age of religiosity, to be ready for the challenges of nationhood? Brandeis
evidently believed that nationhood, sheltered and assisted by American
power, could grow of itself without vitality flowing towards it through
partnership with the Jews of the world. Moreover, he did not appreciate
the spiritual qualities of Zionism, as an ingredient necessary to the psychological completeness of the Jew wherever he might dwell. To Brandeis
there could be no Jew more complete than the Jew of Wilsonian America.
A clash of personalities and policies was inevitable. But first Weizmann
took the precaution of returning to Palestine and re-assessing his Zionist
policy there.

The situation was as menacing as Jabotinsky had predicted. Since Allenby's departure, to administer the conquered empire as a whole, his subordinates were taking no pains to disguise their resentment of Zionist pressures. How serene occupation duties would be without the Jews, and what a pleasant aftermath to the rigours of war! Arab pressures, on the other hand, seemed to them entirely reasonable, and already, Weizmann found, handicaps were being imposed on Jewish immigration.

The year before, he had obtained Allenby's sanction of a plan for the amelioration and utilisation of publicly owned state domain. These substantial areas, suffocating in sand or diseased by long stagnation in swamp, needed the attention of a healing hand. It was a task the Zionist Organisation ought to undertake at once. But it was not allowed to start. Weizmann was uncertain what was more to blame: British hostility concealed beneath insistence upon the *status quo*, or the continued apathy of world Jewry towards Palestine.

The socialist labourers alone seemed aware of the error in delaying the pioneering life until a political settlement was achieved. Quite the contrary: they understood Jewish labour on the soil as Zionist intervention in the making of political decisions. Inspired by Trumpeldor, they sought to occupy any land, no matter how remote, that was in Jewish ownership. Some they possessed was situated in Upper Galilee; no one could say exactly where in this rugged region British writ ended and the French conflict with Feisal began.

Aaronson, who knew Palestine hill and dale, had emphasised to Weizmann that this region, plentiful in water, had to be kept out of the French grasp if the country was to be irrigated and electrified. The agronomist had been lost over the Channel while en route to Paris by aeroplane the year before, but Weizmann had not forgotten the advice. Now, in Jerusalem, he made no secret of the anxiety.

In January, 1920, Trumpeldor and seven comrades, two of them girls, moved into a Zionist encampment in the north. They came to re-stake a claim on Metulla, a Rothschild colony lately abandoned because of the insecurity of the borderlands. It was a gesture by the socialist Left to demonstrate that the Jewish love of this soil must extend to personal commitment to its defence.

The local Beduin were fiercely pro-Feisal. They suspected Trumpeldor and his group of sympathy with the French, for the Jews refused to fly the Shereefian flag. The encampment was attacked. Dotted over this terrain were other tiny settlements where Jews, under guard, stubbornly tilled

their land. Trumpeldor held off the assault while he called for reinforce-
ments, but by the time relief arrived the place was over-run. It was the last
battle of the Port Arthur veteran of the Twenty-Seventh East Siberian
Regiment. He and his comrades lay dead.

The deed of self-sacrifice reverberated through the Jewish world.
Zionism now had the nourishment on which national movements thrive:
a folk-lore. The heroism of Trumpeldor gave inspiration to a hundred
Hebrew poets, and his picture hung in the club-rooms of Zionist youth
movements everywhere. Yet the bravado had been ill-conceived, indicative
of the impetuousness with which the Zionists confronted the slow processes of government.

Worse was soon to come, in Jerusalem: not an incident of derring-do on
an uncharted frontier but an explosion in the capital, with the British Army
well in evidence. The Powers were about to assemble in San Remo to
hammer out at last the peace treaty with Turkey – or more truthfully, a
peace treaty between Britain and France.

Jabotinsky warned of a projected attack upon the tumbledown Jewish
district of the walled town, a huddle of seminaries, synagogues and mean
dwellings occupied by the devout. His prediction of bloodshed was
ignored, so he summoned his volunteers and openly drilled them in sight
of the military. If condoned, this illegal activity would register as tacit
acceptance by the authorities of a Zionist defence force. It was the *Nebi
Moussa* festival, and Moslem pilgrims were crowding into Jerusalem.

The Orthodox Jews, for whom Zionism was heresy, did not seek protection; it had never previously been needed. But these were different
times, and soon the stones were flying. Jabotinsky's men tried to rush the
city's gates, but were held back by the Tommies. Five Jews and four Arabs
were killed and over 200 people, mainly Jews, injured. On the restoration
of order the foiled rescuers were taken into custody. Jabotinsky was
sentenced to fifteen years' prison, to be followed by deportation.

Here, then, was the descent of a noble dream into a sad reality. Arab-
Jewish brotherhood under the British flag had become a triangle of
animosities, with the two Semitic peoples in confrontation and the British
stolidly holding the ring. It was more than Weizmann could tolerate, and
he lost no time in travelling to Cairo to express his disgust to the
Commander-in-Chief, now a Field-Marshal and High Commissioner in
Egypt. Allenby heard him out with characteristic equanimity, though an
angry Weizmann could be an uncomfortable experience. To think that
Jabotinsky, who had braved so many difficulties to bring Britain an army

in the field, could be treated thus! And to witness the sorry spectacle of British impotence in the face of an attack upon the most innocuous of Palestine's citizens!

Allenby calmed the other's temper, but conceded little. The bloodshed was regrettable, he said, though as nothing compared to similar incidents between I.R.A. and Black and Tans in Ireland. Weren't the Jews making too much of the fracas?

'I hope it will definitely be decided at San Remo that we have the Mandate,' Allenby said, 'and then a more solid regime can be established.' But Weizmann saw the problem otherwise. If the Jews numbered 400,000 in Palestine, rather than a miserable 50,000, such happenings would be less likely, he complained. Yet immigration was being throttled from the start.

Waiting for San Remo soon ceased to serve as an excuse. Everything was settled there. Weizmann, with Sokolow and Herbert Samuel, sat in an ante-chamber while the fate of the Ottoman Empire was decided. They had two preoccupations: the northern frontier of Palestine, which they wanted mapped so as to include Trumpeldor's battleground as far as the Litani and the richly-watered Hermon slopes; and to have the Balfour Declaration incorporated in the peace treaty, thus enshrining the British undertaking in international law. Lord Curzon had now succeeded Balfour as Foreign Secretary, and though he had been the reverse of enthusiastic towards the Declaration, he could assuredly be trusted to take a firm stand with the French.

The statesmen's game was to smuggle a Sykes-Picot formula through in another, improved guise for Britain and France, Russia no longer being a factor in the Middle East and Italy a negligible quantity. So it proved: Syria and Lebanon were made into French Mandates, Palestine and Iraq into British. Palestine won a frontier at biblical Dan, but to Weizmann's dismay the French held obdurately to its surrounding terrain, which was destined to become a cemetery for Arabs and Jews still unborn. The Balfour Declaration found its place in Article 95 of the Treaty of Peace. One final ritual remained: endorsement of the Mandates by the new League of Nations. American misgivings, Vatican intrigues, Italy's wounded pride, delayed but could not deny the rubber stamp.

The Zionists left San Remo as fairly satisfied customers. Among the new epoch's auguries was the appointment of Samuel, now out of Parliament and available for any call of duty, as High Commissioner for Palestine. One of his earliest decrees brought an amnesty to political prisoners, and Jabotinsky arrived impishly in London to clear his name, have his sentence quashed, and take his seat on the Zionist Executive as the movement's ill-used man of action vindicated. Could anything go wrong with their affairs now?

Only, thought Weizmann as he faced a great conference in July, 1920, through their own inadequacies. It was the first occasion the Zionists had come together in force since the Congress of 1913, when he had appeared to many as little more than a partisan if dedicated propagandist with a talent for organisation. Delegates recalled him from those days as a representative of the minor planet of Manchester in a Zionist constellation whose sun blazed fiercely from Berlin.

Now London was the fount of their inspiration and energy, and Weizmann their acclaimed statesman and administrator, in their eyes an equal with Lloyd George and Allenby. His perceptions were those of a Russian Jew; his thinking that of an Englishman. He had no equal at that gathering. Max Nordau had returned from the lost, but as a shadow of his former glory. David Wolffsohn was dead, Ussishkin sidetracked. Sokolow was a diplomat, not a statesman. Only Brandeis stole stature from Weizmann, but being entirely an American he could not, to their European minds, be wholly a Jew.

'We stand today,' Weizmann declared, 'on the eve perhaps of our greatest hour, when the possibility is given to us to rebuild our ancient home, and I am perfectly sure that no Jew, whatever his opinion might have been before, will stand aloof at this moment . . . We tell the Arabs plainly and honestly that they have enough room, and that the nations of the world, and the Jewish nation, will contribute as they did before to the building up and regeneration of a great and glorious Arab nation. Did not Arabs and Jews collaborate and produce a great literature at a time when the whole of Europe was plunged in darkness? This will come again, but on one condition: that the Arabs respect the right of the Jews to Palestine, just as we respect the traditions of the Arab nation. If you measure Palestine by the square kilometre it is a small country, but if you measure Palestine by centuries of history it is one of the greatest countries in the world.'

The rhetoric flowed with sweeping gestures towards the morrow. But what of today, and the difficult business of setting Zionism on its immediate tasks? Brandeis and his American group formed a bloc that shone with affluence and vigour, untouched by the ordeals which had aged the continent of Europe and its inhabitants during these past years. Their strength betrayed a condescension, and an innocence. Friends had been urging their leader to take the movement in his keeping, for his prestige would attract others of similar rank to the cause. But Frankfurter's advice was that Brandeis must not compromise his position on the Supreme Court.

The Justice brought a plan to London. It entailed the suspension of the Zionist Congresses, which he saw as a platform for irrelevant controversy. Instead they should form a supreme Executive free of party interests or dependence upon the plethora of committees that had water-logged the organisation before the war.

Weizmann did not intend returning to the system of the old days either. He knew its frailties only too well, and had long lamented the inability of Zionism to attract the best Jewish intellects. But, repeating his earlier admonition to Brandeis, he insisted that they could not widen their platform at the cost of forefeiting Zionism's fundamentally spiritual role. Palestine must not be demoted into a depository of homeless Jews – that was Herzl's mistake. It must be uplifted to radiate inspiration for the universal enrichment of the people, as preached by Ahad Ha'am.

Their first task, in his view, was the creation of a great fund both for reconstruction in Palestine and as a social and political instrument outside. San Remo had demonstrated the need. In those centres of Jewish population where Zionism existed as a force they had been able to lobby their governments to make the will of the Jews known to the assembled Powers, and an orchestrated voice had reached San Remo to provide Weizmann's evidence that British trusteeship was their undivided wish. Such work on the international plane would long be necessary.

In London, every meeting between Brandeis and Weizmann became a study in opposites. One saw in the other a Jewish Woodrow Wilson, full of good intentions no doubt but at the same time sanctimonious and impractical. Brandeis observed a Clemenceau, scheming behind the scenes to get his own way in everything. Weizmann demanded a contribution of two million pounds from an America gross with three lucrative years of wartime neutrality. Brandeis countered with the expectation of a sum not in excess of £100,000; the rest would come as private capital, but only if stringently controlled by men versed in town planning, railroad construction, economics. He was not impressed by Zionism's assemblage of other-worldly Eastern European Jews, lost in their obsessions with Hebrew culture and the eternity of the Jewish soul. Weizmann, on the other hand, saw this as a striving to re-assert their heritage. He refused to abandon the men, and the movement they had cherished in bad times, now that prospects were bright.

Determined to escape this garrulous machine, Brandeis returned to America in a huff. He forbade any American to join the Executive, and threatened an apparatus by-passing London, to deposit funds direct in Palestinian institutions. As a result, the London conference became Weizmann's triumph. He was elected President of the World Zionist Organisation, with Sokolow as Chairman of the Executive. He knew that when the time came to challenge Brandeis for the affiliation of America, he would win.

He announced his credo: the world understood the Balfour Declaration, already subject to so many conflicting interpretations, to mean as much or as little as the Jewish people made of it. If the Jews did nothing, it gave them nothing; if they failed the movement, and their achievement in the first years was insignificant, scepticism would grow both as to Jewry's intentions and capabilities.

If the Arabs became an inferior element in the country, then the Zionist organism ran the danger of being poisoned. The Jews must be committed to raising Arab standards to their own level, for all elements of the population must progress together. And he formally pledged Jewish help to enable the Arabs beyond Palestine to develop their lands too. The Moslem world would thus come to recognise that its fear of the Jews was groundless.

The moment also demanded a gesture towards Jews unable to accept Zionism as a philosophy. Their assistance was necessary, for the project they were embarked upon was an exciting cooperative adventure with repercussions for the whole of Jewry. Hence the new Executive would formulate principles for the recruitment of the so-called assimilationist branches of their people. To some of his hearers this suggested a Brandeisian policy without its progenitor. They reserved their judgment.

The pursuit of this programme during the next decade gave Weizmann little time for science, and he grieved at the weakening of friendships born of his Manchester days. Samuel Alexander in philosophy, Ernest Rutherford in physics, Robert Robinson in chemistry, had constituted with himself a brotherhood of intellects to give the northern university its great reputation for free enquiry. Weizmann was to observe, not without envy, how their undiverted dedication to knowledge enabled them to advance the frontiers of thought while he remained tied to a mission that he felt, at times, to be his prison.

Vera had not been wrong about the impossibility of serving two masters. His work on synthetic rubber remained uncompleted. His development of a fermentation process for a constituent in the vitamin B group was for the present frustrated, and he had long desired to explore the new world of synthetic foods and discover a solution to scarcity and hunger in the laboratory. Zionism denied him access to those secrets, but why should not Zionism make of Palestine a national laboratory, with a younger generation pursuing the experiments he had discontinued?

True, the industry of his earlier years was bringing their harvest – not spectacularly, but life insisted upon its compromises. His butyl alcohol was the solvent that transformed the durability of the automobile, but this was not the satisfaction sought by the pure chemist, who flourished on theoretical challenge. And to the neglect of science he had to compound the neglect of his family. Benjamin, born during those humble Manchester beginnings, was a sensitive child who took badly the constant absence of his father on protracted journeys in the Jewish cause.

Weizmann was as good as his word in taking on the challenge of America. He arrived in April, 1921, to fight Brandeis on his own territory, re-organise the Zionists in the United States as a properly-constituted body within the world movement, and launch his great fund-raising campaign. It required a sure touch, in which his very entry into New York harbour would decide whether he would carry this amorphous, volatile continent with him or whether his visit would pass as a barely-perceived event. America was not unused to the arrival of international personalities bearing their fame in one hand and a begging bowl in the other.

He had enlisted one of the most celebrated men of the day, Albert Einstein, to join him in the mission. The effect was electric. The discoverer of the Theory of Relativity had that year won the Nobel prize for physics, and his disembarkation side-by-side with the victor of the Balfour Declaration sent New York Jewry, assembled in thousands at the water-front, into a delirium of enthusiasm. Einstein's purpose was not to argue the Zionist case but to employ his unparalleled reputation in promoting the Hebrew University. The third member of the mission, Menahem Ussishkin, would address his oratorical powers to problems of colonisation in Palestine, and the acquisition of land for settlement. The Jews had been cheated of state lands, and every acre would have to be purchased. Ussishkin's fire would implant the mystique of agriculture in the minds of the city-tied masses.

The ground was thus well prepared. The visitors fanned out across a country perplexing for its variety of Jewish sects, for its peculiar ambivalence towards Europeans, and for its residues of provincialism in a climate of unmade social frontiers. Contrary to their previous assumptions, Brandeis was not the dictator of American Zionism. Beyond his circle of admirers, and untouched by his reputation as the great jurist, was a more familiar Jewish society, a recent transplant from Eastern Europe. It recognised Weizmann as one of its own.

These were Zionists of the old school, and thorough field work brought them in large numbers to a convention at Cleveland. Here the choice was made as to which leader to follow. It was not Brandeis' way to attend such a gathering in person, and had he done so he might have over-awed the opposition. Instead, his group suffered a resounding defeat. They retired in the hope of fighting another day, and a new Zionist Organisation of America, owing allegiance to the London Executive, was constituted.

Weizmann cast a charm over America, confirming his supremacy in the Jewish world for years to come. Zionism was a weakling in this territory, for Jews devoted themselves to one creed here above all others: Americanisation. He troubled them little with ideology, but proffered the expectation of a new Jewish world arising in the ancient East as this one had arisen in the modern West. He refused to humble himself, or make Zionism into a charity. His Yiddish was as rich and earthy as any to be encountered on Second Avenue, his command of English shamed many of the up-town wealthy, and in academic circles he was greeted as the renowned scientist summoned from the scholar's sanctum to help turn the fortunes of war at the Democracies' front-line. There was no truly international Jewish organisation in existence except the one he headed, and Zionism was Judaism militant.

He was once asked, why should American Jewry concern itself with a few thousand in Palestine, when there were masses of Jewish poor, numbered by the million, in the world, and even here in America?

Weizmann replied: 'In Palestine, for the first time since the Diaspora, we have an opportunity to build up everything – our language, our institutions, our schools, agriculture, the very soul of the Jew, from the ground upward. Here you have only the opportunity to adapt yourselves to a culture that other people have created. When, after a history sanctified by our martyrdom of eighty generations, the world will ask you what a Jew can do when he is free and unhampered, you should be able to point to a beautiful Palestine, where a psalm sung will ring from Dan to Beersheba, a song that might go ringing through the gilded and sordid ghetto of New York. That is the meaning of Palestine to us. It is something so sacred that we shall not barter it away for all the millions of dollars you may possibly offer us.'

America became the provider, and although the flow of funds in no wise equalled the need, it came in sufficient volume to enable the Jews to acquire lands in the Jezreel valley, which was drained of swamp and dotted with neat collective villages, to inaugurate industry, and to raise the buildings of their university on Mount Scopus.

The Congress was revived again in 1921, and along with the frustrations, and the clamour from Jabotinsky's followers for a stronger line towards the British, and from the *Mizrachi* for more deference to the *Torah*, great advances were registered. Tel Aviv sprawled, and from being a suburb became a city. Haifa prospered as Britain's naval alternative to Alexandria, and alert entrepreneurs gave it an industrial hinterland. Ben-Gurion and his comrades, worker-priests that they were in the socialist-Zionist religion, consolidated their position as the pace-makers of the re-birth.

And in this dynamic region of the Middle East, the Arabs too shared in the general prosperity. Under Herbert Samuel they enjoyed the fruits of ordered government denied to their brothers in turbulent Syria. They crossed the frontier and found work in plenty among the Jews, though simultaneously complaining at the creeping Zionisation of the country. Soon the rumblings of unrest began to reach London.

If Weizmann needed a lesson in the poor memory of politicians, he was to receive it now, in the appointment of Winston Churchill as the Colonial Secretary, with responsibility for Palestine. No longer the pushing parliamentarian, Churchill had little need to cultivate the Jews, as during his earlier electioneering days in Manchester. On the other hand, the goodwill of the parvenu Fleet Street barons was necessary to him. They were devoting considerable space in their newspapers to the subject of Palestine.

A campaign was in train to bring the Army home and stop wasting taxpayers' money in protecting the 'Bolsheviks' against the justified wrath of the Arabs. Churchill's fame rested on his crusade against Bolshevism – he presumed to be an expert in the subject – and he had no doubt that the creed had captured the soul of the Jew. Succumbing to the popular cry, he journeyed to the Middle East determined to settle all outstanding problems there: Palestine, Feisal, the entire war-time legacy of promises broken and hopes vanquished.

Churchill's errand, connected as it was with a sense of British guilt, gave the Arabs every right to believe they had found a friend. Feisal, a refugee in Haifa, was now pacified with the kingdom of Iraq, but this left his brother Abdulla unhonoured and unemployed. That part of biblical Palestine lying in Transjordania, embracing Gilead, Moab and Edom, beckoned for the knife. The surgery needed to be performed with despatch, before the League of Nations could sanction the Mandates and fix their frontiers. Churchill awarded the territory to Abdulla as an Arab preserve where the Jews would be denied land purchase or settlement. The Zionist Executive held its fire. What would the Jews be given in return?

Not much, it transpired. The Arabs were advised that Britain had no intention of renouncing the Balfour Declaration, and Churchill insisted that Western Palestine had been excluded from the undertaking given by Sir Henry McMahon to Feisal's father Hussein during their negotiations of 1915. Indeed, the Jews were in Palestine 'as of right and not on sufferance'. But this should cause the Arabs no distress, for, the Colonial Secretary stated, Jews would be allowed to immigrate to Palestine only to the extent of the country's absorptive capacity. Then, with a propitiating reference to the virtues of Zionism and the Jews' historic association with this land, and with hopes that the two peoples would now live in harmony, Churchill embodied his decisions for the future of the area in a government White Paper.

As an illustration of England's traditional prerogative to fashion undisturbed the destinies of nations, this episode lacked nothing in nineteenth century panache. Unhappily, it also bore the stain of failure. Trouble arose in the Holy Land almost on the morrow of Churchill's departure, and Samuel, welcomed by the Jews as a latter-day Messiah when he first appeared at Government House in the plumes and gold braid of his office, lost his *sang-froid* in the gathering storm.

The High Commissioner dreamed of serving George the Fifth in the way that another of his tribe had served the king's grandmother, and bring Palestine to his monarch as a self-governing dominion within a world-system which still thought of itself as an empire surviving to the end of time. But he received a foretaste of what would follow when, in May 1921, a hundred rioters died in an outbreak of savage violence in Jaffa – half of them Jews killed by Arabs, the rest Arabs killed by the military. This indeed was the ghost of Ireland, which had been Samuel's tragic responsibility in 1916, stalking him in the oriental sunshine. He rushed out an edict temporarily suspending all immigration. The Zionists summed up the situation in a cynical phrase: Samuel was just another timid English Jew trying to act the *goy*.

Scenting a continuation of British retreats as heralded by Churchill's visit, the Arabs of Palestine now seemed to find themselves as a people. No longer did they feel dependent upon brother-activists in Damascus for their voice. A leader rose from among their own.

Haj Amin el Husseini had been imprisoned for his complicity in the Jerusalem disorders two years earlier, but amnestied about the same time as Jabotinsky. He was distantly related to the other Hussein, the Shereef of Mecca, and likewise claimed descent from the Prophet.

After long deliberation Samuel decided that the peace of the land demanded that he win this man, a convicted trouble-maker, to his side. He appointed Haj Amin as Mufti of Jerusalem, or Grand Mufti. It was a religious office carrying political responsibilities and guardianship of immense endowments. The High Commissioner had little choice: the office was a family sinecure and no other suitable candidates presented themselves. He therefore made a virtue out of the necessity, to gain the Arab's assurance that his people would be kept in order.

Haj Amin was too wise to break his word during the remainder of Samuel's term of office. Indeed, Palestine was outwardly quiet for eight years, a period employed by the Mufti to consolidate his authority, make Jerusalem the focus of his nation's resurgence, and preach, from the impregnability of the Mosque, the justice of their claim to national independence.

Weizmann had accepted the Churchill White Paper, albeit with heavy heart. But an embargo on immigration, however temporary, was intolerable. It broke a solemn pledge – could there be a national home without people? He asserted that the Jews had not displaced a single Arab. As for the disorders, did not Britain have such troubles in India and Egypt, where Zionism did not exist?

His magisterial tone of reproach, as though to a wayward government that would one day come back to a realisation of its duty, went down very well in London drawing-rooms. But it alarmed his followers awaiting immigration permits in Eastern Europe. Weizmann knew it. Yet he was tired of bluff, and disillusioned not only by the meagre harvest of fund-raising in America, but also by the reluctance of Jews to join the pioneering work while immigration was easier. The movement owned large stretches of uninhabited land, but they had no ploughs to till it, no bricks to build on it.

They had to face the facts: Zionism as then constituted failed to convert the non-committed to their cause. He wanted the support of all their people, not merely a segment, and this would be achieved only by surrendering a place in their councils to the rich and the eminent, cool though such Jews might hitherto have been towards the national movement.

This talk struck Menahem Ussishkin, now of Jerusalem, as a compound of heresy, defeatism and treachery. Just five years since the Balfour Declaration, he thundered, and they were sunk in the humiliation of immigration restriction, and forbidden entry into the larger portion of historic Palestine. Was it for this Weizmann had asked them to place their trust in England? Ussishkin had lost all patience with their leader, whom he saw as a docile instrument of Britain's power, and intimated that the Palestine branch of the Executive, which he headed, was the true summit of the movement.

Ussishkin found a willing ally in Jabotinsky, who regarded Herbert Samuel as the evil genius of the Arab cause. This Jew, he declared, peopled his staff with avowed anti-semites, and the principal reason why money and immigrants were not forthcoming was because the High Commissioner discouraged Zionist initiative at every turn. And as for Weizmann's plan to enlist the non-Zionists, this was a betrayal of Theodor Herzl's legacy.

Strange, Weizmann pondered, the way Herzl's memory was invoked by the very men whose strictures drove their first leader to the grave. He reminded his critics of an inescapable truth: 'Nowhere in Herzl's writings,' he told them in 1922, 'is there a word about the question that is almost the central problem of our movement: the Arab question. In Herzl's time the Arabs did not exist politically. But today there lives in Palestine a people which does not wish the Jews to gain ground there. This is wrong, but it is a fact which you, we, and British statesmen have daily to take into consideration.'

Anxious to avoid a break with the government, and to keep the road open to an accommodation with the people comprising the great majority of the Palestine population, Weizmann demanded loyalty from his dissident colleagues. This could not be, for his relations with Jabotinsky and Ussishkin were clouded by personal feuds and ancient grudges. Sokolow apart, they were the only men around him with claims to the leadership, and their ill-concealed ambitions warned him of the disharmony to come. In 1923 he forced them out of the Executive. Ussishkin departed with vain threats of one day returning at the helm, but Jabotinsky was a more serious contender. He created a power-base of his own, and a political party, the 'Revisionists', out of the fevered atmosphere of Poland, where his demagogy could compensate the Jews for their lowly social situation. Other, lesser fry, followed the two principal rebels into the wilderness, among them Leo Motzkin, and it seemed that Weizmann was at last purged of the burdensome associations of his younger years.

In truth, he had had a narrow shave, and though the test of strength left him in total command, he knew now that every future Zionist Congress would prove an ordeal: the rank and file, denied a real voice in the conduct of the movement, would give vent to biennial outbursts of revolt. But while the momentum was his, he plunged ahead with his plan for a 'Jewish Agency', as it was termed, with broad appeal. It would not, as Brandeis had conceived such a body, replace the Zionist Organisation, but be subservient to it. He already had one candidate in Sir Alfred Mond, later Lord Melchett, of Imperial Chemical Industries. A former Minister in Lloyd George's government, Mond was brought to Palestine by Weizmann, to taste the idealism of the young country's pioneers. And from America he selected Louis Marshall, an outstanding lawyer and public figure in the Brandeis mould.

To Ussishkin and company such recruits, by their remoteness from the Jewish national spirit, sullied Zionism. Weizmann welcomed them on their own terms, trusting that commitment would beget conversion. He had in Baron Edmond their exemplar – a man who could not forbear from working for the cause while professing strong distaste for its objectives.

And an urgency fired the leader, for behind the proud Zionist drum-beating crisis was mounting. Over 30,000 Jews had arrived in Palestine since the end of the war, but few of them could contribute more than their bare hands, and money to start the factories and farms the country hungered for was pitifully inadequate. By the mid-twenties the boom had worked itself out. Unemployment, disease brought on by sudden transfer to a semi-tropical climate, the harsh realities of the life, were giving second thoughts to many. The West retained its lure.

Chasing elusive finance across the world, Weizmann was constantly reminded of the fundamental differences between the psychology of the Diaspora and the mentality of the settlers. Zionism could be conducted as a worthy middle-class relaxation by the Jews of the world, but in Palestine it was a ceaseless struggle, embracing the children's education and personal safety as well as their parents' right to a living wage. This produced an ideologically intensive proletariat, and leaders, like Ussishkin, with Byzantine attitudes of grandeur. As he set out to create his Jewish Agency, Weizmann arranged to protect his rear. He needed his own man to take charge in Palestine.

He sought a Jew familiar with the ways of officialdom, perhaps impeccably British himself. If he had no previous experience of Zionism so much the better. Weizmann's choice fell on a soldier in regular service, Colonel Fred Kisch, then attached to the British Embassy in Paris.

Loyal, urbane and enterprising, Kisch fulfilled his role to the letter. He was as tough as his chief in representing Jewish interests with the authorities, and followed faithfully the command to seek an accommodation with the Arabs. The Jews themselves were none too easy to handle. The workers were strengthening their position, and by creating the *Histadrut* as a trade union complex they moved with confidence in their own initiatives. Animosity between Left and Right in the *Yishuv*, as the Jewish community was biblically termed, rivalry between village and town, contrasts of Orthodoxy and secularism, these fractured solidarity and led to wasteful competition for the funds available. On the international plane the Zionist Congress re-animated these divisions as the frontiersmen of Tel Aviv and Galilee faced the committee-men from the bourgeois Diaspora.

Relations with the Arabs were by no means beyond repair. Kisch enjoyed the confidence of many notables in Jerusalem, but their Grand Mufti refused to speak to him, even formally at the receptions Samuel held at Government House. The two communities were tribally autonomous, but until they could be made to sit together in a Legislative Council overall government would remain a virtual despotism.

To the Zionist leader, no disappointment was so great as the weakness of Palestine's magnetic power upon Jewry. Even in the ghettos of Eastern Europe they continued, while weeping for Zion, to seek visas for New York, where they mostly had relatives, and which they knew to be the golden gateway to opportunity. The direction they travelled was westward until 1924, when America cried 'Enough!' and arrested the flow. Now Palestine had to absorb Jews who were Zionists by *force majeure*, people with nowhere else to go.

In the three years from 1924 to 1926 a substantial proportion of the 60,000 Jews who found their way to the Holy Land were of this category, and Weizmann could not but wonder whether they were the stuff of which nations are made. Instead of taking the pioneer path into agriculture, and the battle against the desert, the majority flocked to the towns, which were now in a condition of slump. The streets of Tel Aviv became choked by the barrows of petty traders, reminding Weizmann, when he arrived with Vera in 1925, of a place he detested, Warsaw, and the Nalewki district there, which spoke to him as being all that was negative about the Diaspora.

'Zionism is nothing if not a protest against Nalewki!' he exclaimed in wrath. Of course, he could not expect the transformation of a centuries-old way of life overnight, but he was determined to voice the danger while the *Yishuv* was young.

Yet that visit with his wife captured one of the shining moments of his dual life as Zionist and scientist: the opening of the Hebrew University at last. A glittering array from the world of scholarship, including old colleagues from Manchester, joined him as he stood on Mount Scopus with Balfour, Allenby and Samuel, those Englishmen chosen by destiny to help him write a new chapter of Jewish endeavour. The seventy-seven year old former Foreign Secretary, in his scarlet robes as Chancellor of Cambridge University and more a philosopher than a statesman, faced a scene of wild enthusiasm under the scorching sun. To the people of Jerusalem he seemed an instrument of the divine will.

It was Samuel's last year as High Commissioner, and together with Balfour, Sokolow and the Weizmanns, he toured the new settlements, those *kibbutzim* which have added a new word to modern vocabulary. To the cheering Jewish bystanders a caravan of Zionist history was passing on its way; to the Arabs observing in silence, it was a procession of their nation's executioners. All went off without incident until Balfour left the country for Syria. There, Damascus told another story. Angry demonstrators besieged his special train, and Balfour ended his visit ignominiously, on board ship and behind the guns of the French navy outside Beirut.

The economic crisis would not cure itself. The agricultural collectives, and the public enterprises sponsored by the *Histadrut*, had prior call upon the Zionist exchequer, so that resentment against Labour attained a groundswell. The best that Kisch could do was not enough, the broad Jewish Agency of Weizmann's hopes had still not materialised, and early in 1927 it seemed as though the entire Zionist experiment might remain just that, and collapse.

Jabotinsky was a gadfly. He staged dramatic entrances into the cities of Europe, bringing audiences to their feet with his cries that the Jewish future be taken out of the compromising hand of Chaim Weizmann. He publicly invited the Arabs to depart from Palestine and fulfil themselves in the limitless expanse of newly-born Arabia.

In the island of calm that was Jerusalem in those days Harry Sacher was cloistered, serenely engaged on a career at the Bar. Society, for the privileged, was not unlike that enjoyed by Englishmen in hill-stations throughout their tropical empire: formal dress, tiffin parties, civilised gossip, the knowledge that anything reproduced à l'anglaise exuded an excellence requiring no advertisement. To Sacher justice had its comedies as well as its challenge, for litigation entailed a meandering progress through a maze of Ottoman law, Rabbinical law, British law.

In 1927 Weizmann called Sacher, his earliest Manchester disciple, back to Zionist service. He must strengthen Kisch's position on the Jerusalem Executive, wrestle against their financial chaos, and conduct affairs as the Zionist leader would himself have done; favouring no party or special interest, restraining expenditure, asserting the rule of reason. Sacher shared authority with Kisch and Henrietta Szold, a remarkable American lady whose life was given to social welfare. On Mount Scopus Rabbi Judah Magnes, of New York, was taking his first steps as President of the new university. Government House was now occupied by Lord Plumer, the victor of Messines.

Sacher counted up the unemployed, to find he had to provide a dole for 7,000 workers and their families; the Jewish community hovered around the 150,000 mark in all. More Jews were leaving than were coming in, so deeply had defeatism eaten into the core of Zionist idealism. The new broom addressed himself to the problem with an application that earned him the reputation of a desiccated bureaucrat, and David Ben-Gurion, the general secretary of the Histadrut, spoke of his regime as tyranny. But he gained government contracts to provide work for the jobless, called a halt to fancy projects undertaken to impress visitors, and stemmed the tide.

For the moment they were saved. America seemed at last to be emerging from its torpor, though Weizmann remained unforgiving towards the Brandeis group for its desertion. He flung a stinging accusation at Felix Frankfurter: 'Brandeis could have been a prophet in Israel. You have in you the makings of a Lassalle. Instead, you choose to be only a professor at Harvard and Brandeis only a judge in the Supreme Court!' And, bitterly reviewing all the complications of their crippled cause, he remarked: 'In our Zionist work we have convinced everybody except the Jews.'

Soon, the truce with the Mufti would be over, and events outside the Jews' control would be doing the persuasion for him.

9

End of the Truce

As the 1920s rolled by in comparative peace, Chaim Weizmann was often given to wonder at the peculiarity of his public position. This movement, of which he was at once the champion, the apologist and the personification, what did it in truth signify? He was constantly confronted with its contradictory elements, each having a life of its own divorced from the others, and leading into byways where he found no place.

He was himself a rationalist, a product of that scientific materialism which he once described as a combination of Hegel and Darwin transformed into the modernism of Einstein and Eddington. But Zionism was by contrast Messianism, borne painfully across time by the Jews in the vessel of their ancient religion. The Zionist Organisation operated as an international network of autonomous associations, some regional, some ideological, enjoying a spasm of excited collective existence every two years at its Congress, where it staged its mutinies and then returned to hibernation.

Palestine, haven from the cruelties of one kind of world yet the frontier of conflict with another, was a reality to which he came as a stranger, for there the *Yishuv* of local Jews constituted a minor self-governing community in a quasi-imperial colony. They were developing social institutions in their own way.

Weizmann was the sole cohesive force in this complicated national edifice. The movement was weak, desperately so, because of its inability to win understanding for all its elements simultaneously among Jewry as a whole. As a result, the Zionists were too few in number, too divisive in their tendencies, and of insufficient resources and talent, to carry the endeavour through. Millions of Jews the world over either feared them for what their success might do to their own situation, or scorned them for the hopeless archaism of their task. The movement would have to change. He alone could do it; in fact, he alone wanted it. Thus Weizmann struggled with his followers for years to win the right to create a Jewish Agency on a broad base, even though he was enjoined to do so by the Articles of the Mandate.

At last, in the summer of 1929, he was able to consummate the preparations he had initiated six years earlier with the British industrialist and Liberal politician Lord Melchett, and with Louis Marshall, who spoke for non-Zionist Jewry in America. All opposition had been worn down, and now only Jabotinsky and his uncompromising Revisionist Party, together with a few so-called 'Radicals', persisted in their objections. According to them, the Agency would place the Zionist fate in the wrong hands for the wrong purpose.

He could now afford to disregard such detractors. The constitution of the new Jewish Agency provided for ultimate control to be invested in whoever was elected President of the World Zionist Organisation. This clause assuaged even a die-hard like Menahem Ussishkin, jealous guardian of Zionist purity though he was.

From the moment the Agency was established, at Zurich immediately following the Congress, the restoration of Jewish nationhood in Palestine ceased to be the obligation only of one great figure, sometimes assisted, sometimes impeded, by the lesser men surrounding him. The tragedy of Zionism had long been the detachment from the ideal of the finest Jewish minds, unable to cross the psychological barrier as demanded by commitment to a sectarian cause. Now, for the first time, Albert Einstein, hitherto restricting himself to avuncular advice on the running of the Hebrew University, identified with the intensifying Judaism of soil and culture. Herbert Samuel came at last to a Zionist gathering as an insider, together with Léon Blum, the French socialist leader whose personal affection for Weizmann prompted him to leap the chasm between Paris and Jerusalem. The old Baron Edmond de Rothschild, eighty-five years of age but still with five more years of active life ahead of him, accepted the office of Honorary President, thus ending, after forty years, the separation of his philanthropy from the movement of national regeneration.

Never before had Jewry achieved so near a healing. Palestine evidently had its message for all, the catalyst of fusion in a people diversified as well as dispersed. Those old enemies of Zionism, the Bund, were represented in the figure of Sholem Asch, the most distinguished Jewish novelist of the day; his presence marked the peace between the two largest Jewish political groupings of modern times.

Weizmann had had to be 'the fisher of men', for none came forward without his personal urging. In practical terms the recruit of highest value to him was Felix Warburg, the German-American banker who carried the substance of the Kuhn, Loeb finance house in his every gesture. Warburg had contributed half a million dollars to the Hebrew University, yet had shrunk from a place in the councils of the movement. With his capture, Weizmann knew that he had achieved for Zionism what could not be done by Brandeis: he had stormed the Teutonic fortress of the American-Jewish establishment in its very citadel of Wall Street.

Such people would never substitute for American Zionists proper. Weizmann freely admitted this, but he was doubly grateful for his success with them because the organised movement in the United States was proving a grievous disappointment. The Cleveland Convention of 1921 had produced a disciple, Louis Lipsky. Weizmann had been counting on this man and his New York supporters to bring him America, but they failed, and he had grown impatient with their political naivety and parochial conflicts. His words seemed powerless to convey to the Americans some appreciation of the plight of their own kin suffering increasing wretchedness and subject to shocking humiliations in Eastern Europe. America gave neither immigrants to Palestine nor whole-hearted political support to the cause. Let it, at least, learn to contribute adequate funds.

The Jewish Agency came not a moment too soon. While many delegates to the Zionist Congress were still completing their summer holidays in the pleasant watering-places of Central Europe that August, 1929, and the High Commissioner was abroad, and Palestine seemed overlaid with a tropical calm, disaster struck again in Jerusalem. The truce with the Arabs was over.

Only one man, Haj Amin el Husseini, was prepared for it. He had observed the growing militancy of the young people organised in Jabotinsky's party, always ready with a fiery demonstration in the Holy City. He had envied the Jews as they worked their farms, though the sight of scantily-clothed women at work alarmed him as a threat to Moslem morality. Little escaped the Grand Mufti: the spectacle of Weizmann constantly harried by his followers for his apparent moderation; a different Britain under the charge of a socialist Prime Minister, Ramsay MacDonald, who cared nothing for the imperial mission of a Power that in any case was gravely weakened by the world slump. Haj Amin had waited for eight years while the army of occupation dispersed. He knew that the Jews, given time, would create a suitable incident. It now arrived, with an apparently petty quarrel before the Wailing Wall in Jerusalem.

A portable canvas screen placed at the Wall by Orthodox Jews to segregate men and women at prayer simmered for nine months as a contest of religious rights and a goad to inter-racial hatreds. Talk in the coffee-houses dwelt on the seemingly inexhaustible supply of Jewish funds, and the newcomers' perverse addiction to toil. Perhaps that screen was the first step in a Jewish bid to possess the shrine entire, including the Mosque of Omar? Did the Jews not maintain that this was the Western Wall of the original Temple area?

The Mufti reminded his people that Weizmann had, in the days of the Zionist Commission, tried to purchase the courtyard in front of the Wall, to clear the rubble, he had claimed, and to render the site more worthy of its Jewish sanctity. Were the Arabs not master in their own capital? In neighbouring Syria and Iraq they were marching proudly towards national independence, while here their prospect was of endless servitude.

Thus began a long, hot summer of rebellion that terminated in a massacre. Choosing their victims with care, bands of Arabs roamed among the Jews in Jerusalem, Hebron, Safed, and selected villages. The 133 they butchered were not new pioneers, who rarely distanced themselves from their shot-guns, but the Orthodox element, ever close to their sacred books. The few British troops encamped in Palestine were evidently in the wrong places, and the violence continued until more soldiers could be brought in from outside. Now it was the Arabs' turn to suffer. In the quelling of the rioting they lost 116 of their young men.

With hundreds more injured or homeless (the Jews never returned to Hebron) the land had not known a disaster of such magnitude, neither in the period of Turkish control nor during the war years. The Jews could think of a parallel only in the Russia of the seventeenth century, and again while the Ukraine bled in the aftermath of the Soviet Revolution.

For the British, it was the long-feared parallel with Ireland, except that the woes of the latter country descended from four centuries of stormy relations, whereas Palestine had been in London's keeping for less than two decades. The Labour government was appalled, and cursed the folies de grandeur of its predecessors for landing them in such a mess.

MacDonald had visited Palestine twice as an Opposition leader, wooed by the Zionist socialists intent upon rendering the Second International into a propaganda platform. He had been carefully steered through the tented communes of the workers, and shown the greening of the desert achieved not by patrician *colons* employing cheap native labour but by the settlers themselves. But here was a picture of a different hue. It was no part of his policy to employ the British army in holding down the Empire. He had been a pacifist during the war and did not want the Empire.

The Prime Minister and his colleagues respected Weizmann, perhaps feared him, but they now hated to be reminded of the Balfour Declaration, which troubled them as a British document originating in a Machiavellian age. They recognised Jewry's right to a homeland in Palestine, especially as anti-semitism was on the increase in Europe, but they were moved also by the justice of the Arab case. The result was a calamitous vacillation of policy.

Perceiving that the general interpretation of the bloody events would be of Arab and Jew in battle for possession of the country, Weizmann returned hurriedly to London from Switzerland, where he too was on holiday with his family. He sought an exchange of assurances with MacDonald. He would calm the Zionist temper provided Britain remained faithful to the Mandate and continued immigration unrestricted by any factor except the economic capacity of Palestine to absorb it. He found the Prime Minister under pressure also from the friends of Zionism in the Labour Party – one of them his own son Malcolm. On the other side stood the Colonial Secretary, Lord Passfield. He was the former Sidney Webb, and he favoured the winding up of the whole burdensome Zionist business, which collapsed as an ideology under the joint scrutiny of himself and his doctrinaire wife Beatrice. As the reigning theoreticians of socialism the Webbs were formidable adversaries.

Weizmann was receiving little help from his own ranks. The riots told Ben-Gurion and Jabotinsky that time was working against them (though political opponents, they were making the same type of speech) and they floated a vision of millions of Jews hastening 'home'. Yet where were the signs, where was the money to finance it, how could the government's hand be forced? Weizmann showed the movement how the Mufti's incitement drew its fire from these empty, melodramatic challenges, that would additionally cost them the sympathies of men of state everywhere.

In Weizmann's view, the Jews' safeguard lay in a reaffirmation of the basic principle inherent in the 1917 Declaration. At his urging, the three surviving members of the War Cabinet, Balfour, Smuts and Lloyd George, all spoke up in its defence; and Churchill too, whose voice had remained silent on the subject of Palestine for seven years, now emerged as a determined friend of Zionism. Balfour was then in his last sickness, but he kept up his messages to Weizmann, encouraging him to resist any bid to disavow the National Home. MacDonald took the step characteristic of an indecisive man: he appointed a Parliamentary Commission, under Sir Walter Shaw, to investigate the causes of unrest in Palestine.

There was nothing to do now except wait. Or so Weizmann thought. In fact two men refused to await the outcome of the Shaw Commission's enquiries. The Colonial Secretary and the High Commissioner, now Sir John Chancellor, agreed between them that once the Zionists had occupied the land already in their ownership there should be no further Jewish agriculture. And the Arabs must have their say in all matters affecting immigration in the future. The Prime Minister was given a memorandum embracing these proposals in January, 1930. The Shaw Commission did not finish its work until March.

Its report was not favourable to the Jews. To Weizmann's dismay it went beyond its appointed task of investigating the immediate circumstances of the disorders, and concluded by repudiating the policies of successive governments since 1917. Though acknowledging the benefits to the country as a whole brought about by the revival of undeveloped land long thought of as unusable, it recommended suspension of all immigration. Rightly or wrongly, the Shaw Report stated, the Arabs identified Jewish growth with Jewish intentions of annexation. The Labour member of the Commission, Harry Snell, disagreed with these conclusions, blaming the trouble on Palestine's inadequate police force and the activities of the Grand Mufti.

In a forthright discussion with the Prime Minister, Weizmann asked whether Britain intended abdication from its functions as laid down in the League of Nations Mandate, and indeed give effect to Shaw's recommendations. It would mark the end not only of the Anglo-Zionist alliance, he warned, but of himself as the leader of the movement. And if he disappeared the result could only be a new, militant direction of their affairs.

Realising the danger, MacDonald agreed to strengthen Weizmann's hand. He made a conciliatory statement in the House of Commons. But far from being an unequivocal repudiation of Shaw, the speech was cautious and ambivalent. The government was in an exposed, minority position and recoiled from an expensive and unpopular reinforcement of the army in Palestine. The Prime Minister announced the despatch of another investigator, Sir John Hope-Simpson, to evaluate the economic situation. Immigration would cease till his return.

What disturbed Weizmann above all was the spread in his own ranks of both defeatism and extremism under the impact of these developments. Disillusionment with Britain, and recognition that the Arabs possessed in the Mufti a skilful and ruthless leader, told many Jews that they must either lower their sights and work for an accommodation by surrendering their hope of an ultimate majority in the country, or fortify their position for the power struggle that must inevitably arise. If the first, then hope was lost of solving the Jewish question in Europe. If the second, they must build a clandestine army for their protection in Palestine and smuggle the Jews in to make up their numbers.

As we have seen, Weizmann could not retain his grip on every outgrowth of Zionism, and in the event both these policies had champions working to put them into effect. Rabbi Judah Magnes, head of the Hebrew University, led a movement of conciliation that upheld Jewish right of entry but conceded to the Arabs ultimate control of the population structure. He gathered around him a group of 'intellectual' Zionists, among them Norman Bentwich, son of Weizmann's early English associate Herbert and now the country's saint-like Attorney-General, and Arthur Ruppin, who was the movement's colonisation chief. Their support was to be found principally in Germany (Einstein was among them), and in the near-Communist *kibbutzim* of the ultra-Left.

Such people were remote from the workaday realities of the country. Not without justification, they were regarded as hopeless visionaries, proclaiming as they did a Jewish humility when they themselves were the embodiment of Jewish ascendancy: Palestine boasted no Arab university, no Arab colonisation expert, no richly-subsidised Arab *kibbutzim*. Weizmann felt that Magnes was making a dupe of Einstein – whose political naivety was monumental – and his contempt for the university's head knew no bounds. He described the rabbi to the physicist as a 'hypocrite, a Tartuffe, lightly abandoning the Balfour Declaration. He didn't bleed for it; he only gained by it.'

Reason, at least, was on the side of those at the other extreme. While they mostly protested socialism and preached a policy of friendship with the Arabs, they quietly consolidated their position as the compact, peace-loving shock-troops of a bloodless conquest. Jabotinsky might be more strident in the Diaspora, but in Palestine his following was weaker in numbers and idealism, and this would be his ultimate undoing. The

Histadrut, however, rested on a strong political infrastructure. Its General Secretary Ben-Gurion could call the workers out on strike, carry their voting strength to the Congress, manage a factory, establish a *kibbutz*, build a hospital, and pay a standing army to wait in the shadows. Weizmann had little except his personality to contain this spectrum of interests within one organisation. He transcended political parties and consequently invoked the wrath of them all. Now the events of 1929 were to prove a watershed. His beloved creation, the Palestine *Yishuv*, was beginning to outgrow its parent. The result was his own surrender to defeatism – momentary only, but disastrous just the same.

Ben-Gurion served notice on the President that the Jews of Palestine could no longer tolerate a system whereby the leader sent his own nominees to Palestine to conduct affairs on their behalf. He wanted Harry Sacher and Fred Kisch removed from the Executive. To him they were Englishmen, not Palestinians, and more nearly government officials of Bentwich's stamp than Jewish spokesmen. More, Ben-Gurion and his comrades could speak to MacDonald the socialist as 'worker to worker'. The *Histadrut* leader therefore demanded representation in London, on Weizmann's 'Cabinet' at their Bloomsbury headquarters in Great Russell Street, and a say in the daily conduct of Zionist business.

This was not intended as a challenge to the leadership. Few people could as yet visualise either the Zionist Organisation or the Jewish Agency without Weizmann's unifying presence. Who else among them could impel Smuts to action in distant Africa with a telegram, or extract an undertaking from Lloyd George to oppose government policy in Parliament, or travel the world with the dignity, almost the authority, of a Prime Minister? Who could win money from the non-committed as he could, merely by shaking the hand of a rich man and promising in return only another visit, the year after, for a further donation?

Nevertheless Weizmann's era seemed to be drawing to its close. Nothing marked its end so vividly as the scene at Lord Balfour's death-bed, described by Blanche Dugdale, niece and biographer of the Declaration's author, when the Jew came to make his farewells to the man he had placed within the Zionist scheme in 1906. This was twenty-four years later:

A few days before the end he received for a few moments a visitor from outside the circle of his family. This was Dr Chaim Weizmann, the Zionist leader. No one but myself saw the brief and silent farewell between these two, so diverse from one another, whose mutual sympathy had been so powerful an instrument in the history of a nation . . . No words passed between them, or could pass, for Balfour was very weak and Dr Weizmann much overcome. But I, who saw the look with which Balfour moved his hand and touched the bowed head of the other, have no doubt at all that he realised the nature of the emotion which for the first, and only, time showed itself in his sick-room.

The government still hesitated from a declaration of intent. Weizmann believed his doctrine of partnership with Britain and the Arabs might be given fresh life if he could satisfy the Arabs that their fear of the Jews was a chimera. He chose a conference in Berlin, in August, 1930, to expunge formally and specifically the concept of an exclusively Jewish State from the Zionist vocabulary. 'The Jewish State,' he said, 'was never an aim in itself, only a means to an end. Nothing is said about the Jewish State in the Balfour Declaration. The essence of Zionism is to create a number of important material foundations upon which an autonomous, compact and productive community can be built.' Relations with the Arabs, he went on, could be bound in friendship if they worked together towards bi-national government, in which both races could enjoy independence without one dominating the other.

The Arabs would not have it. Without replying directly, the Mufti declared through his newspapers that he had one demand only – complete independence in the whole of Palestine. In October Hope-Simpson's report was published, and with it the Passfield White Paper on government policy.

The first document voiced the fear that further Jewish settlement would reduce the living standard of the *fellah*, the Arab peasant. The second fore-shadowed the 'crystallisation' of Zionist enterprise, with the early forma-tion of a Legislative Council. This would give the Arabs the voting strength to stifle Jewish growth. And although the Jews repudiated Hope-Simpson's statistics, as did later the Permanent Mandates Commission of the League of Nations, compelling a government offer to re-examine the facts, there was little hope of a reprieve.

Passfield's White Paper was a lamentable apologetic for the colonial officials in Palestine, who had their own failures to justify. They had been warned time and again of the threatening clouds but had chosen to ignore them. Jewish pleas for an expansion of the police force by increased enrol-ment from their own people had gone unheeded. Many officials adopted a cynical front towards Zionist rehabilitation of the soil, ascribing the disparity between Jewish and Arab living standards not to the traditional Arab tempo of serenity (insensitively described as inertia by the Jews) or to exploitation by their absentee *effendi* landlords, but to a carefully systematised Jewish invasion. The White Paper decided Weizmann. He publicly renounced his trust in Great Britain and resigned his leadership. Lord Melchett and Felix Warburg, the two principal officers of the Jewish Agency, resigned with him.

Now the Weizmann method came into play. When required he could be an adroit politician, and he had developed machinery for just such a time. Blanche ('Baffy') Dugdale was on his staff, and her family connections and personal friendships gave her extraordinary influence in the Conservative Party. She was now put to work. She induced the Conservative leader, Stanley Baldwin, and his lieutenants, among them Austen Chamberlain, Leopold Amery and Winston Churchill, to condemn the government in the strongest terms. Churchill, exponent though he might be of the imperial mission, tempted the fates in a challenge he was destined to repeat to a later Labour government: 'From the moment that we recognise and proclaim that we have departed from our undertakings regarding the Zionist cause, we are bound to return the Mandate to the League of Nations and forgo the strategic, moral and material advantages arising from British control of, and association with, the Holy Land.'

The strands of agitation at Weizmann's command stretched in all directions, and he released a cataract of protest – on the Continent, in America, throughout the British Empire. A word to the Labour Party intellectual Harold Laski, who by no measure could be termed a Zionist, and to Felix Frankfurter, and the campaign was taken up by academic and legal luminaries of the entire English-speaking world. The emotion thus generated came to MacDonald as a startling revelation. He blamed Passfield for bringing his government so low in international esteem, and hurriedly arranged for Weizmann to come to luncheon in Downing Street.

The Prime Minister's son Malcolm was also present, and Weizmann listened in admiration while this young man categorised to his father the errors of the White Paper, both in its ignorance of the terms of the Mandate and in its assessment of the Zionist impact upon the Arab situation. And when the Prime Minister, in retreat, himself spoke disparagingly of Passfield, Weizmann demanded the White Paper's formal repudiation.

This was not possible, MacDonald told him, but he would 'interpret' the document in a public statement. Further, in response to Weizmann's persistent complaints against the administrators on the spot in Palestine, he undertook to replace High Commissioner Chancellor, on termination of his service, with a man more friendly to Zionism.

The government's surrender took the form of a letter from the Prime Minister to Weizmann, in February, 1931, which was read from the front bench of the House of Commons and communicated to the Mandates Commission in Geneva. MacDonald stated therein:

It is recognised that the constructive work done by the Jewish people in Palestine has had beneficent effects on the development and well-being of the country as a whole . . . Obligations to facilitate Jewish immigration and to encourage close settlement on the land remains a positive obligation of the Mandate and it can be fulfilled without prejudice to the rights and position of other sections of the population of Palestine.

Though the letter contained implications and qualifications not likely fully to reassure its recipient, Weizmann nevertheless felt justified in producing it to his followers as re-endorsement of their cause. This brought him to the difficult question: should he, then offer himself for re-election as their President?

Now that he was, technically, no longer leader of the movement, he deliberated over the prospect of not assuming office again, for some years at least. The thought of establishing a home in Jerusalem, and spending six months of the year at the Hebrew University, seemed particularly attractive. He had acquired a house for his mother at Haifa, where her eldest and youngest sons were employed by Melchett's Imperial Chemical Industries, and most of their large family was now reunited in Palestine. At fifty-six years of age, Weizmann was feeling the pull of science again. He must respond now or never.

Moreover, the Hebrew University demanded the attention of an expert academic hand. The position was delicate. Magnes was a man of great, almost painful, integrity. Born on San Francisco Bay, he was connected with wealthy American families, and was by vocation a theologian, so that he even saw ritual purification in his passionate devotion to baseball. But his conduct of the university did not suggest that he fully understood the true functions of such an institution. Difficulties had arisen from his inexperience as an administrator and his tendency to use his office as a pulpit to advance his political views. In discussion with Einstein, Weizmann saw that he was not alone in his misgivings about the university.

If only that most renowned thinker were available for service in Jerusalem!

Meanwhile, in July, 1931, the delegates assembled for their Congress in Basle. It seemed that barely a week had passed without Palestine reaching the world's headlines since they had last come together two years earlier. Their appearance was of an army in disarray. A brooding sense of impotence, an atmosphere of righteous indignation, resentment against Britain; these had their effect on Weizmann as he proceeded to the rostrum and scanned the hall to read the expressions of friend and foe.

Time had dealt roughly with him since that proud day in neighbouring Zurich when, at the inauguration of the Jewish Agency, he was acclaimed as the architect of the people's unity. What could he bring to the Congress now, except an avalanche of state papers – they excused and accused – emanating with wearying rapidity from Whitehall?

He was stripped of great sources of strength. Both Louis Marshall, who was to have been his American right arm, and Lord Melchett, had died suddenly. Sacher, unable to sustain a Draconian role in Jerusalem, had yielded to the workers' demand and returned to England. Kisch too had had enough, and was retiring to private life. The Wall Street crash had torpedoed Weizmann's calculations regarding transatlantic funds, and soon every Jewish village in Palestine would feel the loss. It was the movement's prerogative to select a scapegoat, and he had already dared to voice the unthinkable in his resignation. On what terms would the movement have him back? He would not speak of defiance; he could not counsel patience.

The Congress detected this lack of decision in his survey of his years of stewardship, masterful though it was as an assessment of the forces balancing each other in framing the destiny of Palestine. Recognition of the Arab case, he insisted, did not one whit diminish the Jewish case. They must have faith in their own constructive toil; it would make them an unassailable economic unit, and he reminded those of his hearers clamouring for release from the British straitjacket that, in the time of Cyrus, only 40,000 Jews in Babylon had responded to the Zionist call. Yet they were sufficient to re-create the nation.

The speech gave small comfort to the Left, whose loyalty he always professed to value and was now claiming as his due. Jabotinsky, speaking not only for his own delegation but also for many without party affiliation, pronounced it a confession of failure. The militant Right was demanding that they at last abandon their hypocritical mask and state an unequivocal objective for Zionism. Terms like 'National Home' could neither appease nor deceive, Jabotinsky charged. Their aim was nothing less than a Jewish majority in a Jewish State on both sides of the Jordan – that is, to include Abdulla's Emirate beyond the river.

The corridors buzzed for days afterwards as the Congress simulated attention to its bulky agenda. Budgets had to be agreed, sub-committees elected, education, propaganda, fund-raising, all required discussion – two years' business was being compressed into two weeks. Believing that he might yet produce tangible evidence of the Prime Minister's undertaking of a new start, Weizmann despatched Ben-Gurion to MacDonald in London. They would see what the *Histadrut* leader could achieve when 'worker spoke to worker'.

But Weizmann was being pressed for his reply to Jabotinsky's challenge. If it failed to satisfy the Congress this other Russian (their personal rapport still survived) could well become their new leader, and rapprochement with either Britain or the Arabs would prove impossible. He gave an interview to the reporter of a Jewish news service, and in an outburst of impatience was driven to state: 'I have no understanding of, and no sympathy for, the demand for a Jewish majority in Palestine. Majority does not guarantee security, majority is not necessary for the development of Jewish civilisation and culture. The world will construe this demand only in the sense that we wish to acquire a majority in order to drive out the Arabs.'

The words were read almost with incredulity in the bulletins the following morning, and Weizmann's friends vainly protested that he had been misreported. But the damage was done. If this was their leader's view they might just as well have Magnes, against whom they had just passed a vote of non-confidence, as their leader. Weizmann, it seemed, was intent upon political hara-kiri.

Ben-Gurion came hastening back to Basle. He had good news. MacDonald had reiterated his promise that Palestine would be given a new High Commissioner with instructions to keep faith with the Balfour Declaration and all it signified. Furthermore, Ben-Gurion reported, the Prime Minister had hinted that the Jews might indeed be permitted to colonise in Transjordan, for the Arabs, with freedom in the immense territories they had won during the war, had surely achieved every aspiration to which they had a right.

It was too late. In Ben-Gurion's absence there had been a furore, and it brought into prominence two younger men of the post-war Zionist generation, both disciples more or less of Weizmann. Chaim Arlosoroff, the political secretary of the *Histadrut*, stood apart from his comrades of that body as its sole Central European intellectual with a western education. Nahum Goldmann, of the tiny 'Radical' group, was busily making a name for himself in the German Zionist Federation. They took up the protest in 'parliamentary' language, before the full assembly.

In response to a question from Arlosoroff, doubtless by prior arrangement, Weizmann amended his statement, diluted it with qualifications, by-passed it in biting aspersion to the absurdity of the militants' stance. Arlosoroff declared himself satisfied, and proposed that they proceed with the agenda. This the Congress refused to do. It desired a formula; not Jabotinsky's of course, but one that would adequately embody the ultimate objectives of Zionism: a new Basle Programme, in fact, to supplant the formulation made in this same city at Herzl's first Congress of 1897.

Goldmann, chairman of the political sub-committee, moved a vote of censure against the President on the grounds that his reply to Arlosoroff was unacceptable. The latter sprang to Weizmann's defence, but to no avail. The vote of censure received only a small majority, but enough to signify to Weizmann that he could not stand for re-election. Stunned, he took Vera's arm and departed, followed by his immediate retinue of British supporters.

Now all was confusion. The Congress refused to believe what it had done: Israel, in the words of Jeremiah, devouring its own prophet. The Revisionists tried to force their maximalist motion through while the Left howled them down, singing the Zionist anthem *Hatikvah* as though the proceedings were over. Leo Motzkin, in the Chair, hammered in vain with his gavel, and Jabotinsky strode from the hall, theatrically tearing up his delegate card as he went.

Jabotinsky could still win election to the Presidency. But having dismissed Weizmann the Congress drew away from the consequences. It finally conferred the leadership on Nahum Sokolow, his life-long Zionist comrade. On hearing the news Weizmann could not suppress a sardonic satisfaction. He had long considered Sokolow a sleeping, rather than an active, partner; it was as though the Zionist Organisation had dissolved itself.

While his resignation had been issued as a proud challenge, his rejection was a humiliation, and made worse by his being beaten by the party system, which he always despised. He had not worked enough to secure a power base, and in fostering his American group he had overlooked the resilience of the Brandeis faction. This old guard had stolen supremacy from Lipsky. It was led by Stephen Wise, who had largely engineered Weizmann's downfall. He was also paying for his long neglect of Poland, which since the war had become the quarry where rival election agents mined votes for Right or Left.

Certainly Weizmann was justified in his morose verdict on the Sokolow regime. Of new blood there was little; of new ideas there were none. The British mathematician Selig Brodetsky sought Weizmann's express sanction before joining the Executive. A *Mizrachi* member was appointed for the first time, ostensibly to give Poland a voice. Wise placed one American representative on the Executive, and the Left-wing two Palestinians, including Arlosoroff. Ben-Gurion remained aloof, biding his moment, which would come when he had achieved undisputed mastery of the *Yishuv*. The great problem remained the Jewish Agency. Could it survive its creator's departure? In fact the Agency quietly died as an independent body, for its leading members were virtually Weizmann's nominees. By default, its powers were vested in the Zionist Executive, which had started life in Herzl's day as the Smaller Actions Committee and now assumed the title of Jewish Agency Executive.

True to his word, MacDonald sent a different kind of official to occupy Government House in Jerusalem, selecting Sir Arthur Wauchope, an ex-general like Plumer and the antithesis of the traditional colonial servant. The new man seemed well-disposed to the Jews and soon made a warm friend of Arlosoroff who, just as perversely, liked the British, though without crediting their political intentions with his trust. Almost imperceptibly, immigration ceased to be a source of contention, 10,000 Jews arriving in 1932.

A universal preoccupation with international problems now removed Palestine from newspaper headlines. The deepening economic crisis sent Britain off the gold standard and compelled MacDonald to form a National Government. The Jews could hardly complain now of hostility in high places. Perhaps the new immigration trend was not unconnected with the brief presence in the Cabinet of Herbert Samuel as Home Secretary, Lord Reading as Foreign Secretary, and Lord Crewe, whose mother-in-law was a Rothschild, as War Minister. Britain had two million unemployed, but Palestine, due to the immigrants' need for housing and an upsurge in citrus production, was experiencing another boom.

The storm over, Weizmann recovered from his sense of betrayal. He could give more time now to his family. Benjamin was at Cambridge; Michael, a boarder at Rugby, was developing more definitely the traits of a typical upper-class English youth at the establishment immortalised by *Tom Brown's Schooldays*. Vera's beauty was undiminished. She dressed regally, and was in great demand as a speaker for the Women's International Zionist Organisation, which she had founded together with their dear friend Rebecca, wife of Israel Sieff. Chaim loved nothing more than to accompany Vera at her meetings, and when called upon for a few words his pungent humour rarely deserted him. Usually the family travelled to Palestine for the Passover, and there at old Rachel Weizmann's crowded table slipped naturally into Russian, but the boys neither knew that language nor Hebrew. Paradoxically, they were being drawn into the very assimiliation against which their father's life was a protest. Benjamin seemed more his father's son, Michael his mother's. The younger boy was easier to handle, jollier company, than had been his brother, progeny of a more difficult period in the parents' relationship. In a family ever surrounded by admirers, who regarded the lowliest errands they were privileged to undertake as a Zionist service, Michael was the spoilt darling, the other a remote introvert. To Benjamin the domestic atmosphere was distasteful. His father understood the reasons better than Vera, but she governed the home and her first-born disappointed her in not conforming to her image of the fine English gentleman.

Pending the fulfilment of his promise to himself to work at the Hebrew University, Weizmann opened a laboratory in London and plunged happily into a new routine. It was anticipated that he would head the School of Agriculture and develop the Department of Chemistry at Jerusalem, and this meant brushing up on the requisite scientific literature.

The mood for Palestine was optimistic, and hopes were high. But he refused to allow complacency, nor would he subscribe to false heroics about Jewish achievements there, striking though they were. 'In the last twelve years,' he never tired of repeating, 'we have poured something like £40 millions into Palestine. It would have been a cause for wonder and misfortune if this had not achieved the present results . . . Palestine will not be built up on dividends received from oranges, but on the sustained efforts of those unfashionable people called idealists.'

Sokolow, for all his virtues, failed to carry the movement along the coordinated strategy demanded by its complementary forces: the disunity of the Diaspora, the singularity of the *Yishuv*. A man of the widest culture, he possessed integrity, personal humility, compassion and shrewdness. But he lacked the fire of a restless conscience. Weizmann, for all his weaknesses, was indispensable in guiding Zionism from the periphery of the world's attention to the centre. In contrast with the easy-going Sokolow, he could be suspicious of the motives of others, secretive, domineering, quick to anger. Weizmann was not beyond petty deceptions; yet he inspired loyalty, made dreams seem everyday realities, and gave to their national struggle a nobility of intent vital if it was to succeed in attracting recruits from the post-war generation.

Only a man of his adaptability could manage so complicated a people as the Jews, who merged servility with aggressiveness and played their minority condition like a violin, alternating pathos with chords of grandeur. The moment Sokolow took office the Zionists worked, nay intrigued, to get Weizmann back.

He was now in no great hurry to return. His influence on the movement was almost undiminished, for he was consulted both by the London Executive and Arlosoroff, who worked from Jerusalem to restrain Wauchope from pressing summarily forward with the Legislative Council plan. With Weizmann's encouragement, Arlosoroff poured out his confidences, although he was fully aware that the fallen leader was almost alone in giving guarded support to the Legislative Council.

Weizmann's view was that they might succeed in negotiating parity of representation with the Arabs in such an assembly, the first step towards self-government. But Arlosoroff, since the 1929 riots a pessimist like Ben-Gurion about Arab intentions, saw little purpose in talk. More likely, he wrote, the Jews would one day have to resort to open rebellion to gain their objectives, for under the evolutionary system they were losing the race.

This was a young man's fantasy, Weizmann thought, and he dismissed the sentiment as belonging to the emotionalism invariably generated by the Palestinians in discussion. Hitlerism had not yet arrived as the overwhelming factor of Jewish life, and he was more concerned with quality than with quantity in the growth of the *Yishuv*. He tested their ability and determination to effect the Jewish revival on two aspects of their work: the pioneer agricultural base, with Jewish labour on Jewish soil avoiding all the pitfalls of traditional colonialism, and their cultural development, with the Hebrew University as its pinnacle.

His faith in the pioneers was vindicated in the evidence everywhere of desert and marsh dramatically transformed. But the university remained a worry. Einstein had resigned from the Board of Governors, refusing any longer to associate his name with the institution.

Having enlisted the physicist's interest in the university with their joint onslaught upon America in 1921, Weizmann sorrowed at the implications of his withdrawal. Einstein had given the inaugural lecture at the university, well before its formal inauguration in 1925. This in itself reflected something of its inherent weakness – a tendency towards self-glamorisation in advance of real progress. Einstein readily forgave the exploitation of his name in any cause he supported, and was accustomed to the practice. But he would no longer allow his name to be coupled with the university while Magnes reigned unchallenged as Chancellor on Mount Scopus.

The American rabbi assumed responsibility for all activities: curriculum, administration, choice of personnel, fund-raising. This was in part inevitable, as Weizmann knew only too well – sadly, Jewish scholars of the front rank could only rarely be attracted to Palestine against competition from more luxuriant pastures. But Magnes was deaf to pleas that another hand take over his purely academic duties. He convinced himself that Weizmann and Einstein were intriguing against his position, even though his ability to extract large sums from his American faithfuls made him almost unassailable.

Apart from its School of Jewish Studies (embracing Archeology, Sociology, Philosophy and Oriental subjects) a field in which neither Einstein nor Weizmann professed expertise, the university had so far established Departments of Chemistry, Physics and Mathematics. These were basically the research institutes foreshadowed in Weizmann's original scheme of 1914, and would soon be due for expansion with an in-take of students and the award of first degrees.

With this in mind, Weizmann had recommended Brodetsky, whose distinguished record in mathematics had been crowned with a professorship at Leeds, for the post of Academic Head. But Brodetsky had refused the appointment, anticipating conflict with Magnes, whose scholastic approach he regarded as no more acceptable than his Zionist views. Hence Einstein's impatience with the politics of scholarship in Jerusalem.

Weizmann could not shrug off responsibility for the university, and while arrangements for his appointment to the School of Agriculture were gestating he decided to open his own laboratory there, and renew his association with chemistry. He had a standing invitation to do so, and it would enable him to stay close by and ensure general scientific progress on recognised lines. His requirements would be modest, and perhaps be understood as an example of the Zionist pioneering he was preaching to the Jews of the world.

Magnes saw his opportunity to repay Weizmann in kind and, amazingly, a place was refused to the deposed leader. Magnes pleaded lack of funds.

He thus denied entry to the university of its own Chairman of Governors, whose mere presence would enhance the status of the institution! Moreover, Magnes announced·shortly afterwards that the university was about to initiate a degree course in Biology. Weizmann had not been consulted and reacted in horror at the news.

Of course it was impossible, as Brodetsky had discerned, to dissociate Magnes the politician from Magnes the Chancellor. He had started in Zionism as an ally of Weizmann, but the two men had taken opposite roads: one was preoccupied with the guilt in Jewish nationalism, the other represented its exaltation. Suddenly everything associated with the university provoked notoriety. A Chair had been found for Norman Bentwich, the Jewish Attorney-General forced out of his post by Colonial Office displeasure. His inaugural lecture, on international peace of all subjects, had to be conducted under police protection, because Revisionist students threatened violence as Bentwich began to speak.

However, politics were far from Weizmann's mind now. He could visualise no course of study at the university to justify a degree in Biology, for the subject could have no academic meaning in an institution so modest. Sadly, for he regarded science as the key to a thriving Palestine, he confessed to Felix Warburg, the university's most generous patron: 'It would be an irreparable error to set up a series of second-rate subjects which serve as window-dressing for the public but which, in substance, would be of no service to any scientific institution.'

He was determined to harness science to Zionism. He knew he must himself work in Palestine. But not in Jerusalem. Pending a change in the situation there he would find a home for his laboratory elsewhere. The place he had in mind was south of Tel Aviv, among the citrus plantations where the Jewish Agency already maintained an agricultural research station. He would found a new institute and keep it to the highest rigorous standards. But where would he obtain the money, where find the scientists to staff it? The year 1933, the year of Adolf Hitler, provided answers in plenty.

10

Gathering Clouds

WEIZMANN WAS WORKING IN HIS STUDY ON A SPEECH WHEN, IN February, 1933, the report came through that Germany had voted Adolf Hitler absolute powers to deal with the problems of his country. He threw his draft away and began afresh. This was news of a magnitude that even a Zionist, accustomed to the lurid language of catastrophe, could not readily assess.

By striking first at a Jewry of great talent, identified with the *esprit* of their fatherland, deeply patriotic and fast progressing to voluntary extinction, Hitlerism changed the character of this people as a whole. Before its advent the justification for Zionism was debatable. Now the argument whether the Jews were indeed a people became a theoretical luxury. A western leader, acclaimed enthusiastically among his own, covertly applauded by many others besides, had resolved that ancient controversy with a deadening finality. According to Hitler, the Jews did not belong to European civilisation.

Such an assertion, the Jews protested, was a blasphemy against history; it disqualified Germany from the right to be counted a civilised nation. Nevertheless they were now more effectively converted to Zionism than by any speech, any event, since the time, still recalled with humiliation by the Jews, when a charlatan Messiah arose to lead the straying tribes home in the seventeenth century.

Immediately, Palestine received a significance hardly anticipated by the authors of the Balfour Declaration. It became the land that every Jew, whether enjoying freedom or existing in pariahdom, would now, in his fears and fantasies, recognise in his heart as the refuge of last resort. Not that their conversion was at once apparent to them; some would resist its implications even as they lined up to enter the concentration camps. Weizmann was at a loss as to how to refer to the news in his speech. The German Jews themselves would not be grateful to premature champions leaping to their defence from remote parts.

He was due to address a great banquet in London 'in honour of the friends of Palestine in Parliament' – one of those events devised by professional fund-raisers eternally engaged in the invidious task of making such occasions attractive to guests with the right-size purses. Inevitably, he could not give his mind to it. He had served both his Zionist and scientific apprenticeship in Germany, and the country had strongly influenced his cultural development also. Life-long friendships had been formed there.

His thoughts dwelt on the numerous German scholars he had coveted for Palestine. Surely Hitler would now do his persuading for him. He wondered at the emotions being experienced by Martin Buber, for example, comrade of his younger years, the leading twentieth century philosopher of Judaism then teaching at Frankfurt. What fate would befall Richard Willstätter, the great organic chemist of Munich, and Fritz Haber, whose war work for Germany was similar to Weizmann's for England? And Einstein himself, who on Hitler's accession to power was lecturing in Los Angeles? German Jewry had produced more Nobel prize winners than any group, and here were three of them, the élite of the world's unemployed, though victims of a moral rather than an economic slump. Now, rejected by their native land, they could come to the true home of the wandering Jew, and, in the phrase made famous by Churchill in 1921, 'not on sufferance, but as of right'.

Money would surely be available as never before. Was there an American Morgenthau, Warburg, Schiff, Straus, whose family-tree did not extend to some impecunious victim of the Nazis? And beyond these Weizmann thought of the thousands of others, the doctors, lawyers, civil servants, to be re-trained for a new life – Palestine had little need of so many professional people, but it could find a place for everyone on farms and in factories, at tasks that were honoured for being performed in the Holy Land. Germany, it soon transpired, was amenable to a sad bargain: Jews leaving the fatherland would not forfeit their assets provided these were translated into German goods.

The Zionists established their emergency committees. The *Yishuv* waited expectantly. Despite Jewish cynicism at the MacDonald Letter, the British Prime Minister remained faithful to his undertaking, so Passfield was just a wry memory. Arlosoroff prepared the way for the newcomers, and he and High Commissioner Wauchope together inspected locations for villages of the orphaned who would be leaving their German institutions.

Arab land-owners, braving the Mufti's surveillance (reinforced by threats), beat a path to the Jewish Agency's headquarters in Jerusalem with offers to sell. Weizmann arrived in Palestine in the spring of 1933, buoyant with anticipation of the fruitful union of Germany's Jews with the homeland. He was ushered by Arlosoroff to the King David Hotel, where a group of Transjordan chieftains waited to convey the greetings of their Emir, Abdulla. And not only greetings. They had land in plenty to lease, and Abdulla would be pleased, Weizmann was told, to welcome the Jews to his territory. MacDonald had intimated such a possibility to Ben-Gurion. Agreements were signed, dignified photographs taken. But it was one of those strange lapses of judgment on Weizmann's part. Wauchope refused to approve the transaction. He knew nothing of a change of policy regarding Jewish settlement in Transjordan. Why indulge in needless provocation?

Weizmann was still smarting under Magnes's rebuff over the university business, though many problems would surely be solved in time by recruitment of scholars from Germany. He remained impatient to effect his own reconciliation with science. His laboratory in London was merely one of many; here it would be a sapling to help change the desert, a focus for European scientists determined on a new life.

He had thought long the previous year about his ambitious plan, but had refrained from seeking funds for it in apparent competition with the university, whose needs must take precedence. But the German situation had fired him afresh, and in recent weeks he had seen a way out of his dilemma through his relationship with the brothers-in-law and business partners Simon Marks and Israel Sieff.

These two had been inseparables since their Manchester schooldays, and by the thirties their partnership had blossomed into an empire. The third brother-in-law, Harry Sacher, was likewise associated with them since his departure from Palestine. Few family groups could be so happily united spiritually, and under Weizmann's spell they felt their lives enriched by Zionism, to turn them into a middle-class version of the aristocratic Rothschilds. Established since the war in London, they formed a ring around the leader, sustaining him in good times and bad. The Sieffs' son Daniel and the Weizmanns' son Michael seemed to be reproducing in their own friendship the pattern set by their elders. But tragedy intervened, for early in 1933 Daniel Sieff, at the age of seventeen, committed suicide. In their grief the bereaved parents recalled the boy's enthusiasm for science, and searched for a means to perpetuate his name in a way that could benefit the Jewish people and Palestine. Weizmann came to them with his dream of an institute of scientific research. Promptly, the family made it their financial responsibility.

Thus it was, shortly after the meeting with Abdulla's chieftains, that Vera and Chaim Weizmann, accompanied by the devoted Arlosoroff, drove westward out of Jerusalem and along the historic route to Jaffa. Soon they were past Motza, a Jewish settlement despoiled in the violence of 1929, and were descending to the lowlands. Judea and the picturesque Arab villages contoured into its slopes were left behind as they arrived at Latrun, where the Trappists had their monastery. This was the Valley of Ajalon, unchanged, apparently, since Joshua commanded the moon to be still, and before them rose Ramleh's Tower of the Forty Martyrs, guarding entry to the Plain of Sharon. They had barely crossed a Jewish habitation on their way, but now their motor-car swerved to the south, into the sand-brushed heart of the citrus belt. Barely a half-dozen miles from Ramleh stood their destination: a wayside railway halt, a cluster of cottages, a few plantations, a small agricultural station. When the Jews first settled this place, in 1890, they went to the Bible for a name – Rehovot.

The little party walked a hundred yards off the road, and all was sand again. Here a modest ceremony was enacted, the placing of a marker to register the location of what was to be the Daniel Sieff Research Institute. Speeches seemed inappropriate, and whereas a similar occasion on Mount Scopus fifteen years earlier had been witnessed by a host of dignitaries, and authority as represented by the British Commander-in-Chief, now just a few local villagers were roused to curiosity. But inconspicuous among the party was Ben-Gurion's friend and comrade, the 'quiet one' of the Labour movement, Isaac Ben-Zvi, who one day would step into the shoes of Chaim Weizmann as the second President of the State of Israel.

Rehovot had a gentle gradient, and the scientist escorted his wife along the full extent of its upward sweep. From where they stood, the great dunes washed by the Mediterranean lay to the west; to the east a glimpse, hazed but uninterrupted, of Ramleh. All was silent. On this spot, he promised Vera, they would build their house; and Rehovot, the place he recalled so vividly from his first visit to Palestine the year after their marriage, would become his scientific and spiritual retreat. So it transpired. The gift of the Daniel Sieff Institute by his closest friends grew over the years into the Weizmann Institute of Science, unequalled in Asia and a priceless gift to Israel.

Weizmann returned to London, to engage in discussions with the leaders of Anglo-Jewry, men with whom he had crossed swords in the struggle for the Balfour Declaration. Now feuds were forgotten in their anxieties for the Jews of Germany. The task was to organise world-wide a project of rescue and rehabilitation. Arlosoroff travelled direct to Berlin, to forge their compact with the enemy and receive what Germany discarded. When the list of contributions to the special fund was published, Weizmann's name appeared among the highest. His chemist's royalties were going to his people's ransom.

The Jewish world was astir with conjecture: would he take his place again at the head of the movement, as many agreed was its need and his right? Immigrants were flocking to Palestine, though as yet those coming from Germany were few: the Jews there entertained the desperate belief that Hitler was an ephemeral aberration. Wilstätter thought of Germany as a beloved mother fallen ill, and not to be rejected by her children. Arthur Ruppin, himself a resident of Jerusalem, described Hitler's policy speech to the Reichstag as 'significant, interesting and absorbing'.

The first Congress since Hitler's arrival was shortly due. Its character would be determined not by events in London, or Berlin, or even in Jerusalem, but in the cities of Eastern Europe, from the Baltic to Bessarabia. In Warsaw the Jews, nearly forty per cent of the population, had their own representatives in Parliament, and a dozen daily newspapers. The Polish and Rumanian governments vigorously encouraged the movement that they hoped would succeed in emptying the ghettos. Ben-Gurion and Jabotinsky came to Warsaw in 1933 to win over the masses for their respective points of view. Both leaders were intent on a final reckoning, and now that Communist Russia was beyond reach the three million Jews of Poland would provide a majority of Congress delegates.

It was an election campaign of unparalleled intensity. In the West, delegate cards were distributed to time-servers on committees almost as a ritual, but in Warsaw feeling ran high. Bricks were hurled at Ben-Gurion as he addressed a packed meeting in the Nowosci Theatre, and he had a similar stormy reception in Riga. Jabotinsky canvassed in the streets accompanied by bodyguards in resplendent uniform. When the votes were counted it was found that one half had gone to Labour, with the Revision-ists a poor second. So the seats on the Jewish Agency Executive could be filled by Ben-Gurion's party at the Congress.

To some leaders of the Left this would be a prize of doubtful worth. Through the *Histadrut* they were already entrenched in Palestine, which was a battlefield they understood. But they saw the London Executive in an unflattering light, particularly without Weizmann. Should they join those timorous Diaspora Jews regularly proceeding cap in hand to the British Colonial Office? Yes, Ben-Gurion said, it was time they assumed a role in the political struggle. What of Arlosoroff, more a European, less a proletarian, than the others?

They would never know. Two days after his return from Germany, and while on an evening's walk with his wife on the Tel Aviv promenade, the thirty-four year old political secretary of the *Histadrut*, a man frequently spoken of as a future leader of the movement, was shot dead by an unidentified assailant. Now a new element of drama transformed the atmosphere of perennial tedium in Zionist conflict. For suspicion rested on a young Polish follower of Jabotinsky discovered hiding in the Tel Aviv home of a Revisionist journalist. The courts dismissed the charges brought against him for lack of evidence. But in the opinion of many, not wholly of the Left, the man was guilty.

It could not now be the usual Zionist Congress. Scarred by the self-inflicted wounds of its deep animosities, the movement took fright. The call went out for Weizmann.

Three weeks before Arlosoroff's assassination the former President had left for Chicago, and if ever a man required testimony of his people's affection Weizmann found it there, at the World's Fair, on what the organisers had scheduled as 'Jewish Day'. Until then this exposition, purporting to commemorate a 'century of progress', had struggled unsuccessfully for the public's attention. 'Jewish Day' appeared doomed to pass as any other day. They were to stage a pageant, to be produced by the only functionary in American Zionism with a theatrical sense, Meyer Weisgal. Rashly, he had undertaken to fill Soldier Field, the lake-side arena with space for 100,000 spectators.

Weisgal had won Weizmann's admiration for his service during the Brandeis conflict, marshalling with Louis Lipsky the East Side votes that defeated Brandeis at Cleveland. A bond, almost metaphysical, had sprung up between the two men, born perhaps of nothing greater than Weizmann's love of Yiddish humour, of which the other was an acknowledged master. But Weisgal was no mere court jester to Weizmann, as an unkind gossip would have it. Polish-born, he cherished the culture of the pre-war ghettos of the Old World, which in his estimation the Zionist leader exemplified, and ennobled. 'Some men are elected,' he said, 'but Weizmann is of the elect.'

Anxious to retrieve his 'Day' from threatening disaster, Weisgal tele-phoned London from Chicago (a rare happening in the thirties) beseeching Weizmann to come to the World's Fair, and deliver just one speech. He promised 100,000 dollars for the German fund in return. It was an ir-resistible invitation, and the result was a swarming of American and Canadian Jews by the coach-load towards Chicago. Accommodation had to be found in Soldier Field for over 130,000. The scene belonged uniquely in America, and then perhaps only in the Depression era: an exercise in collective adoration approaching religious hysteria. What had begun as a publicity stunt terminated as a political *tour de force*.

Of course, the Chicago demonstration revealed that transatlantic Zion-ism was still an America-Jewish pastime, lending itself, like the notorious spectacle of pole-squatting, to escapist marathons. By contrast, the Zionist Congress met in Prague the same year much sobered by premonitions of tragedy, and sought escape in impassioned appeals for the unattainable. It demanded *carte blanche* for immigration to Palestine, and this was beyond Britain's power to grant; it sent out a call to the world for help to protect the Jews of Germany by forcing a general economic boycott of the Reich, but the cry went unheard; it ordered its own investigation of Arlosoroff's assassination, as though Zionist justice might satisfy where British justice had failed. Labour delegates vacated the hall in a body whenever a Re-visionist rose to speak, so a rational agenda was out of the question. And all this time Weizmann was pointedly marking his absence by setting up a holiday headquarters in Zermatt, Switzerland, not a day's journey from Prague.

Messengers shuttled back and forth entreating him to return – let him only name his terms. He would not make it easy for them. 'All that was needed was a little political geography to throw me out,' he confided to a friend, 'but to bring me back requires a moral force.'

The Congress refused to place its trust in Sokolow's continued steward-ship, yet could not achieve a united voice for Weizmann. In a little American Civil War, Lipsky canvassed for a general summons to Zermatt while Stephen Wise fought just as strenuously to keep Weizmann away; they produced no suitable compromise candidate of their own. Some spoke of the young Lord Melchett, a few of Brodetsky. But Labour wanted the fallen leader, and at this Congress they were the effective masters.

Weizmann intimated his readiness to resume the Presidency provided the Jabotinsky party were excluded from the Zionist Organisation. His supporters were dumbfounded. That Weizmann, of all people, should reveal so little regard for the democratic machinery of the movement! Weren't the Revisionist representatives elected as had been all others?

It was a ploy, in fact, to give him a further respite from office. The Presidency would entail daily apologetics, and he made the discovery that he commanded more authority in an elder-statesman role than as an active participant. He wished before everything to serve Palestine through the cause of German Jewry, and he could do so now without having to justify his every move. The current Zionist mood was to fight Britain. He would not subscribe to it, or fall victim to it. Sokolow was left in command for a further term, but real direction was taken at last into the workers' grasp. Ben-Gurion, with three other Labour leaders, formed the Jerusalem end of the Executive. The arrival of Palestine's most accomplished organiser onto the international Zionist stage signalled the demise of an old-style, bourgeois Jewish movement and the birth of a guerilla nationalism with its fist in the field.

Weizmann would not deny the *Yishuv* its right to ascendancy. Neither did he wholly condemn Jabotinsky, for the Revisionist had form, policies, a Zionist background. He allocated to Wise, however, the role of dangerous adversary; the rabbi purported to speak (with what authority no one could discern) on behalf of millions of American Jews. Wise was ready to launch a full-scale attack on Britain for denying them colonisation rights in Trans-jordan. Well, he too had once shared this aspiration, but was now converted to the opposite view. Wauchope had been correct. Why press such a claim when barren land in abundance awaited cultivation west of the Jordan? Who would guarantee security to the few villages they could plant on the other side?

Weizmann had his own assessment of Zionism's priority, born in part no doubt of the role he now saw for himself. He had once been a graceless *Ostjude* despised by these cultivated Germans. Now the situation was reversed: they were despised in their own country, he could be the saviour of their pride. It would have been inhuman not to experience a secret triumph in his emergence as champion of the fallen. He would charge the Jewish world, rather than Britain, with responsibility for the new refugees. He would make preparations in Palestine to absorb the most substantial number, but the rest must be taken by the U.S.A. principally, and the British Empire. Perhaps Argentina too would be persuaded. They could solve the German problem if the Jews acted swiftly, and in concert, and with a minimum of polemic.

Leadership of the international campaign for German Jewry was given to him, as he desired. He was ready to travel the continents yet again with his begging-bowl. But some rather rough speaking was required also among the Germans themselves. Unfortunately, many were deceived as to the precariousness of their situation. Others could not bring themselves to face a Zionist trek to the Orient and entry into an atmosphere of positive Judaism.

The rich were naturally able to look after themselves, while fierce competition among the academic institutions of the world developed for the privilege of sheltering the eminent. It was not so easy to find a welcome for those lower down the professional scale. As for the humblest refugees, shop-keepers, craftsmen, pensioners, they would in the end learn to be grateful for a resting-place anywhere. The League of Nations appointed James McDonald, an American, as High Commissioner for Refugees, and he was assisted by Norman Bentwich as his Jewish expert. Viscount Cecil of Chelwood, 'Baffy' Dugdale's cousin, who in 1917 had, as Lord Robert Cecil, been Balfour's deputy and Weizmann's strong arm at the Foreign Office, was accorded overall supervision of the programme. Evidently the international community would not shirk its responsibilities. Or so it appeared.

Palestine extended its hand, but the immediate response of the refugees was to turn their backs. To McDonald's consternation, and the Jews' own, Argentina and fourteen other governments offered homes only to a minute few. Soon a floating population of refugees clutching transit visas were wandering over the face of Europe with nowhere permanent to settle. This was just the beginning.

Hitler's Jewish policy brought repercussions in heightened anti-semitism throughout Europe. Switzerland was the scene of a *cause célèbre* necessitating Weizmann's and Sokolow's presence to demolish that notorious forgery, *The Protocols of the Elders of Zion*. The Refugee Commissioner struggled on for two years, until in 1935 he resigned in protest against the hesitancy of the nations to open their doors. The experience made McDonald, like other public figures, into a Zionist. For Palestine accepted 30,000 in 1933, and 42,000 in 1934. Sad to state, of Germans they were largely the very young and the very old, in the care of institutions. Accepted by the Zionists through love, they had been rejected by powerful states through self-interest.

It was an ironical situation. Every country save England spoke of Palestine as the solution to the refugee problem, thus evading a real

A *kibbutz*, with tower and stockade, is born in the Jordan Valley.

Weizmann inspecting Jewish volunteers during World War II.
Meyer Weisgal (with spectacles) in the background.

Neville Chamberlain opens St James's Palace Conference, 1939. On his right, Lord Halifax; on his left, Malcolm MacDonald. Foreground shows (second from left) Nahum Goldmann, Selig Brodetsky, Weizmann, Ben-Gurion, Rose Jacobs, the American representative, and Shertok (Sharett).

contribution of its own. England, in her fear of stirring renewed unrest in Palestine, brought the largest proportion to her own shores. The economic slump was not yet over, and the nations' hospitality, if extended at all, remained frigid.

Weizmann was impatiently waiting for the most distinguished refugee of them all to prove by his example that the Jewish National Home was indeed what it proclaimed to be. He wanted Albert Einstein to turn from the deceptive life of Diaspora and enjoy the honoured reception that was his due in Palestine. He rarely omitted a reference to the savant in any speech he made on Germany's Jews, on the Hebrew University, on science harnessed to the Jewish revival. And while the author of the Theory of Relativity was being showered with invitations the world over, Weizmann proffered him 'pencil and paper and a quiet corner' on Mount Scopus.

Einstein, much irritated, was reluctant to reply publicly to the invitation: he had no wish to damage the Hebrew University by openly admitting his contempt for its mediocrity. He merely restricted himself to a statement to the effect that Weizmann 'knows in what circumstances I would undertake work for the university'.

He did not specify what work that would be. A return to active participation on the Board of Governors? The delivery of an occasional lecture? Or the permanent occupation of a 'quiet corner'? But Weizmann had spent his life converting 'no' into 'perhaps', and 'perhaps' into 'yes'. He seized on Einstein's words as implying that the latter would settle in Jerusalem once reforms were made. Eagerly, he declared that Einstein's criticisms would be met: Magnes would be made to conform. This infuriated Einstein all the more. In truth, he was no different from the majority of Central European Jewish intellectuals; he was unable to cross the Jewish Rubicon. Undismayed, Weizmann approached Einstein again as the Daniel Sieff Institute at Rehovot neared its opening, but with no greater success.

Rehovot, Weizmann was convinced, would live to stand comparison with the great research centres of the West. Nothing less would be worthy of Palestine and the genius of the Jewish people. He would consolidate it step by step, avoiding pretentiousness, the way he wished the National Home itself to be built. But when he scoured Germany he failed to recruit a single scientist of international repute. Willstätter helped him plan the institute, and delivered its inaugural lecture. He then returned to Germany – only to be ignominiously expelled in 1939. Fritz Haber, perhaps the personification of the German-Jewish tragedy, did eventually consent to work in Rehovot, but professional and social ruin had shattered his health, and he did not survive the journey to Palestine.

Weizmann's approaches to the younger generation were happier, and in April, 1934, a modest beginning was made. One of his earliest captures was David Bergmann, a biochemist like himself and already with an expanding reputation. He came to Rehovot with his brother Felix to set up shop. They were joined by Weizmann's sister Anna. She had studied in Manchester before the war, and then been swallowed up in Russia. When heard of again she was serving the Moscow Institute of Biochemistry. Anna found her way to Palestine in 1933. Altogether, eight scientists assumed positions at Rehovot, and Weizmann directed them along the paths from which he had had to branch off when summoned in 1915 to the Admiralty.

Research began from the classic starting-point, coal-tar. The synthetics they sought would be principally for pharmaceutical use. Soon a programme was initiated to find uses for the waste in citriculture, and to conserve and 'stabilise' the natural juice to retain its vitamin C under adverse conditions. They laboured over the improvement by selective breeding of plants rich in oils, and they built on their chief's own discoveries in bacteriology and fermentation, with the conversion of the sugar content in vegetation into substances of greater value. Weizmann was never happier than in the brief periods he could personally spend in this familiar territory. What they were starting might well have been regarded as common-place in Boston or Oxford; in this region such work exuded the exciting pioneer atmosphere of the *kibbutz*.

Simultaneously, the rift was healed with Magnes over his stewardship of the university. He bowed to a critical investigation, and agreed at last to the appointment of an Academic Head. With the inauguration of new courses it became possible to enrol a host of refugee students. But one shortcoming of the university was not in the power of Weizmann and Magnes to overcome: the meagre response from Arab students to their invitation to study on Mount Scopus. The Arabs remained hostile as the entire world applauded Zion in triumph: innovation everywhere, and the desert in retreat before a people to whom this land acted as a healing hand.

The times were in a condition of sorry paradox. In 1935, the year of the Nuremberg Laws, passivity disappeared from the Zionist vocabulary. For that year the United States of America, with a President largely carried into power by the Jewish vote, the White House crowded with Jewish advisers, the Governorate of New York occupied by the German-Jew Herbert Lehman, with frontierlands under-developed in the South and

West, opened its doors to just 6,000 European Jewish refugees. The Argentine took 3,000, South Africa 1,000, Canada a mighty 600, and Australia so few that it was ashamed to publish the figure. In the same year over 62,000 Jews were welcomed into Palestine. The contrast was not lost on the Mufti of Jerusalem.

These were the legal immigrants, officially counted. Others arrived without permits or under a masquerade: if they could not smuggle themselves in they came as tourists, students, spouses of convenience. The Jewish Agency was now anything but the body created by Weizmann in the form visualised by Article Four of the Palestine Mandate. It was a government in miniature, dominated by activists under the leadership of Ben-Gurion. It had agents procuring arms from anyone in Europe ready to sell; one of its assembly-shops, unknown to Weizmann, lay buried below ground on the property of the Daniel Sieff Research Institute.

As always, the Zionist movement operated with cohesion in Palestine alone. The Revisionists had finally quitted the organisation, to proceed along an independent path embracing agitation, arms purchase, illegal immigration. Their leader, ever catching the headlines with his own representations to the statesmen of the world (including a plan for the mass transfer of Poland's Jews to Palestine in a single operation), flirted with the possibility of securing Mussolini's support against Britain.

The Jews as a whole could not identify with Jabotinsky. Nor could they identify with Ben-Gurion, whose extraordinarily long speeches stretched even further for being made by preference in Hebrew. They were still underestimating the man, a mistake not being made by the Mufti. Ben-Gurion was not yet the antithesis of Weizmann. But already he had determined that the fate of Palestine would ultimately be decided not through concessions by foreign governments, nor through intercession by overseas Jews. He foresaw a collision of local forces, in which the community that was better organised, physically more enterprising, ideologically more committed, must emerge the victor.

The Mufti's was the one clear Arab voice. He spread his net from Palestine into any place where his disunited people, largely illiterate, oppressed by local landlords, indentured to foreign capitalism, searched for a national spirit. His travels through the Islamic world, including India, brought him acclaim as the leader who had revived the Arab Revolution and set it on its march. Hitler had termed the Jews an Oriental menace; Haj Amin spoke of them as the European menace threatening the Moslem way of life, the colonialism of old in a particularly insidious form. And for the present the Jews could see their answer to him in one man only: Chaim Weizmann. For even the Zionists who opposed Weizmann could not think of another who so completely fitted all the requirements of their cause.

Again the thorny question: the terms of his return to leadership. Could the movement learn to live with his determination to see British policy in its most positive light, and cheer the immigrants allowed in rather than reproach the government for those left behind? Hitler had converted him to the necessity of ultimate Jewish independence, but could they agree to keep such a goal out of their debates while their paucity of numbers in Palestine rendered talk of it a dangerous vanity? Many schemes were in the air: a Jewish State, a Near-Eastern Federation, partition of the country, a covenant of union with the Arabs. But he refused to be ensnared into formulating a definitive aim for Zionism, or into breaking the Anglo-Zionist alliance.

His belief in the alliance was enhanced, for he respected Britain for struggling to maintain the democratic way of life in a period when country after country in Europe was succumbing to dictatorship. The Jews needed democracy more perhaps than any other people, so they should not play with the traditional friendship of the only Power that seemed able to resist the tide.

As for Mussolini, Weizmann placed little credence in his overtures to the Zionists. The Italian leader was not yet an ally of Germany, and his military advisers included several generals who still acknowledged their Jewish origins. Doubtless, as they pored over the map and dreamed with the Duce of turning the Mediterranean into Mare Nostrum, their fingers lingered on Palestine, to stimulate thoughts of their idol in the poise of honest broker. Weizmann, who felt he must promote Zionism to any interested statesmen was glad of an opportunity to put his case to the Italian leader, but when Mussolini cajoled him with schemes for a Jewish State in the southern part of Palestine he informed the dictator unequivocally that statehood was not part of his programme.

It was easier to make such a declaration to Mussolini than to the Zionist Congress. Could he therefore build an Executive loyal to his sense of restraint? Even without the Revisionists the organisation luxuriated in a plethora of interests uneasily juxtaposed. The only support he could count upon in the centre, marshalled by Lipsky in America and Brodetsky in England, was dwarfed by the forces of Stephen Wise. The latter reflected the views of the Palestine Right, which had a local champion in Menahem

Ussishkin, now holding everything that did not belong to the *Histadrut* in his grasp.

Propose moderation to such people and he would be arraigned for public defiance of the Almighty, whose defender in the Zionist Organisation, withal, was the *Mizrachi* party. He must therefore look to Labour. But he was by no means certain of total loyalty from the Left. Although united beneath its trade union umbrella, the Left was itself fractured into infinity by differing concepts of socialism and guilt feelings towards the Arabs.

Could he carry so motley an Executive with him in his efforts to work in harmony with the British? The Colonial Secretary in 1935 was Malcolm MacDonald, and though government office was cooling his Zionist ardour, Ramsay's son still venerated Weizmann. Of course, his officials in Palestine were carved in a different mould. A friendly statement in London, Weizmann knew from long experience, had a quite different complexion over there, even when communicated to a High Commissioner as amenable as Wauchope. Jewish energy and enterprise discomforted the British, while the courtly Arab, with his tranquillising mystique, reinforced their sense of superiority.

These complex factors gave Weizmann pause as he contemplated another period as President, and all it would entail in battles with emotionalism and coalitions with the irreconcilable. If he came back he must be allowed to choose his own Executive and to fight Britain in his own way – not by empty pronouncements but by the moral pressure of their case. 'The walls of Jericho fell at the blowing of trumpets', he told the Congress of 1931 as it dismissed him, 'but I have never heard of walls being erected by such means.' He would exclude the die-hards of the Right, Ussishkin especially, from his Executive; similarly the *Mizrachi*. But he was prepared to work with Labour, and felt he could achieve a working relationship with their leader, who spoke of Britain's curb on unrestricted immigration as 'committing robbery'.

The Congress met in Lucerne. This time they were left in no suspense as to whether Weizmann would play his full part in their proceedings or hover in the background. He was elected amid scenes of elation to the role of Congress Chairman, traditionally accorded to Motzkin, who had died since their last meeting. But a few delegates muttered their misgivings: this master of science and manoeuvre would seek over-riding powers, and this they must not permit. All thoughts were on Germany. Some delegates intended using the forum for fiery speeches to attack Hitler as the Haman of the twentieth century. They were not, however, allowed the luxury, for the German delegates feared reprisal against their families remaining at home. But for the first time, the German language was not publicly heard at a Zionist Congress.

Of Hitler, Weizmann said: 'The only dignified and really effective reply to all that is being inflicted upon the Jews in Germany is the edifice erected by our great and beautiful work in the Land of Israel. This alone is the real, proper, comforting and redeeming response to this tragedy . . . Something is being created that will transform the woe we all suffer into songs and legends for our grandchildren.'

And to Britain: 'Our colonisation work has been achieved without firing a shot. We did not build our home on other people's backs. We have revived and re-cultivated swampy, sandy and malaria-infested regions. And it is not true that we have uprooted the Arabs. We have shown them the way to a better life, and we shall continue to do so, until they will understand that we have a common interest in reviving the Middle East and that this task can be achieved only on the basis of a strong Jewish Palestine. The Mandatory Power may make it easier or more difficult for us, and our quarrels may prolong this Congress by two days or shorten it by one, but the work proceeds.'

They cheered. But behind the scenes discussion of his terms for return to the Presidency was fierce. His opponents refused to accept banishment to the wilderness at Weizmann's whim. Then Ben-Gurion devised a compromise: a small Executive of Weizmann supporters, and a broad coalition of party representatives with lesser, though substantial, authority. After long deliberation Ussishkin agreed, and this made it easier for Wise to secure the concurrence of his American delegation. The religious forces took with good grace the proposal that they occupy posts which restricted their activities to within Palestine itself. Sokolow, now much aged (he was thirteen years older than Weizmann), went into virtual retirement.

'This is my Sabbath of Repentence,' Wise announced. He and the President would, on occasion, differ still, but he became a devoted supporter in America, closing at last the schism opened in the days of Brandeis. Almost imperceptibly, Ben-Gurion slipped into a newly-created post: Chairman of the Jewish Agency. Not a man to be silenced, he voiced to the Congress an intention of bringing to Palestine a million families in five years – it was a fantasy, five million Jews in all. Weizmann's hope was 50,000 families. However, Ben-Gurion was the tiger he had agreed to ride.

Weizmann almost had the best of both his worlds, given that such a phrase was appropriate. With the problems of the university approaching solution, he was appointed Dean of its Faculty of Science, an office ideally complementing his work at the Sieff Institute. So he could impose his stamp on Mount Scopus at last. Now he felt justified in making one last bid for the services of Albert Einstein. The latter, clinging as always to his child-like faith in the essential nobility of the human race, would not admit to being a Jew in need of a refuge. He was supping at High Table at Oxford, and in the end turned his back on Jerusalem in favour of Princeton. Palestine still had to beg for such immigrants, and most frequently in vain. Even Martin Buber had so far refrained from answering the call.

England was bedecked with flags that summer of 1935 in honour of King George the Fifth's Silver Jubilee, and the Zionists marked their association with the British Empire by planting a forest in Galilee. Weizmann became a familiar figure in Whitehall once more, and British politicians were frequent guests at his Kensington home. Nevertheless he would not betray the trust the Congress had placed in him. He resisted every attempt at restriction of the National Home, and rejected any scheme for a Legislative Council aimed to perpetuate Arab domination in Palestine.

Flags across the Empire, patriotic speeches in London, a colourful array of foreign dignitaries proceeding with their sentiments of goodwill to Buckingham Palace – none of it could conceal disquiet at the growing menace from Europe. Hitler marched into the Rhineland, Mussolini into Abyssinia. Even as Britain began her reluctant rearmament she was re-minded of her gravest weakness: the Suez route to the East, her Mediter-ranean naval bases, her sources of oil, all located within the territory of Arabia. How long could this old country's domination endure?

Weizmann had referred in Lucerne to 'a certain weariness in the British Empire', implying a readiness for retrenchment, perhaps surrender. And William Ormsby-Gore (inevitably, another of Baffy Dugdale's relatives), in taking his place in 1936 as Colonial Secretary, must surely have trembled at the change in those far-flung possessions since, as a young Tory aristocrat, he had accompanied the Zionist Commission on its expedition to Palestine. How reassuring it had then been to camp with Weizmann in the sun and gaze upon the Land of Promise, with its spacious, mineral-rich Arabian hinterland where the natives could be relied upon to do as they were told!

II

Between Eton and the Dictators

IT MAY HAVE BEEN AT THAT ANNUAL SUMMER FETE OF THE BRITISH privileged, the Eton and Harrow cricket match, or on the Members' Terrace overlooking the Thames at the Palace of Westminster, or in the midnight intimacy of a *tête-à-tête* supper with a friend or kinsman in the Cabinet. But wherever she found herself, Baffy Dugdale's ear zealously gathered intelligence for her chief at Zionist headquarters.

Mrs Dugdale's world divided evenly into its halves, and thanks to her accommodating husband, a wealthy coal-mine owner whose interests lay elsewhere, she gave herself to it twenty-four hours of every day. Politics were an obsession with her, like the family gossip with which it was tightly interwoven. Her relatives were mostly high Tory, and generously sprinkled over both Houses of Parliament. Her instincts were socialist, but the split in the Labour Party produced by the economic crisis of 1931 placed her inside the rump faithful to Ramsay MacDonald under the banner of National Labour. This faction attracted a fair proportion of aristocratic Left-wingers all looking to the heir apparent, Malcolm MacDonald, as their potential future leader.

Baffy saw in Zionism the finger of God moving across the twentieth century – every true believer could discern the portents in the pages of the Bible. Her ancestral name was thus joined by the Balfour Declaration to the divine purpose, and in her frequent visits to the incipient Jewish nation in Palestine she renewed her gratitude and faith. When the historian Lewis Namier, himself an uneasy combination of twilight Polish Judaism and British Tory prejudice, introduced her to Weizmann in 1923 she entered what seemed an exotic and wonderful world.

Namier, together with his colleague Leonard Stein at Great Russell

Street, brought to the Zionist leader convictions about the English mind that could only be the result of an Oxford training. Their interpretation of the governing classes sprang from their enchantment with that university. In serving Weizmann, both these much-tried men found their lives harnessed to a Jew vastly different from themselves, one who was simultaneously an exacting employer and a difficult colleague. They were intimate with all the theories associated with Zionism, demolishing its adversaries with consummate skill and true scholarship. But they were worlds away from personal identification with the people motivated to build the Jewish homeland with their own hands, or who surrendered their intellects exclusively to this ideal.

In controversies with the government neither Namier nor Stein could fail to concede merit to the English point of view. Baffy however lent to the Zionist headquarters a personality so naturally British that she could without difficulty condemn her country's policies as stupid or evil, or both. Weizmann represented something higher than England: she described him in her diary as 'one of God's great instruments'.

Not that she was blind to his imperfections. No doe-eyed sentimentalist, Baffy was a clinical observer of her Zionist colleagues. Conversely, she was the neutral outsider to whom they could whisper complaints about each other, and lament the weaknesses of the chief. Ben-Gurion she found 'a great and noble fellow, but without common-sense.' When Selig Brodetsky grieved that Weizmann was giving him short shrift, and regarded him as a 'fifth wheel', she could not but admit that the Leeds professor indeed was without real function on the Executive. Namier suffered for his pedantry and frustrated ambition, and though she protected the man, she saw justification in Weizmann's severity towards him. She sided with Vera against Chaim when necessary, for she rightly comprehended that the wife was better than the husband at keeping cool in a crisis.

The impression of Weizmann received by the outside world was of a Zionist leader of autocratic authority. In fact, he leaned heavily upon his colleagues, two of whom, Ben-Gurion and Moshe Shertok (the latter would, as Sharett, succeed the other as Israeli Prime Minister), saw their function specifically as arresting the Anglicisation of the Executive. If Weizmann's Memoirs give little credit to their role, it was because *Trial and Error* was composed during and subsequent to the Second World War, and was influenced by later American advisers for whom the thirties were of subordinate interest. Shertok, who occupied Arlosoroff's place, succumbed before the charm and strength of their leader; Ben-Gurion never.

Weizmann's resumption of office in 1935 served as a cue to American Jewry to descend once again into Zionist ineffectuality. Having accepted Weizmann personally, Rabbi Stephen Wise neither disputed his policies nor vigorously promoted them, and as a consequence President Roosevelt was troubled little by the Jewish condition in Europe, and was left in the White House with his hostility to Zionism unassailed. The Jewish national movement was now also the Jewish rescue movement, with its rhythm of activity dictated by the Congress, and constituent bodies required a year to recover from the last one and another year to prepare for the next.

In Palestine, however, Zionism was a daily endurance test, and the Jewish situation in Europe an agonising preoccupation. Relations with the Arabs were moving alarmingly towards the point of no return, for every new immigrant affronted the pride of the old inhabitants and sapped their feeling of security. Judah Magnes was urged by the march of events to bring his friends among the Arabs into contact with the Jewish Agency. Ben-Gurion was deputed to conduct negotiations with them. He appeared reasonable; they seemed friendly. Both sides were united in their condemnation of England and in voicing misgivings at the ambitions of Mussolini. The Arabs countered Ben-Gurion's acceptance of their right to self-determination with a generous admission of the Jews' connection with Palestine. It was stimulating to exchange views on the future character of the Near East, and much coffee was consumed as to whether this should be in the form of separate states or a confederation. But these were pleasantries. The real subject at issue was a Jewish majority in western Palestine, and this the Arab moderates would not concede on their own behalf, let alone on behalf of the Mufti of Jerusalem.

Desperate for an accommodation, Weizmann sanctioned use of what he considered the ultimate weapon in Oriental persuasion: bribery. Ben-Gurion's discussions were with men of probity: the Christian scholar George Antonius, the land-owner Musa Alami, the nationalist leader Auni bey Abdul Hadi, all of them in the confidence of the Mufti and the Husseini oligarchs. But others, notably members of the Nashashibi family, rivals to the Husseinis in Jerusalem, were encouraged with gifts to hinder the Mufti in his schemes for an Arab revolt. Money also passed to Abdulla in Amman, and to the Foreign Minister of Iraq, Nuri es Said.

Undertakings were given, and thousands of pounds changed hands. But the only figure to impress the Mufti was the 62,500 Jews arriving in 1935. He demanded the handing over of control to the Arabs while there was still time. The harassed High Commissioner, Wauchope, undertook to see the Legislative Council through, on the likely eventual ratio of forty per cent Jewish representation to sixty per cent Arab. Weizmann declared, sorrowfully, that he could not accept a Council that would leave the Jews too weak. The Mufti rejected it imperiously for making the Jews too strong. Wauchope pressed London for action nevertheless.

Action in this case involved a Bill in the British Parliament, whose by-ways none knew better than Baffy Dugdale. She and Weizmann began priming the right politicians. Together they had 'chosen' Sir Neill Malcolm to succeed the American James McDonald as League of Nations Commissioner for Refugees – easily achieved through Baffy's intercession with her relatives Viscount Cecil and Lord Cranbourne ('Bobbity' to her). Weizmann informed Malcolm of the need to bring 100,000 Jews to Palestine annually for ten years, with the more distant future making its own decisions. It was a bargaining figure, greater than he then anticipated in British permits or even Jewish desire, and he halved it in discussion with Wauchope. His real anxiety was to ensure that nothing was done to foreclose on the National Home.

'When Jews come to Palestine they create space for others, they do not fill the space of others', he insisted to Malcolm. Meanwhile his work among parliamentarians was gaining fruit, and the Legislative Council laboured forward like a snail against the speeches of friends in both Commons and Lords. But he could not stop the clock ticking away in Palestine. The Arabs launched their war against the Jews, and British officialdom, on April 19, 1936.

While the disorders seven years earlier bore the character of a spontaneous display of suddenly-released tribal anger, this time the Arabs revealed considerable capacity in advanced planning, for their objective was the dismantling of the National Home at its very base. Their various political parties, rudimentary though they might be, formed a union and coalesced with all other Arab groups, including the Greek Orthodox and Catholic communities. A pact of defiance and sacrifice was sealed at Nablus, and out of it emerged the Arab Higher Committee.

The goal was national independence; the strategy sabotage and terrorism, with a general strike and guerilla warfare on a grand scale, waged by professional bands thousands strong from across the border. England's reaction was slow. The whole might have been contained by the institution of martial law, but to Wauchope such a move would herald the final collapse of Arab-British-Jewish relations, and he resisted.

Immigration continued. Sales of land to the Jews went unrestricted. The rebels' reply was to derail trains, mine the roads, and fire the oil pipe-line to Haifa. The government, now under Stanley Baldwin, gambled with its defence requirements for the home country by rushing 20,000 troops to Palestine – a large force at a time when England was seeking to reduce her military expenditure while simultaneously negotiating a treaty with Egypt and keeping troubled watch on the beginnings of a civil war in Spain. In Tel Aviv the Jews were staging a Levant Fair as proud shop-window of their economic progress, but behind this facade of confidence the sound of machine-gun fire told another story. Soon the dead and wounded numbered in thousands, mainly among the guerillas.

The Weizmanns arrived in the country and were given a night and day guard by the Jewish self-defence organisation, *Haganah*, which lined the road with retiring-looking sharp-shooters wherever the leader travelled. Baffy Dugdale accompanied them on this visit, spending much time with her friend Antonius, conveying messages as it were from Weizmann for onward delivery to the Mufti. Vera busied herself with her German refugee architect in planning their Rehovot home, and was having the grounds landscaped like a typical English garden. But her kitchen equipment stayed boxed up in strike-bound Jaffa harbour.

The *Haganah*, like so much else in Palestine an off-shoot of the Labour sector, was under strict orders to fire only in self-defence. However, its commanders had no control over the Revisionists, and rumour quickly spread that Jewish reprisals were responsible for some Arab casualties. Weizmann disavowed all knowledge of such operations. To him every round of ammunition expended in Palestine threatened his creed, and mythology, of a Zionism whose existence in this land nobody need fear.

Information reached him, indirectly, of a government intention to send another Commission out to investigate the situation. Wauchope had not been man enough to tell him outright, for he anticipated Weizmann's angry reaction at the prospect of being dragged through another of those inquisitions, and its inevitable trail of restrictions, and annulments, and ambiguities. It would be victory for the Mufti. Cutting his visit short, Weizmann returned home, threatening to organise a Jewish boycott of the enquiry. Then the government took the steam out of his protests by announcing the Commission together with a statement that immigration would proceed as before. Bombs were now exploding in Jewish cinemas. How long could the Agency's policy of self-restraint hold? Why didn't the government put the Mufti in jail?

Nuri es Said, the fervent mediator, followed Weizmann to London. The

Arab Higher Committee, he assured the Jew, would call off the strike, and with profound relief, if only Weizmann would make a gesture of reconciliation. The strike was proving injurious to the Arabs, and it was time to gather in the citrus crop. It was common knowledge that back-door trading with the Jews had never ceased.

What gesture, Weizmann asked? The Jews should themselves suspend immigration, Nuri replied. He was repeating a request already made by William Ormsby-Gore. The Colonial Secretary believed he had done his part, by warning the Arabs that no Commission would be sent out until their revolt ceased. Now it was up to the Jews. Volunteer this concession, difficult though he knew it to be, Nuri implored Weizmann, and peace could return to the Holy Land. With heavy heart, the man who all his life had fought for the right of free entry of Jews to their land now intimated his acceptance of the proposal.

Consternation greeted Weizmann's report of his talk with the Iraqi Foreign Minister when he met colleagues in Great Russell Street. While his 'English' advisers sat tight-lipped with their thoughts, Ben-Gurion, pale with anger, launched into a tirade against their chief. Surrender in London if you will, he told Weizmann, but this would produce the Arab-Jewish war they were struggling to avoid! Ben-Gurion left the other in no doubt where he would stand in that event. In an open fight he, Ben-Gurion, could call upon 3,000 trained men permanently mobilised. He intended this to be only a beginning. In Palestine the Jews had no security without immigration; if Weizmann took this from them many would place their destiny in the hands of Jabotinsky and the Revisionists.

A typical Ben-Gurion exaggeration, Weizmann thought. Better voluntary suspension than government prohibition, which would turn a gesture into a defeat. Perhaps he had blundered, but he was convinced he could keep the Yishuv's loyalty, and in any case he had committed himself. Through a Quaker intermediary he sent a message to the Mufti: the Jews would suspend immigration in return for peace and further talks.

The reply was an icy blast. The Quaker telegraphed back: 'Haj Amin deems it a shame on the Arabs and on himself to accept any compromise coming from a Jew. Who is this Weizmann who will offer us a compromise and we to accept it? No, we refuse it. We need stoppage of immigration, and from the government.'

Since the encounter at Zionist headquarters, Ben-Gurion was trailing Weizmann to every meeting with Ormsby-Gore. Unobtrusively, the Histadrut leader began taking precautions of his own. He picked up some

money from James de Rothschild in London and Felix Warburg in New
York to strengthen the *Haganah*. Neither could refuse a call to protect
innocent Jewish life.

Weizmann for his part recovered from what he spoke of as a lapse. Now
he rejected Ormsby-Gore's plea too that the Jews voluntarily halt immigration. Angrily, the latter demanded Cabinet sanction to stop the
arrivals by edict. While the discussion proceeded in Downing Street, Baffy
waited anxiously at her telephone. Soon Walter Elliot came on the line. He
was Secretary of State for Scotland, and her intimate friend. Elliot put her
mind at rest. The Cabinet would not give 'Billy' his way; immigration
would proceed.

Sputtering like a candle-end, the strike ceased at last in October, 1936.
It was Nuri's work. A Royal Commission, under Lord Peel, sailed for
Palestine. Grimly, Weizmann began drafting his opening speech on behalf
of the Jewish agency.

Palestine presented a sorry picture to the Peel Commission. Marauders
had destroyed many of the Jews' orange groves and the infant forests with
which they were lovingly clothing the desert. Murder still occurred, almost
daily, while the happy scenes, once so frequent, of Arab and Jew working
together, had changed into frigid confrontation between the two communities. Palestine's martyrdom was only just beginning. In the hills
above Nazareth the Jews replanted their King George Forest, but if they
entered the town itself it was at risk to their lives.

Once he had decided to accept the Royal Commission, Weizmann's
attitude towards it changed. He ceased to view it as a tribunal, but as a
platform. Whatever its ultimate findings, and he had no illusions on that
score, its sessions could avail him the opportunity to address the Jewish
world at large, not to mention international public opinion. He would
employ every weapon of his oratorical armoury to reach his greatest
audience ever. He believed Jewish history was its own case for the Return,
so he would not stoop to polemic with the Mufti.

He arrived in a mood of sober optimism to give his evidence. A well-
made phrase would resound through the world, a slip could be snatched
out of context and come back to haunt the remainder of his life. He would
leave to others the details of their case – facts to prove that Zionism was
not displacing the Arabs, that it had instead brought the industrial revolution to the Near East, that world Jewry, not the British taxpayer, was
enabling Britain to develop an outpost of Empire which his people wanted
strengthened, not destroyed.

Zionism alone offered hope that the Jewish question, which had obsessed mankind through the centuries, could be given a solution. In the event Weizmann's evidence constitutes one of the great statements of contemporary Jewish history. And not one word but it came from his personal experience, and his troubled odyssey as leader of a nation without resting-place, uncertain of its future, incapable of speaking with a single voice.

He reminded the Commission of a recent Polish announcement that there were a million Jews too many in that country. 'Why exactly a million *Jews*? They are citizens of Poland, their fate and their destinies have been bound up with the fate and destinies of Poland for well-nigh a thousand years. They have passed through all the vicissitudes of the Polish nation. They desire to make their contribution, good, bad or indifferent – like everybody else – to Polish development. Why should they be singled out as being a million too many? . . . Where can they go?'

Enumerating his people's plight in that country, in Germany, in the Baltic states and Rumania, he found that, excluding the Soviet Union, 'there are in this part of the world six million people pent up in places where they are not wanted, and for whom the world is divided into places where they cannot live and places where they may not enter'. In a few brief years those six million would be branded into the conscience of the Christian world.

Britain too, he observed, had depressed areas, unemployment. 'It is tragic enough, but at least a man may feel in Durham or Newcastle that there is a state that takes care of him as far as it can. There is hope. There may be an opportunity. But that is not applicable to the millions in Central and Eastern Europe. They cannot go out, they cannot find employment, they are not surrounded by a friendly atmosphere, there is nobody who is concerned for them. They are doomed, they are in despair.'

And of the dangers: 'Since my early youth I have fought destructive tendencies in Jewry, but it is almost impossible to avoid destructive tendencies among a younger generation which lives in the state I have described, unless some hope is given to the young people that one day, in some distant future, one in five, one in ten, one in twenty, will find a refuge somewhere where he can work, where he can live, and where he can straighten himself up and look with open eyes at the world and at his fellow men and women.'

He referred to the impossibility of containing anti-semitism: 'That uneasy feeling which used to stop at the Vistula has now reached the Rhine, and crossed the Rhine. It infiltrates across the Channel and across the Atlantic. It has not become so acute as to make our life unbearable, but it is there, and what has happened in Germany is the writing on the wall even for the Western democracies . . . Only recently, on the appointment of M. Blum in France [as Premier] I walked through the streets of Paris and heard the familiar cry, *Mort aux Juifs*. It may be only talk, but it is not pleasant.'

Such manifestations gave to many Jews, though by no means all, the urge for an identity: 'When one speaks of the English or the French or the German nation, one refers to a definite State, a definite organisation, a language, a literature, a history, a common destiny. But it is clear that when one speaks of the Jewish people, one speaks of a people which is a minority everywhere, a majority nowhere, which is to some extent identified with the races among which it lives, but still not quite identical. It is . . . a disembodied ghost of a race and therefore inspires suspicion, and suspicion breeds hatred.'

The mentality of the Jews, he thought, came from their relationship to Palestine: 'Whether it is our misfortune or whether it is our good fortune, we have never forgotten Palestine, and this steadfastness, which has preserved the Jew throughout the ages, and throughout a career that is almost one long chain of inhuman suffering, is primarily due to some physiological or psychological attachment to Palestine. We have never forgotten nor given it up . . . During the nineteen centuries which have passed since the destruction of Palestine as a Jewish political entity, there was not a single century in which the Jews did not attempt to come back.'

Had the Jews exaggerated or distorted the memory of the Balfour Declaration when it was issued during the war? 'We read into the Declaration,' Weizmann said, 'what the statesmen of Great Britain told us it meant: a National Home. "National" meaning that we should be able to live like a nation in Palestine, and "Home" a place where we might live as free men in contradistinction to living on sufferance everywhere else . . . Perhaps the German government considered it a piece of propaganda, but neither the British government nor the Jews ever conceived it as such. There was nobody to win over . . . It meant nothing to the rich Jews, and the poor Jews had nothing to give.'

But then, what of the Arabs? 'The Arab race emerged out of the war more conscious of itself, and rightly so; and they look upon Palestine as an Arab country and upon us as intruders . . . It may perhaps be interesting to read to you a quotation from the late Lord Milner [Orsmby-Gore's earliest political mentor] in a House of Lords debate in 1923: "If the Arabs go to

Rehovot: the village as Weizmann saw it in 1907 (above), and some of the buildings of the
Institute of Science today.

The damaged refugee ship
Exodus being towed into
Haifa port, 1947.

Vera and Chaim Weizman
are met by scientist David
Bergmann at London Airp
1946.

the length of claiming Palestine as one of their countries in the same sense as Mesopotamia or Arabia proper is an Arab country, then I think they are flying in the face of facts, of all history, of all tradition and all associations of the most important character. The future of Palestine cannot possibly be left to be determined by the temporary impressions and feelings of the Arab majority in the country at the present day.'' I should like to add that as soon as the Balfour Declaration was issued, and even before that, British statesmen and those who had negotiated with British statesmen were well aware both of Arab susceptibilities and the necessity for making our position clear to the Arabs. The difficulty with which we were faced, and are unfortunately still faced today, is that there were and are very few Arabs who can really speak authoritatively on behalf of the Arab people.'

Of course, Weizmann had recognised Feisal as a true Arab leader, and had reached an accord with him. He told the Commission about it. But he could be pardoned for now ignoring the Mufti. Haj Amin was then boycotting the Royal Commission, and was preventing other Arabs from testifying. Only two months after Weizmann had spoken was the Mufti persuaded to appear, together with others of the Arab Higher Committee. By this time Lord Peel and his colleagues had worked their way through the labyrinth, and had decided on their recommendations.

At a session conducted *in camera* Weizmann was taken into the Commission's confidence. He had made out a strong case, he was told. But so had the Arabs. What hope could be given, therefore, to this territory in which a million people of one race were arrayed against 400,000 of another? What common ground existed between them? They then put a startling suggestion to him: What would he say to the division of the country into two separate, independent states?

The Commission had not yet considered the details. But the implication of its proposal was that England would retire from the scene, the Jews would receive an area in which to work out their own destiny, decide their own immigration capacity, enact their own laws. It would mean, Weizmann recognised, the termination of the old Jewish history: the sense of homelessness gone, peace with the Arabs, two thousand years of wrong righted. He replied, with care, that he could not as yet speak for the Zionist Organisation, which must discuss any scheme at its Congress. But he indicated that, for him, such a solution would be a relief. Secretly, his heart was singing.

Weizmann had no indication then that partition as the Peel Commission visualised it would include a generous slice for Britain too. Professor Coupland, of the Commission, had been warm and pro-Zionist when he saw Weizmann just before returning to England, though of course he could give no hint that Jerusalem and its environs, being hallowed by multitudes, could be allocated neither to Jews nor Arabs, but would have to be held by Britain, for ever perhaps – together with a corridor to Jaffa and the sea. And Haifa, fortuitously, could not be allocated as its population was almost equally Jew and Arab; it would best remain what it had become, a British naval station. No, what Weizmann understood was an honest division of the territory between the two parties sharing title to it, not a sly endeavour by Britain to keep for herself all that was of value to her, nor the presentation of the Arab area to her puppet in Eastern Palestine, Abdulla.

This was not to be known for months. But soon the secret of the surface scheme – simple division – was out. And even on that basis Weizmann, who affected innocence, at first had just one supporter: Baffy Dugdale. She thought the Jews should take what they were given while they could, even if it was the size of a pocket handkerchief. No one else had a good word to say for partition, so Weizmann determined to maintain his discreet silence and cross that bridge when he came to it.

Now the Arabs renewed their campaign of violent disruption, and Weizmann found himself in agreement with Ormsby-Gore on one issue only – the urgency of ridding Palestine of Wauchope. The High Commissioner's reign had begun auspiciously, but his later prevarications had turned into an unmitigated disaster for the entire population of the Holy Land. The Royal Commission's report was published in July, 1937, one month before the Twentieth Zionist Congress was due to convene in Zurich.

Once in black and white, the proposals seemed worse than the Jews feared even in their most pessimistic forebodings. Peel's map granted the Jews only one city, Tel Aviv; all their other urban concentrations were retained under British control. Their state would embrace a narrow coastal strip plus Upper Galilee, one fifth of the total area of Western Palestine, and they were particularly stung by the suggestion that immigration be held to the limit of 60,000 over the next five years. The Arabs, of course, dismissed the plan as unworthy of discussion. As for the government, Elliot, the Zionists' strongest advocate in the Cabinet, whispered to Baffy that it regarded the report merely as a set of recommendations, a basis for discussion. Naturally, Abdulla did not raise his voice against a partition scheme of which he would be by far the greatest beneficiary, though Ibn Saud let it be known that he would not tolerate so dramatic an accretion of strength to his traditional Hashemite enemy.

From Weizmann there came not a sound, but Ben-Gurion, helped by the mood of pre-Congress fever, led a campaign from inside the Jewish Agency to abort the plan. Resolutions pouring into London from overseas Zionist federations spoke of instructing their delegates to vote against it. The British federation, of which Weizman was nominally head, joined them. Brandeis emerged from seclusion to work against partition, the Catholic newspapers in Ireland spoke of the plan as a typical British felony against a country's identity, and Winston Churchill foretold in an article that partition would bring about an armed collision. 'Where is Weizmann in all this!' the *Jewish Chronicle* cried. 'Why does he fail to give a lead in Peel's denunciation?'

Weizmann was playing a subtle game. He had no intention of accepting the map as it stood, but he exuded triumph. For the utterance by an official tribunal of the 'Ineffable Name' as he termed it – an independent Jewish State – gave the British little room for retreat. It suited him that the agitation should come from quarters other than himself. By Congress time all the arguments would have worked themselves to a standstill, allowing him to win authorisation to negotiate an improved scheme.

Then the incredible happened: the conversion of Ben-Gurion. He now agreed with Weizmann that the very insertion of the term 'Jewish State' in the Peel Report rendered unthinkable the resumption of the old-style Mandate. They could fight for a re-drawn map. Furthermore, with Abdulla replacing the Mufti as the dominant Arab personality in Palestine, hope revived of Jewish colonisation across the Jordan.

Weizmann applauded the logic, and confided to his colleague: 'They have given the Negev to the Arabs, but why worry, it won't run away.' And Ben-Gurion now realised the great advantage the coastal plain offered them – already he was launching a thousand Jewish ships. Now to tackle Ormsby-Gore. The Congress would be carried, Weizmann stated, if he could assure delegates that Peel's diminutive Jewish State was not the final word. The Colonial Secretary, who was dreading the Cabinet's dismissal of partition in principle, needed the Jews' endorsement to help it along. He readily conceded that a plan more favourable to the Zionists could be negotiated.

Battle-lines were drawn in Zurich, with Weizmann and Ben-Gurion quietly confident of their combined ability to quell the Nay-sayers, and turn hostility into acceptance. Still the fight was bitter, all the more so for the discussion being conducted behind closed doors – the only outsider present being Baffy Dugdale. She had learnt, with difficulty, to follow the Yiddish speeches, though Ben-Gurion, whose advocacy would be crucial, scorned the language and spoke for an hour in Hebrew. The Americans were under orders from Brandeis, and most of them, including Wise, strenuously resisted negotiating a partition scheme, as did some of Ben-Gurion's closest socialist comrades. Among its opponents was a little-known woman delegate, Golda Meir.

This was Uganda come again, with Weizmann in Theodor Herzl's 1903 role and Menahem Ussishkin his old intransigent self – 'Palestine, the whole of Palestine, and nothing but Palestine!' And when their leader pleaded only for the right to begin negotiating, a voice from the rear of the hall protested: 'But that's what you've been doing!' The interrupter was the former Jabotinsky lieutenant Meir Grossman, and he hoisted a sheaf of papers as evidence that the President was already discussing a partition scheme with Britain as if the Congress had already empowered him. Weizmann was taken aback: Grossman was waving a résumé of his last discussion with Ormsby-Gore – purloined, it transpired, from Ben-Gurion's room in Great Russell Street. Soon the worst of it was out: nowhere did the document mention a demand for the Negev, uncolonisable except by Jewish devotion, uninhabited except by the restless Beduin.

The delegates were outraged, but Weizmann cajoled them with the advantages: 'The choice lies between a Jewish minority in the whole of Palestine or a compact Jewish State in a part.' The mood changed, the breast-beating ceased, and they voted. It was by roll-call, each delegate speaking his Nay or Yea individually. In favour of negotiation were 300, against negotiation, 158. Weizmann, in victory, felt drained. He had his eyes closed tight and shielded from the light as Ussishkin, also on the platform, pointed a warning finger at him. He was to negotiate only on the basis of the resolution, the old man emphasised, and bring a better scheme to the next Congress, not a garden-plot of a state as an accomplished fact.

Weizmann was convinced he could do it. How he ached to carry off a real achievement for these, his people, many of whom had spent forty years talking out their hearts at gatherings such as this! Their one desire was to be able to make decisions for themselves, instead of eternally suffering the decisions of others. When he first addressed this Congress, almost a fortnight earlier, his words were about those six millions, and his response to Lord Peel's question whether he expected to bring such a number into Palestine.

'I replied: No. I am acquainted with the laws of physics and chemistry, and I know the force of material factors. In our generation I divide the figure by three, and you can see in that the depth of the Jewish tragedy – two millions of youth, with their lives before them, who have lost the most elementary of rights, the right to work.' He hesitated for a moment before continuing: 'The old ones will pass, they will bear their fate or they will not. They are dust, economic and moral dust in a cruel world. Only a remnant will survive.' Fate would soon decide which of his hearers would number among the remnant.

He returned home to find Ormsby-Gore highly incensed that their confidential discussion had been shuttle-cocked around Zurich. In the interim the Palestine situation had worsened. Militant elements among the Jews increased reprisal action. The Arabs saw that partition was now a step nearer, and began assassinating high government officials, among them the Acting District Commissioner for Galilee. The irregulars continued to terrorise their own people to scotch undertones of a possible accommodation with the Jews. Ormsby-Gore now took his courage into his hands. He dissolved the Arab Higher Committee, deporting its leaders to the Seychelles. The Mufti, together with members of his family, escaped to the Lebanon. Wauchope was brought home. Weizmann breathed a sigh of relief, but it was naive to think any other High Commissioner could have done better.

The British at last concurred with the view, frequently pressed on them by the Jews, that Mussolini was financing the Arab rebellion. This, to Ormsby-Gore, was reason enough to hurry a partition scheme through, build up Haifa and surround it with a friendly Jewish population. Mrs Dugdale noted in her diary a conversation between the Colonial Secretary and Lord Melchett, faithful Zionist messenger of Weizmann in the House of Lords and antidote to the less committed Samuel. 'Henry Melchett came bursting from an interview with Billy Gore today,' she wrote. 'Billy had told him he would *like* us to begin now working up a demand for a Jewish State to become part of the British Empire. There is a *great change.*'

In fact Billy could not have been more wrong. The great change lay in Britain's determination now to abandon partition, keep Palestine the way it was, and woo the Arab majority there. Anthony Eden, the Foreign Secretary, was inaugurating his Middle East policy and had picked Ibn

Saud to lead that part of the world under British aegis. He had made a fool of Ormsby-Gore, who was now tired of Palestine, tired of politics in general, and impatient to withdraw to his Welsh estates. The struggle for dominance in the Mediterranean by the European dictators against Eton and Harrow had already begun.

But what to tell Weizmann? The Cabinet took recourse in the usual charade: another Commission, under Sir John Woodhead, to explore partition in detail, produce definite frontiers perhaps. And perhaps not. It was some time before the Zionist leader saw through the plan, and he could tell the Prime Minister (Neville Chamberlain, son of the author of the Uganda scheme): 'You have produced the Woodhead Report to give the Peel Report a second-class burial!'

Not yet, however. The Jews had still to eat their bread of affliction, the British their humble pie. The refugee problem, serious a few years before, now swelled to assume the dimensions of a major world crisis (see chart p. 264). Hitler's march into Austria, and the consequent atrocities in Vienna, home of nearly 200,000 Jews, infected Germany anew with the antisemitic virus. Soon the disease spread in malignant form, to all of Eastern and Central Europe – everywhere except in Czechoslovakia.

The sacrificial process was in train, demonstrating with sickening accuracy Weizmann's thesis as described to the Peel Commission. Britain could not allow the fleeing tribe into Palestine – how could she, she maintained, while the country was in a virtual state of war, and a large part of her army, needed at home, was deployed against guerillas crossing the border in waves? Germany tried to transport her foreign-born Jews (mainly Polish and Russian) forcibly across the frontier, but they were turned back. The stretching queues forming outside the consulates, particularly the American, strangled this people's faith in human nature. Roosevelt still would take only a few, but his self-respect was activated sufficiently in July, 1938, to assuage local and international opinion by organising the Evian Conference. Hungary, Rumania and Poland sent observers, their sole function being to implore for help to rid them of this human detritus.

Nobody would help; not even American Jewry, infatuated as ever with the New Deal, and still reluctant to agitate against Roosevelt or exert pressure against Chamberlain. The world remained silent – except for one leader, Chaim Weizmann, and one group, the Zionists. They had a policy, and were not lacking in the will. All they needed was the power.

It was as though two men were locked in a *danse macabre* while millions stood in line waiting to be consumed by the flames licking at their feet.

The two were the Zionist leader and the new Colonial Secretary of Great Britain, Malcolm MacDonald, summoned once again to that thankless office. He assumed his task from Ormsby-Gore as Weizmann's friend; he would relinquish it as his enemy.

The week before Munich MacDonald suddenly arriving at the Weizmann home just as dinner, with Ben-Gurion and Baffy as guests, was over. The disillusioned Baffy barely acknowledged the man she once hoped would be her parliamentary leader, for he was associated, as to her grief was Walter Elliot, with the shame of setting Czechoslovakia on the altar of appeasement. She and Vera continued at their bezique while Weizmann escorted the Minister to another room. Ben-Gurion joined them; he was studying his chief's every expression.

MacDonald broke the news to them. Partition was indeed dead. Arab opposition was intensifying, and embraced not only the neighbouring states but also the Moslems of India. 'But not Ibn Saud,' Weizmann shot back, having long been in contact with St John Philby, the king's adviser. MacDonald withheld comment, reiterating instead that Britain could not afford to immobilise her forces in a Near Eastern rebellion when she faced a more serious threat from Germany and Italy. It would be better for the Jews in the long run to accept a minority situation; they could rely on Britain to help, for she was the best friend the Jews had.

Weizmann saw the Minister to the door. He said nothing. Later, in deliberate tones, Ben-Gurion observed: 'Now we shall have to fight the British.'

Czechoslovakian independence died. Weizmann had a front seat, as it were, at the execution, for Jan Masaryk was in and out of his house describing the painful mechanism by which the dismemberment of a nation-state could be conducted. Weizmann felt the Jews were next. Hitler had successfully forced the pace with Czechoslovakia, and they also must force the pace, in reverse. 'We have to do everything, by fair means or foul, to bring about our state within two to four years,' he declared.

MacDonald too felt tormented. His status in the Cabinet was not great, and for months he had tried to win partition from colleagues who all but refused him a hearing. A man he admired now looked upon him as a viper. He was given the errand of informing Weizmann of the government's last bid for Arab-Jewish compromise and agreement: a Round Table Conference in London. A young Jew had recently murdered a German diplomat in Paris, and pogroms reigned wherever Hitler dominated. Would Weizmann bring his people to such a conference? 'Will you allow at least the immigration into Palestine of 10,000 children from Germany and Austria?' Malcolm was asked.

'We cannot do it. But you will have my support if you wish to bring them to England instead.' And later? He could give no assurance that they would eventually proceed to Palestine.

Weizmann refused the offer. 'We shall fight you all the way, from here to San Francisco,' he said.

In the course of this argument, ten thousand children were condemned to certain death. MacDonald never forgot the incident. It must have been on his mind thirty-four years later, after his long subsequent career as a British administrator overseas, when in a television interview he confessed to his regrets at having failed the Jews in the hour of their direst need.

But, in the agonising dilemma, was he the guiltier of the two?

12

Churchill, Roosevelt, and a White Paper

WHILE THE POLITICIANS DELIBERATED, THE JEWS WERE THEMSELVES partitioning Palestine, their methods reminiscent of Hollywood-style colonisation in the American West. They owned more land than they could as yet cultivate, and they determined to sit on it lest one day another Commission take it from them. Joseph Trumpeldor had shown the way in the early pioneering days. He had not died in vain.

A convoy of trucks with young families would assemble at first light, and steal across the desert paths unperceived except by the lone Arab shepherd. Broad, flat timbers, ready shaped and bolted, were picked up at pre-arranged halts, together with tents, field kitchens, a generator. Settlers from various *kibbutzim* would join the convoy, and a *Haganah* detachment. Difficult terrain was approached by pack-horse. Towards nightfall a stockade would be thrown around an encampment, a searchlight combed the neighbourhood from the skeleton of a tower, and another village was started on its life.

In 1938 two hundred Jews died in Arab attacks, but that year the Lebanese frontier was secured, and the whole of Upper Galilee. The Beisan lands, once national domain, then given by Samuel to the Beduin, later sold to the Jews, were now settled, to guard the east against guerillas infiltrating from across the Jordan. Samarian hill-country, a redoubt of fierce Arabism, was largely ignored, as were the Judean uplands leading to Jerusalem. The Zionists planted encampments close to Beersheba, and a solitary *kibbutz* on the eastern shore of Lake Tiberias, though they aimed for contiguous settlement wherever they could.

Filling the country with people in the teeth of the immigration laws engaged young men and women holed up in modest hotels throughout

Europe. Well-rehearsed in swift access to the Mediterranean, they were plentifully supplied with cash, which changed furtive hands at sea-ports and sent ships through the night under the Panamanian ensign towards remote stretches of the Palestine shore. Sometimes the British cooperated in this game of nautical hide and seek, and picked up the refugees later, subtracting a corresponding figure from the immigration quota.

Settlement entailed subterfuge, and immigration deception. Yet both activities won a measure of acquiescence from the administration, which needed the Jews' armed units to help in countering the terror. Their small regular force was trained and led from Ein Harod *kibbutz*, in the Vale of Jezreel, by Orde Wingate, the British intelligence officer whose passion for Zionism involved him in frequent brushes with his own superiors. To his young *Haganah* disciples, principally Moshe Dayan and Yigal Allon, he was a heroic figure out of the Bible, a book he carried everywhere. He frequently stayed at Rehovot when the Weizmanns were in residence. Chaim on occasion found Wingate's unbridled behaviour exasperating, while to Baffy Dugdale, long familiar with Scottish low church religiosity, it could be intolerable fanaticism.

The *Haganah's* potential extended to the Jewish police supernumeraries, in which Dayan was a sergeant, and beyond them to a host of reserves in innocent employment, so the British knew that here was a community capable of substantial call-up, and engaging in operations over which they had little control. Rightly, they gauged the chain of command in militant Zionism, embracing settlement, immigration and defence, as leading to David Ben-Gurion. He moved with ease from his office in the Jewish Agency's London headquarters to a lonely stronghold in the wilds of Palestine, or to a secret refugee assembly-point in Europe.

More problematical, the *Irgun Zvai Leumi* claimed 2,000 members in Palestine sworn to war against the Arabs, and the British too if necessary. Linked to the Revisionists, outlawed by the Jewish Agency, the *Irgun* ignored the official Zionist apparatus and fostered illegal immigration through its own representatives in Eastern Europe, where anti-semitic governments approved and facilitated their endeavours. When Weizmann threatened Malcolm MacDonald with a fight 'from here to San Francisco' his words could be taken as encompassing all the activities of both wings of Zionism. Perhaps he intended them to convey a serious challenge. Perhaps they were heard as such.

In fact his threat was the rhetoric of anger, not enmity. He believed England to be the Power most likely to act, if any would, to stop Hitler.

Without her the Jews of Europe would go to certain doom. He intended MacDonald to fear his indignation, in its own way a weapon more potent than the guns of the *Haganah*, or the bombs of the *Irgun*.

With war against Germany so close – Weizmann was informed of Chamberlain's dread of its sudden eruption upon this ill-prepared nation – he dreamed once again of making a Jewish contribution to the protection of England. In the First World War his scientific work had put him on the road to the Balfour Declaration. If the worst happened again, war could bring him to the Jewish State. The Jews as a spread of separate elements throughout the world were pitifully weak. As a coordinated Zionist movement, however, they had become, since the rise of Hitler, a force not to be despised when democracy had few allies and was at bay. He felt he could tap resources beyond the reach of the British Empire, and marshal them in directions where the interests of Britain and the Jews coincided. In Turkey, for example.

In the Western Mediterranean Spain was lost; a partner, active or passive, of the dictators. But at the opposite end Turkey stood as a cipher, wavering between the rival blandishments of Britain and Germany, unwilling to link herself with the latter, afraid lest closer ties with the former drew the hostility of Russia. Weizmann believed he could place his weight, as the Jewish leader whose magic had raised many millions of dollars for Zionism in America, in the scales. Herzl could have 'bought' Palestine from Turkey if he had the money to finance a loan. Well, he could obtain the money, and buy Turkey's friendship for Britain and the Jews at the same time.

He discussed the subject with Lord Halifax, Eden's successor as Foreign Secretary, and was not discouraged. He travelled to Istanbul and Ankara late in November, 1938, soon after the death of Ataturk. His mission promised success, though it would require lengthy preparation. Would there be time?

Ben-Gurion dismissed this foray as a wild-goose chase; Jewish money should be raised for the coming struggle in Palestine, and Weizmann had no business squandering his energies elsewhere: it was further evidence of the leader's ambivalence, the Englishman battling with the Jew in him for possession of his personality. And the Jewish Agency chairman wanted Weizmann's undivided concentration on the forthcoming Round Table Conference, which the government held out as the last chance of a negotiated peace with the Arabs.

Weizmann returned with the beginnings of a possible understanding

with Turkey – it would be no more than that – and argued with his colleagues that he now had a carrot with which to entice the British. But the
London conference proved a total disaster. It was to end in an open breach
with the government, and no talk of Turkey could save the situation for
the Jews in Palestine, or for those waiting at the European consulates for
a permit to enter the gateways of the world.

The conference, at St James's Palace, mocked all ideas of a round table.
Arabs would not sit with Jews, Arabs of the Husseini clan denied equal
rights of representation to the Nashashibis. Britain refused to accept the
Mufti as a spokesman, but there would have been no conference at all had
she not released members of his Arab Higher Committee from their
Seychelles exile. Representatives of the independent Arab states, and non-
Zionist Jews prominent in British affairs, were in attendance, ostensibly to
blunt the daggers of the principal adversaries.

For three weeks the conference sustained uneasy life, Weizmann's
brilliant advocacy facing the unseen, greater strength of the absent Mufti.
MacDonald hurried from one delegation to the other, the civil servants
were in confusion over protocol, and confidential documents reached the
wrong address. Reason was at its last. Chamberlain lost interest when
Hitler moved into Prague, and the conference collapsed in recrimination
and impasse.

Sadly, MacDonald ended the proceedings with the announcement that
the government would now impose its own solution, intimating that the
Arab-Jewish problem, if it could not be settled, would at least be buried.
Weizmann was not too displeased, thinking that a return to partition was
inevitable. His last words to Stephen Wise, representing the American
Zionists at the talks, were: 'Don't make anti-British propaganda when
you get home.'

In the event, the finality of the government's solution dumbfounded the
Jews. With or without agreement between the parties, Britain decided,
Palestine would receive independence in a decade. The Jews could have
75,000 immigrants during the next five years, and after that only with
Arab consent. So it was to be perpetual minority status, never exceeding
one-third of the total population. Now the *coup de grâce*: regulations would
be enacted to restrict Jewish land purchase to one-twentieth the area of
Western Palestine. All this was incorporated in the White Paper of 1939,
henceforth regarded by the Jews as the most infamous policy statement
ever issued by a British government.

To Weizmann it was the ultimate betrayal. He was an aging man, prematurely so, with the scars of life's disappointments marking his temperament, his gait, his face. Could he start again? Dare he? He struggled against constant bronchial attacks. A painful infection of his eyes, which first troubled him in 1917 and increased with years of strain at the microscope, now cruelly impaired his vision. His life seemed to be ebbing away in an atmosphere of defeat, or defeatism. Through his intervention in Jewish history a half-million of his people had come to Palestine. What would befall them in a country to be dominated by the Mufti? At best they would be relegated as 'Arabs of the Mosaic persuasion', the fiction that had brought down Germany's Jews. At worst, they could escape extermination only in flight. He imagined his cherished science institute at Rehovot a derelict ruin, to be engulfed by the sands as the wilderness invaded the shoots of Jewish life once again, like the relics of Aztec civilisation in the dust of Mexico. The clamour 'Down with Weizmann!' rang through the ghettos from Warsaw to Bucharest. He was sixty-five.

Perhaps a brief respite in Palestine would restore him. He and Ben-Gurion, with a large party including Vera, their son Michael with a bosom friend Michael Clark, sailed together with Baffy Dugdale. To his immense relief, Weizmann received a tumultuous welcome. The country was under curfew, the situation was tense and British armoured cars scoured the land. But spirits were high – and in secluded corners Arabs were talking to Jews of their hopes of overturning the Mufti's men.

As so often before, Weizmann's astonishing resilience came to his rescue. Outside the portals of St James's Palace in London he had been brought face-to-face with Egyptian and Iraqi leaders by MacDonald, and they had received him without hostility. Now, in another bid for their intercession he visited Prime Minister Ali Maher in Cairo. He urged for a truce in the Arab-Jewish conflict, at least for the period of the international crisis. He would pacify the Revisionists if only Egypt and Iraq would restrain the forces of the Mufti. Politely, it was put to him that the European situation was not unwelcome to the Arabs. With her back to the wall Britain would be in the mood to concede more to them than otherwise.

But he was his old fighting self again. Leaving his family in Rehovot, he flew to London to brief his parliamentary supporters in readiness for the House of Commons debate on the White Paper. He laid his position before the American Ambassador, Joseph Kennedy, for he yearned for encouragement from Washington. Soon he must be in Geneva. Nothing would be left undone to stop the government. If the Permanent Mandates Commission declared the White Paper an infringement of Britain's trust, the League of Nations must reject it as illegal. As he prepared his notes, a message reached him from Vera in Rehovot: their son's friend Michael Clark had been killed by an Arab sniper while riding his motor-bike to Tel Aviv. Palestine's tragedy now chilled the heart of this Russian Jew as he made his assault upon the Mother of Parliaments.

Chamberlain could normally count on a majority of 250, for the Labour Party Opposition under Attlee was still in the doldrums. Weizmann knew he had their support. If only he could slice Conservative loyalty to the Prime Minister! If only Winston Churchill, whose voice could fill the chamber, would speak! It was to be a two-day debate, and the Government Whips had sent out an order for full attendance.

On the second day Churchill decided to intervene, and at a lunch-time meeting received a private, comprehensive briefing from Weizmann. Then, in the House, he launched into the attack. This was May 23, 1939, and Parliament was treated to a masterpiece of polemic – the best Churchill performance for years. It won him a following in his party that would, one year later, destroy Chamberlain and carry him to the Premiership.

'I should have thought that the plan put forward by the Colonial Secretary in his White Paper, with its arid constitutional ideas and safety-catches at every point, and with its vagueness overlaying it and through all of it, combines, so far as we can understand it at present, the disadvantages of all courses without the advantages of any. The triumphant Arabs have rejected it. The despairing Jews will resist it. What will the world think about it? What will those who have been stirring up these agitators think? Will they not be encouraged by our confession of recoil? Will they not be tempted to say: "They are on the run again. This is another Munich . . ." What about these five years? Who shall say where we are going to be in five years from now? Europe is more than two-thirds mobilised tonight . . . Long before those five years are past, either there will be a Britain which knows how to keep its word on the Balfour Declaration and is not afraid to do so, or, believe me, we shall find ourselves relieved of many more overseas responsibilities other than those comprised with the Palestine Mandate.'

When the votes were counted, the government won a miserable majority of eighty-nine. A hundred members abstained, two Cabinet Ministers among them – Walter Elliot, and Leslie Hore-Belisha, the only Jew in the Chamberlain administration. It was almost unpardonable in a three-line Whip. Within seventy-two hours, the Zionist pioneers flung up the stockades of six more settlements.

Now for the Permanent Mandates Commission. Weizmann canvassed every representative individually, and by four votes to three they determined that the White Paper was incompatible with the trust vested in Great Britain. It must come up before a full meeting of the League of Nations itself.

The League? It was now a hollow shell, destined never to convene in authority again. With Britain and France in prevarication over their next step in Europe, and the world incredulous, Hitler signed his pact with Stalin and began moving towards the Baltic. Palestine ceased to be a preoccupation even of the Zionists.

Yet here they were, reluctantly, almost aimlessly, assembled for another of their Congresses. Weizmann was back in Geneva, though on this occasion Swiss Nazis were demonstrating outside the Grand Theatre as he was speaking.

Nothing from his lips could dispel the pessimism cast by the shadow over Europe. Of the British White Paper, he stated: 'The sorrow is ours, the shame is theirs.' And, imploringly, he told of the need for a renewal of approaches to the Arabs. Suddenly the entire Congress realised the huge omission in their twenty years, nay forty years of diplomacy. Never had they earnestly developed a policy of reconciliation towards the people they expected to reside beside them in friendly neighbourliness. The Zionists could speak languages in profusion, but few understood Arabic. They had zealously wooed politicians in all the capitals of the world, but their agents in Cairo, Baghdad and Damascus had grievously underestimated Arab pride, for they had found points of contact only with the corrupt. Now, when they themselves were reduced to the least significant people in Europe, and their loneliness as a race became emphasised with every new move on the international chequerboard, they discovered that all they could harvest from the Arabs was hatred.

Weizmann had observed the process over two decades, apparently helpless. True, the Arab national spirit had dogged his path, but only as a haunting phantom. Now it was materialising as a colossus. And the Jewish side of the equation produced a phantom too: fear of their own terrorism. Delegates found on their seats leaflets warning them that their future would be decided not by persuasion, nor by compromise, but by a clash of arms. This was the first time many of them had so much as encountered the term *Irgun*.

To the last the aging leader urged that nothing be spoken at the Congress that would sunder with finality his remaining links with the British. He wanted no public discussion of illegal immigration: it would drive the government further into the Arabs' arms. Ben-Gurion brushed these sensitivities aside. He was ready to close down the Jewish Agency's headquarters in London at once, and transfer to New York.

Britain began calling up her reservists, and still the Jews were gathered in this unreal atmosphere of Geneva, held to a discussion that was itself unreal. Anxious eyes drifted through the endless pages of their agenda. Better they should disperse now, and return to their families while there was still time. It was Sabbath Eve, and many delegates could not but note the unhappy symbolism of a departure on the day commanded by the Lord as a time of rest. Other gods were taking over.

Weizmann had already bidden the Congress farewell the day before. Beside him on the platform was Ussishkin, in succession teacher, comrade and adversary of almost fifty years, whom he would never meet again, and the much younger Ben-Gurion. He addressed a few words to the assembly on their faith that the democratic forces of the world would prevail, then he embraced his two colleagues as though their quarrels were a luxury belonging to another age. Outside, his English chauffeur waited at the wheel of his Rolls.

He departed into the night towards the French frontier. Soon he would be like so many other national leaders in London: as it were an exile. He would not see Palestine again for five years, and then, because of the incapacity of his eyes, he would barely see it. He came to Paris, and Léon Blum informed him he expected war on the Wednesday. In fact Poland was to have two further days of peace.

Surely there could be no intention of fulfilling the White Paper now! Britain should cherish all her allies, and who would be more faithful than the Jews, earliest object of Hitler's hatred, and his greatest enemy still. Weizmann felt that all conflict with the government must be forgotten in the higher purpose. His first act on reaching London was to instruct Lewis Namier, aided by Baffy Dugdale, to draft a message to the Prime Minister accordingly.

It went as follows:

In this hour of supreme crisis, the consciousness that the Jews have a contribution to make to the defence of sacred values impels me to write this letter. I wish to confirm, in the most explicit manner, the declarations which I and my colleagues have made during the last months, and especially in the last week, that the Jews stand by Great Britain and will fight on the side of the Democracies. Our urgent desire is to give effect to these declarations. We wish to do so in a way entirely consonant with the general scheme of British action, and therefore would place ourselves, in matters big and small, under the coordinating direction of His Majesty's Government. The Jewish Agency is ready to enter into immediate arrangements for utilising Jewish man-power, technical ability, resources, etc. The Jewish Agency has recently had differences in the political field with the Mandatory Power. We would like these differences to give way before the greater and more pressing necessities of the time.

For himself personally, and for his family, war when it came involved them wholly in the struggle. His sons joined up. Michael, ten years younger than Benjamin, could have stayed at his studies but chose to enlist immediately in the R.A.F., and his brother, now married, was posted to an anti-aircraft detachment at Chatham, in the Thames estuary. Vera volunteered for service as a doctor, and worked in the East End during the bombing of London. Weizmann wished fervently to be in the fight in the way he understood best, with his chemistry, and in fact within a matter of weeks he was asked to undertake a mission abroad. He spoke of re-opening his London laboratory for war-work.

He appeared remote to his colleagues at the Zionist office. He in turn reproached them for their failure to understand the connection between his science and his philosophy. That 'Via Dolorosa' he had been constantly plying to the Colonial Office was not Zionism, he complained. But Ben-Gurion was impatient. On the outbreak of hostilities he summed up their attitude towards Britain in a classic phrase: 'We shall fight the war as if there were no White Paper, and the White Paper as if there were no war.'

More accurately than Weizmann, he perceived the ending of an era. The Mandatory Power, emasculated by its economic ills, in retreat from its imperial stance, would be unable to re-assert its former hegemony. Europe would emerge from the war exhausted. Britain would be unable to restrain the Arabs; only America could do that. Moreover, Ben-Gurion refused to treat the *Yishuv's* internal strains with Weizmann's apparent complacency. As a party man he knew the relentlessness of its disputes.

The prohibition on transfers of land from Arab to Jew was due to be enforced early in 1940. This would be the test. If the government went through with it, the Jews would find themselves confined to a Tzarist-style Pale of Settlement under the British flag. Ben-Gurion demanded that the

Agency show its claws, for toleration of this hated edict would benefit only the extremists of *Irgun*.

Weizmann dismissed ideas of revolt as the theatricality of a practised demagogue who confused a brave speech with a brave act. An open confrontation with the government was surely out of the question; they would achieve more behind the scenes. First, they should rid themselves of MacDonald, and he whispered to friends in high places that Palestine should be taken out of Colonial Office control, assuming MacDonald was to remain there. Churchill, fresh from his triumph in the White Paper debate, his warnings about Hitler vindicated, was now in the Cabinet, and conducting the Admiralty as though his department was in charge of the entire war. He would not be the Zionists' man if they started a fight on the side.

As though proving the point, Churchill invited Weizmann to meet him at dinner. It was the beginning of a war-time association that was to survive many a crisis. What, asked Churchill, did Weizmann want from Britain?

Nothing *from* Britain, the other responded, but to give Britain the full strength of Palestine's potential. They should enrol a Jewish army to take over the defence of Palestine, and to join in all battlefronts against the Nazi enemy. As a first step, 200 selected young men should come to England for officer training and service in the formations as they were raised. Weizmann sought approval to establish an arms factory in Palestine, develop the local chemical industry, and as a start convert the Daniel Sieff Institute for pharmaceuticals.

He revived for Churchill his dream of making the Zionist Organisation a substantial ally. It had excellent contacts in the neutral countries and could gather vital intelligence. For example, Weizmann had received information through Switzerland as quickly as had the Foreign Office of an anti-Hitler plot in the German army.

Churchill reacted hopefully, and instructed Brendan Bracken to be his liaison with the Zionists. It was shortly afterwards that Weizmann received his first government assignment: a mission to old Willstätter in Geneva, to learn all he could of Germany's advances in chemical warfare. Publicly, he described the journey as relating to the needs of refugees from Poland.

He found himself the travelling salesman of his people's talents. In discussion with the Minister of Armaments in Paris he hinted at some modest victories of the Palestine Jews in harnessing science to warfare. Pressed to be more explicit, he disclosed that his young colleague at the

Rehovot Institute, David Bergmann, was confidential adviser on chemicals to the *Haganah*, and had produced, illegally, of course, an explosive unknown to the Allies. Also, under Weizmann's guidance Bergmann had achieved the direct production of aromatic hydrocarbons through the 'cracking' of petroleum, with all that this promised in the manufacture of dye-stuffs, drugs, plastics and T.N.T.

Within days Bergmann was summoned by telegram to a government laboratory in Paris. But it came as a shock to him to discover that his French colleagues, far from having their hearts in their work, were fatalistically awaiting what they regarded as an inevitable German victory. He took the first opportunity to apprise Weizmann of the mood, with the result that collaboration with the French abruptly terminated.

As to the so-called phony war, it had no counterpart in Palestine. The administration, still half-opposing, half-acknowledging the *Haganah,* kept an eagle eye on all the Jews' activities, and as a precaution Wingate was posted back to England, out of harm's way. He haunted the Zionist offices, pressing all and sundry to agitate for the immediate creation of a Jewish Fighting Force. He persuaded Weizmann and Ben-Gurion that he was the right man to command it – in fact he was the wrong man if ever they were to win approval for such a force from the War Office. The brass hats regarded Wingate as quite uncontrollable, not beyond leading his army against themselves. And Moshe Dayan, far from having British trust now, was locked in Acre jail with forty-two comrades; they had been ambushed while training in a remote wadi.

The swift conquest of Poland, and its division between Germany and Russia, shut off another three million Jews from contact with their brothers, and from making a contribution to Zionism. Weizmann's European constituency was dwindling to the Western fringe of the Continent. Instinctively, his thoughts moved across the Atlantic. American Jewry, now his only substantial reservoir of support, must be revived. His injunction of restraint to Wise after the breakdown of the St James's Conference no longer applied: it was before they knew the terms of the White Paper. Weizmann determined to put his case personally to Roosevelt.

The President received him early in February, 1940, and he found the American leader well-briefed on all the elements of the Palestine situation, but from sources which Weizmann immediately regarded as suspect: the Near Eastern division of the State Department, transatlantic twin of the British Colonial Office. Carefully weighing his words, Weizmann informed the President of his hope for a Jewish-Arab federation in Palestine, with 'considerable' immigration, and as part of a Confederation of Arab States.

Roosevelt remained non-committal. He had no wish to embarrass a Britain at war, and was anxious to safeguard her oil supplies; his Administration was fighting shy of influencing events in Palestine. Furthermore, the President had no evidence of American Jewry's displeasure with this policy.

If anything, he was understating the case. To the Jewish-American mass, Zionists included, Roosevelt was the saviour who would wave a wand for their people in his own way, and in his own time. The Zionists may have felt this with less conviction than other Jews, but they were largely a disregarded body still, without standing in the great labour unions, and held in contempt by the quasi-Communist ideologues of the New York intelligentsia. Though Wise was no inconsiderable personality in Democratic Party politics, enjoying direct access to the President, he was unlikely to expose himself against the tide. And the movement Wise and Louis Lipsky ruled between them in America was little else than a farrago of sterile factions sustained by each other's incompetence.

As with the nation as a whole, the Jews' preoccupation with neutrality had achieved the sanctity of a religion. The extent of their commitment to Europe ran as far as philanthropy. Relief funds for Poland, 'Bundles for Britain', the Jews were conspicuous in every such campaign, and if the *New York Times* was a guide Weizmann had come to America solely to platitudinise on the heroism and indestructibility of the Jewish spirit. As emissary of a desperately-concerned protagonist in the European war few wished to know him.

He had a friendly meeting with Brandeis, both men recognising that the past was passed. But privately, Weizmann was caustic about the isolationist mood. Every contact with a prominent American Jew reinforced his impression that this great community was not ready for the leadership of the people that must sooner or later fall to it.

What hopes, then, for his mission succeeding here? Who in the United States would conduct his agitation against MacDonald's White Paper, let alone promote the concept of a Jewish Fighting Force, for which he had intimated to Churchill and the British War Office (shades of 1917!) the prospects of large-scale American volunteering? Despite his frequent visits since the Great War he had no permanent foothold in this country, and with each arrival he found himself engaged in patching up parochial differences, which on his departure would obstinately re-emerge.

An immediate necessity, therefore, was to plant his standard on American soil, and he appointed Meyer Weisgal as his personal representative. Weisgal's multifarious activities included procuring support for the Rehovot Institute, which could not survive as hitherto, purely on the generosity of the Marks-Sieff-Sacher group; and to hold a watching brief over Weizmann's expanding chemical interests in an America girding her might. As a corollary to these, the leader desired Weisgal to forge what he termed a *Union sacrée* of all forces, so as to propel American Jewry, now five million strong and powerfully concentrated in prosperity in the Eastern states, to rise to its new responsibilities – European Jewry being, as he put it, 'practically blotted out'.

Weisgal had to disengage himself from another of those enterprises of showmanship for which he seemed to have been specially created: the Palestine Pavilion of the New York World's Fair. Certainly, he was an adept fund-raiser. Whether he could contruct the *Union sacrée* was another matter. Some American Zionists could not stomach his florid style. Notable among these was a man long in the backwoods, but now a rising star: Rabbi Hillel Silver. A superb orator, he had made a striking defence of Weizmann's stewardship at the 1939 Congress. Silver occupied a pulpit in distant Cleveland, and like his brother cleric Stephen Wise affected a national political role – but as a dedicated Republican. The rabbis sat uncomfortably together in Zionism.

However, none of this was of great consequence until Germany's spring offensive, which over-ran Western Europe and carried Mussolini into the war. Britain, with her Suez base in danger, decided to choose this moment to put the Palestine Land Transfer Ordinances into effect, despite Weizmann's eleventh-hour appeals to Churchill and Smuts to have them postponed. It was as though the only automatic ally of the beleagured champion of democracy was being spat upon, smothered in anonymity, and fenced off. To the War Office, Arab indifference to the struggle was natural, while Jewish zeal was suspect.

In this atmosphere the Jewish Agency prepared the *Yishuv* for national service, believing the distrust could only be a passing phase. Soon 85,000 men and 50,000 women, over a quarter of the entire Jewish population of Palestine, had filled in volunteer forms. Churchill, Prime Minister and war leader at last, knew of these figures. MacDonald, to Weizmann's relief, was shifted from the Colonial Office. Of course the Jewish Fighting Force could not be long delayed now. Weizmann was soon proceeding on his Via Dolorosa again, for his first discussion with the new Minister, Lord Lloyd.

Lloyd was frank about the government's dilemma. He recognised the Jews' desire to play their part, but feared their contribution would entail obligations which could become a weapon against general policy for the future of Palestine. Lloyd admitted that the Arabs were detached from the struggle, at best neutral, at worst hostile. So how would they see the *Yishuv* in khaki – except as a means of gaining eventual control of the country?

Against Weizmann's protests Lloyd offered to enrol Jews strictly under a system of parity with the Arabs: once an Arab joined up a Jew could join; an Arab platoon would be matched by a Jewish platoon. Few proposals could have been more insulting to a man who had just been appointed honorary chemical adviser to the Ministry of Supply. In Palestine the Agency advised Jews for the present to join purely British regiments.

Weizmann returned disconsolate to his newly-opened laboratory in Knightsbridge. He had installed Bergmann and a group of English scientists there to help him solve two problems likely to become of over-riding importance as the siege of Britain intensified. One of them related to the investigation of fermentation processes for the manufacture of high-octane aviation fuel. The other was to improve on existing (German) methods of producing synthetic rubber. Here he was master, and the challenge revived him.

The work proceeded with some success. It pointed to answers to questions far beyond the purposes of war. He thought again of his ambition to create foodstuffs in the laboratory by imitating nature. Britain was an island, dependent on distant continents for so many commodities in times of crisis. She could not hope to dominate the oil-fields of the Middle East, nor the plantations of the Far East, indefinitely. She must look elsewhere: not to America, but to Africa and the inexhaustible vegetation of its jungles. Weizmann failed at that time to visualise the independence of the Black Continent (who did?) except in a form associating it with Britain. And Africa's carbohydrates, sugar, starch, cellulose, reproduced themselves in plenty each year. Whatever the world needed in food and fuel could be made from these substances.

He was now engaged on the most exciting scientific research of his dramatic and versatile career. Perhaps, as a Hebrew sage of old had put it, it would not be given to him to complete the work, but neither was it for him to desist from it. Understandably, his battles over Palestine in Whitehall assumed lesser importance than this battle for new ways to feed the world.

Understandably also, Ben-Gurion felt otherwise. He allowed nothing to enter his life that might dislodge Zionism for a single moment. While Weizmann had his chemistry, Brodetsky had mathematics, Namier history, and those American rabbis their pulpits. But the war against the White Paper must be waged unrelentingly, and so must the war to put the Jewish people in the war. Ben-Gurion's relations with Weizmann grew cooler, and frequently, when the latter arrived at Great Russell Street for a meeting with his colleagues, he expressed disapproval of the leader by going off to the cinema.

Unceasing pressure upon Churchill to create the Jewish Army, Ben-Gurion demanded, must be accompanied by the specification that the force be reserved for service in Palestine only.

'But the war hasn't reached Palestine!' Weizmann, who was applying no conditions, objected.

'If Palestine is over-run, and we have no force there, the *Yishuv* will face massacre by the Arabs, protected by the Nazis and Italians.'

Weizmann persuaded the War Office at last. But, against his better judgment, he committed himself to raising the Jewish force not only from the *Yishuv*, but also from America and elsewhere. He offered 'several divisions' of fighting men, of which two could be brought partially trained from Palestine at once. European refugees would, doubtless, help to make the numbers up, but of course it was a fantasy to see regiments of volunteers crossing the Atlantic.

Lord Lloyd knew this no less than Weizmann. However, this war was far different in character from the last, so he intended putting the claim to the test. He spoke of a proposal, not to be made public before the 1940 American Presidential Election, to incorporate 10,000 men in specifically Jewish units of His Majesty's Forces, of which not more than 3,000 must be raised in Palestine. This formation would come to England for training. No one would be recruited without a guarantee of acceptance by his country of origin after the war. Further, it was entirely for the War Office to determine the theatre of operations in which they would be employed.

Well, thought Weizmann, this was hardly his original offer to the Prime Minister of 50,000 fighting men from Palestine, but the beginnings of a victory nevertheless. It would be his task, once Roosevelt was safely back in the White House, to return to the United States and find his American volunteers. It was easily said. Assuming the Jews of the New World overcame Washington's resistance and their own reluctance, they could still produce another excuse: British policy in Palestine. The Land Transfer Ordinances stuck in the throat.

The government was of course merely palliating Weizmann while it played for time. The prospect of all those conjectural recruits being brought to England, when the shipping situation was so exiguous, was remote indeed. In fact Anthony Eden took one look at the entire proposition and refused to be party to the fiction. Weizmann was bought off in the spring of 1941 with a six-month postponement.

By this time some 9,000 Palestinian Jews had joined the British forces, anonymously as it were, without special insignia or designation. A handful found their way into infantry regiments, the majority being shunted to lines-of-communication units: labourers, stevedores, maintenance men. Over a thousand of these would shortly be left as prisoners-of-war in the evacuation of Greece and Crete.

Shrewdly, the *Haganah* Command decided against wasting its key personnel in non-combatant services, and kept its best people back. The Jewish Fighting Force as such, visualised as a formation similar to the Czechs, Poles and Free French, was left to gather dust in a War Office pigeon-hole. Orde Wingate was posted to Egypt, never to appear in Palestine again.

And Chaim Weizmann, taut with the duality of his existence, sped between his Zionist and scientific headquarters. He must fight the country which failed to recognise the Jews as a factor in the war; he must protest at their harassment in Palestine, where stern police operations had lately resulted in a young Jew's death. He was also the boffin striving to bring Britain's victory closer, for this government, which opposed his people, would also be their saviour, and every day gained could mean a Jew rescued.

In some ways he was more English than before, in others less. He closed down his Kensington home, as though mentally he was already living in Palestine. Vera improvised their residence in a suite at the Dorchester Hotel. But London under bombardment, the strain of war reflected in the tired faces of its citizens, the sense that under Churchill this nation was indomitable, filled him with pride. In a long report to Moshe Shertok categorising his grievances against England he could not forbear to include a postscript on British courage in its ordeal – 'it is a grandiose spectacle to see'.

He suffered private pain. His son Benjamin, in the front-line of the island's defence with his coastal anti-aircraft battery, sustained severe shell-shock. Despite long hospitalisation he barely recovered, to remain a constant anxiety. Bergmann, loyal in all things to his chief, took Benjamin into his faithful care during the Weizmanns' frequent absences from London.

War raged on the Egyptian frontier, and trembled in Vichy-held Syria and in Iraq, where Raschid Ali was conspiring with the Mufti, but Palestine itself enjoyed an eerie peace. Jewish internal politics flourished as argumentatively as before. Refugees still approached the coast after long, harrowing voyages in unseaworthy transports.

The British wished, apparently, to preserve the Jews as inert, blank onlookers of the battle. Newspaper articles inoffensive enough for publications in Britain were banned from the local Press; and *Haganah* members, considered fit to guide the army into Syria one day, found themselves imprisoned for holding a gun the next. Reason was abandoned on both sides – some *Haganah* escapades seemed to be without point except to demonstrate the triumph of bravado over stupidity.

But in Europe tragedy piled on unbelievable tragedy. Reports of German atrocities were reaching the outside world, though so terrible they were classed as Zionist propaganda. Surely such concentration camps as were described could not really exist! And these accounts of deported Rumanian Jews drowning in the Dniester could only spring from the minds of deranged refugees.

An explosion in Haifa Bay told that these were no mere horror stories. The Jews were daring their lives to get to Palestine. The explosion sank the *Patria* – it was a sabotage operation by a *Haganah* unit to destroy the vessel's seaworthiness – and 200 lives were lost. But 1,700 survivors were taken ashore, to speak of their harrowing experiences in occupied Europe.

They were illegals nevertheless, to be assembled for deportation to Mauritius. Now it was the turn of an inflamed Weizmann in his capacity as the opponent of Britain. When Lloyd refused his plea to keep them in Palestine, he demanded an interview with the Prime Minister. Hurriedly, Lord Halifax was sent to appease him. Yes, the refugees could remain. Soon Weizmann was his other self again, working on a paper for Churchill on the utilisation of Indian molasses for purposes of war.

An air of despairing urgency now surrounded his plans for another appeal to America. He could not conduct this degenerating struggle alone, without the political leverage to be gained in New York and Washington. In March, 1941, with the Jewish Army in cold storage, he settled his personal affairs lest this be his last journey – both he and Vera had been carrying cyanide at all times since the fall of France. His scientific interests now ranged over the world, not only in England and America, and he entrusted those on this side of the Atlantic to James Malcolm, the Armenian merchant who had been Weizmann's earliest link with Sir Mark Sykes. Then he went off to Downing Street to take farewell of Brendan Bracken, hoping at the same time for brief minutes with the Prime Minister.

Hitler had not as yet struck in Greece, and it seemed that General Wavell's Eighth Army would soon clear North Africa. Roosevelt had just willed great economic strength to Britain's cause with the Lend-Lease agreement. It was perhaps the last moment in history when this country could sense undisturbed its imperial mastery – Russia was still not an ally, nor China. Churchill was in expansive mood as he called Weizmann to his room.

Bidding his visitor Godspeed, the Prime Minister gave his reassurance that the Jewish Army was indeed merely postponed. He spoke confidently of a Palestine settlement after the war, and promised to use his good offices to promote an agreement between Weizmann and Ibn Saud. The latter, said the Prime Minister, would be made lord of the Arabian countries, 'the boss of bosses'.*

This confirmed Weizmann's instinct, long held, on the coming role of the desert king. He had told MacDonald as much in 1938, for Ibn Saud had no aspiration to lord it over the Mediterranean littoral. St John Philby, doubtless at his master's instigation, had spoken out in favour of the Peel partition scheme, and had only lately intimated to Weizmann that a Jewish loan to Saudi Arabia might be exchanged for acceptance of Jewish statehood in Western Palestine. It was therefore in high hope that Weizmann proceeded on his journey. His aim was to conquer Washington for Zionism, and reproduce there the atmosphere that gave him access to the springs of power in London.

He remained in America four months, concentrating on men who to a considerable degree determined the character of Roosevelt's Presidency. Two of them he revived as Zionist faithfuls after their long separation from the scene: Felix Frankfurter, now a Justice of the Supreme Court, and Benjamin V. Cohen, the former's protégé and an architect of the New Deal. He was more of a stranger to Samuel Rosenman, who had organised Roosevelt's Brains Trust and would shortly be appointed his Counsel, while

---

* The discussion is given slightly differently in *Trial and Error* where it is wrongly dated one year later and includes also a reference to Roosevelt, who does not feature in the note of the talk Weizmann made immediately afterwards.

he hardly knew Henry Morgenthau, junior, a man of far different calibre from the father given such short shrift by Weizmann during his Gibraltar mission of 1917.

The message Weizmann brought to these Americans secured them as willing allies. He seemed to be a statesman representing an Old World still acknowledged in many respects as the teacher of the New. They admired his frankness, appreciated his astringency. Zionism as they saw it organised in New York left them, even the once-committed Frankfurter and Cohen, unmoved. But this leader ennobled the cause. He penetrated the chill corridors of the State Department and worked a similar spell over Sumner Welles.

Of course he had also to place himself on public exhibition throughout the country, and ginger up backward contributors for the movement's bread and butter. There could be no immigration without funds, no university, no irrigation. But it was with relief that he settled down for a short holiday in California, and to collect his thoughts.

In a letter to Frankfurter he voiced his disappointment at the state of Zionist awareness in this country. The speeches to which he had been treated, he wrote, were 'spread-eagled emotional outpourings . . . There is not a single book on Zionism which is up-to-date and can be placed in the hands of the intelligent reader.' He lamented the failure of young talented people to take over in public life, comparing the Jewish situation to the state of England herself. Numbering himself among those who should be passing on, he pointed out that in England 'the war rests primarily on Churchill, and Lloyd George is still discussed as a possible candidate for a Cabinet post'. He had seen Hollywood, 'controlled by Jews', and its vulgarity disturbed him: 'The others would not have made Hollywood any better, but they are the majority who are always right – we are the minority, and are always wrong.' As for Washington, he was now convinced that Roosevelt and Sumner Welles would act more positively to advance the Zionist cause were it not for the people in charge of Middle East affairs in the State Department.

Here Weizmann was doing his duty as a Zionist. However, in writing to Lord Moyne, who had succeeded Lloyd at the Colonial Office on the latter's sudden death that year, he spoke also as an Englishman. He reported that England had no better friend in the United States than Secretary of the Treasury Morgenthau, who 'risked the reproach of working as a Jew and not merely as a patriotic American'. Britain had only two whole-hearted supporters among American ethnic groups, Weizmann declared: the Jews and the Anglo-Saxons. Of the others, he told Moyne, the Irish and the Germans were in the main hostile, and perhaps friendly to the dictators. Many of the Italians were fascist in outlook.

He criticised British propaganda in America as being conducted by the wrong people, who were unable to dissipate among intellectuals and workers the idea that this war was not the old imperialism in a new guise. And not for the first time, he advised that more working-class speakers be sent over, to tour colleges and factories. Labour problems were enormous, and his investigation of the armaments and chemical industries told him that these had not reached more than thirty per cent of their potential.

Now for that old demand for a Jewish Fighting Force. The Jews of America, he suggested to Moyne, felt that appeasement, which may have disappeared from the English mind as far as world politics were concerned, had its last stronghold in the attitude to the Jews. 'The Arabs have betrayed, are betraying; therefore they must be appeased.'

His plea had little effect. Back in England he was stalled yet again on the Jewish Army issue. Eden revealed a cruel insensitivity to the life or death situation of the Jews, stricken as no other people in Europe. He was sending messages of encouragement to the Arabs, the Czechs, the Poles; but not a word of sympathy or hope to the greatest casualty of Hitler's oppression. Harold Macmillan, at the Ministry of Supply, was urging Weizmann to return yet again to America, to consult with the Baruch Committee in Washington and contribute his experience on synthetic rubber research and the replacement of scarce materials. As he considered the prospect he was informed, regretfully but with finality, that the Jewish Army scheme must be abandoned.

So, Weizmann was compelled to admit, Ben-Gurion had been right all along. They should have made a public issue of it, no matter the embarrassment this might have caused the government. Months of confidential dinner-talk, reams of secret memoranda, had been so much wasted effort. He wired to Weisgal in New York: 'A word from the White House and we would get the Army.' Alas, the word did not come.

Now, at last, the Jewish Agency convened a conference in London at which the two leaders disclosed how the long, tortuous negotiations had given them nothing but frustrating prevarication, until this final, humiliating blow. The world must know how Great Britain, standing alone, could have had an ally, yet had refused to tempt the post-war fates in Palestine by inviting Zionist partnership in the prosecution of the war. And all this despite Churchill's support.

America, America! He had to face that continent again, for reasons of his own besides England's reasons. This time it would be a long trip. He must impel the Jews there to bury their differences and come out openly for what was in their hearts. Weisgal must prepare the ground for a great demonstration, in the form of a conference embracing Zionists of every hue, to be addressed by himself and Ben-Gurion. There had never been such a conference on that side of the Atlantic. It would proclaim the Jewish right in Palestine, and to defend Palestine, to a nation upon which Britain depended for her survival.

Weizmann did not envisage an easy passage in New York. He knew that anti-Zionist American Jews were not beyond branding the movement as a war-mongering party in the United States. And he would be giving a platform also to the extremists on his own side, shrill with indignation against Britain. Suddenly, in December, 1941, controversy surrounding America's role in the struggle against despotism was stilled. The Japanese had bombed Pearl Harbour.

On Friday, February 19, 1942, Chaim and Vera Weizmann were once again in Bristol for the flight to Portugal, where they would board the transatlantic clipper. The routine was familiar – all departures from England had to be officially cleared, seat priorities arranged, with perhaps days of waiting again in Lisbon. This time it was to be different. A call from London brought him to the telephone. It was Simon Marks, to inform him that young Michael, twenty-six years of age, had not returned with his Whitley bomber from U-boat patrol in the Bay of Biscay.

The plane departed without them. The public figure and his lady now shrank into their parenthood, which carries only personal joys and private sufferings.

13

New World in Harness

By SUCKING AMERICA INTO THE WHIRLWIND, PEARL HARBOUR ENABLED the Jews of the United States to bare their breasts. Prudent isolationism in the nation was giving way to a heady activism, so the fear of incurring hostility as a war party ceased to haunt them. When Weizmann arrived in the country in April, 1942, he discovered that his whispered pleas of earlier visits were now being reproduced as trumpet-blasts. However, the Jews' transformation was so sudden that he was bound, despite his gratification, to suspect its intensity as counterfeit. He had raised Jewish nationalism from the vasty deep within an amorphous community five million strong, and clutching its American identity like a *Barmitzvah* gift; but he could not tell whether he would be able to govern this new spirit, or whether it would assume the form of a monster and possess him in its embrace. Organisations long moribund were at last fired into a sense of purpose, persuaded by their own slogans and declarations: a Jewish Army forthwith, to defend the Holy Land against Rommel's advance across the desert and to join in the liberation of Europe; maximum immigration into Palestine; the urgency of creating a Jewish State. No editor could ignore the imperious Press releases arriving with every post.

Capitol Hill was speedily convinced that Zionism was now the respectable, all-American movement. Unfortunately, Franklin D. Roosevelt was far from this mind. While basking in Jewish adoration, and welcoming Rabbi Wise ('friend Stevie') to the White House with an affectionate slap on the shoulder, the President kept his own counsel. Compassionate messages to his Jewish fellow-citizens by all means, lamenting with them, hoping with them, trusting with them in God's infinite mercy; but radiating as much and as little sincerity as his annual Columbus Day greeting to the Italians. And any discussion of bringing a substantial number of refugees to America was taboo.

The previous February, a further episode in the European Jewish agony had been enacted on the Black Sea. The *Struma*, ruin of a Danubian cattle-barge, sank beneath the weight of its 760 Rumanian refugees. Denied landing-rights in Turkey, refused entry permits to Palestine, all but one drowned. This did not move Roosevelt to brave the nation's displeasure and offer future candidates for such a fate a haven in the United States, nor inspire him to lodge protest with his British ally for barring them from Palestine.

Roosevelt had expert opinion before him that America's oil reserves would run dry by 1958, when his country would become dependent upon Arabian supplies. So he determined to conduct the war as though the unwanted Jews of Europe were non-existent. Full-page advertisements in the *New York Times* proved an offensive reminder to the contrary from time to time, both to him and the British Ambassador, the former Foreign Secretary Lord Halifax.

In their complex psychology the Jews of the United States had their charms and mysteries. They could be at once stridently vocal and demurely reticent: confident though they might be in their voting strength, they nevertheless betrayed the inhibitions of their earlier tribal insecurity. They lacked a leader of substance capable of standing up to their President, or of voicing their own guilt, over the failure of America to give shelter in this vast and still under-populated land to more of their stricken European brethren. Neither had they produced a man to chastise Roosevelt for his inaction over Palestine. Weizmann realised that if he campaigned against America's reluctance to open her own doors he would not receive a hearing. His arrangement with American Jewry was unspoken but clear: they would help him to castigate perfidious Albion provided he left them alone about heartless America.

As we have seen, he had not waited for these more propitious times before putting his case to America; the process was already begun, at the fount of influence, with Roosevelt's White House entourage. Now this had to be complemented by popular action in the field. Hence his instruction to Meyer Weisgal to set the machinery in motion (and how laborious!) for his 'extraordinary conference' in New York: Zionists of every shade actually meeting under a single roof. Now at last it was achieved. And while Weizmann sought to direct American energies to an assault upon

Washington, his lieutenant Ben-Gurion was steering American fire towards Whitehall.

Weizmann was now a broken man, accompanied by a wife in a state of shock. They had returned briefly to London on receiving the news about their son, to nurse the faint hope of word arriving of his rescue. They had remained at home a month, their personal loss swallowed in the collective tragedy of the *Struma*. Ministers of the Crown, and the head of the R.A.F., came to voice their condolences to him as a father; he responded with the anger of a betrayed leader. He had appeared at a great demonstration of revulsion at the *Struma* catastrophe, and railed against the men ruling Palestine, whom he described as being without understanding, or pity. 'What a mockery,' he cried, 'to read the high-sounding phrases mouthed by the leaders of democracy, when their regulations are sending people deliberately to their death! Regulations applied only to Jews, and applied particularly to Jews in their National Home.'

Now this patriarchal ire was being ventilated in New York. Would it be more effective here? It must. Over 600 delegates came to the Biltmore Hotel to hear him, and observe him in this first public bid to unite American Jewry and take it under his command. The ground Weizmann trod was none too firm, for in the months just gone Ben-Gurion, who had preceded him to America, had been spreading discontent. He let it be known that the Weizmann method did not win endorsement from people like himself who, he maintained, more exactly reflected the views of the *Yishuv*. Zionism was being crippled by personal rule, Ben-Gurion complained, with Weizmann 'holding court' rather than accepting advice. The leader's career of weakness was reaping a harvest of broken promises. Ben-Gurion might have been describing Neville Chamberlain.

Not surprisingly, therefore, mutterings were heard against the Zionist President when he made his appearance. A voice that had dogged him over the years at Congresses in Europe, Meir Grossman's, was raised in a demand for change at the helm. 'We can no longer rely on people with a chronicle of failures and defeats behind them,' Grossman called. He was an echo of Jabotinsky, who had recently died.

Weizmann took up the suggestion. 'I agree,' he retorted from the platform, 'that we need a changing leadership in a changing world. But where are the leaders? I would be the first to vote for them.'

He had dressed his last speech in London with fierce condemnation of the Mandatory Power. Yet here, amazingly, to an audience that regarded England from a traditionally critical posture, he leapt to defend the country that had time and again let him down. He refused to allow any American to forget that, but for that island outpost of freedom in the Old World, the Jews would by now be enslaved, and Palestine would be occupied by their enemy.

'Attacking the British government has become something of a sport. I recognise the right but deplore the tendency . . . As long as British policy in Palestine permits us to buy land and bring in Jews, I am ready to put up with everything.' The words were intended for Churchill. Weizmann was gambling on his conviction that the goodwill of this one man was worth retaining against a rebellion from his own multitude.

He failed to carry the meeting his way. American Zionists were not wholly impressed by the finer gradations of his argument, and though Weizmann was not repudiated, the message that went out from the Biltmore Conference flung a challenge to Britain and delivered a warning to the leader still capable of a good word for her. The conference terminated on a demand for all of Palestine as a Jewish Commonwealth, with control of immigration vested in the Jewish Agency and, by implication, the dismissal of the British. This was wild country indeed for a Zionist diplomat. Ben-Gurion was exultant.

There was little Weizmann could do but accept the verdict, embodied though it was in a formula that no statesman versed in the history of Arab-Jewish relations would ever discuss. The official policy of the movement, as he had guided it and the Zionist Congress of 1937 had approved it, was to recognise Arab rights and negotiate a favourable partition of the country. How could he go back on his word? He therefore decided that he would privately repudiate what he publicly endorsed.

Ben-Gurion travelled direct to Jerusalem, to enclose himself in the clandestine work of a local chieftain preparing his road to power. He represented Biltmore to his comrades as vindicating his challenge to the leader, though without making it the occasion for his usurpation of the leadership. Weizmann's misgivings grew. If the Biltmore resolution was now official Zionist policy, and in default of a Congress it had to be considered so, then it would be transparent to the British that his demand for the Jewish Army was a ruse to arm the Jews with the means to take Palestine, if necessary, by force. In fact Moyne intimated as much in the House of Lords. Ben-Gurion was publicly demanding the immediate transfer of two million Jews to the homeland, and adding this to his clamour for a defence force that might one day have to fight the Arabs or British, or both.

W.—15

Despairingly, Weizmann described such talk in a letter to Baffy Dugdale as reflecting 'fascist tendencies and megalomania'. Perhaps Shertok could keep the Agency chairman in rein? It was a futile thought. Shertok was no match for his colleague, especially now that Jews and British regarded each other in Palestine with mutual contempt, and an arrogant British police officer would be spoken of as a Nazi in disguise.

Biltmore and its famous 'Programme' might have been lost among the many fits and starts which then punctuated Zionism in America, were it not for the news filtering to the outside world of Hitler's latest intentions towards the Jews. He had been prepared to ship them all out of the Continent had there been a readiness to accept them elsewhere. There was nowhere. The result was the Wannsee decision of January, 1942, which initiated the final solution of the Jewish problem through physical extermination in the gas chambers. When Under-Secretary of State Sumner Welles gave Stephen Wise, Roosevelt's man among the Jews, official confirmation of this in November, 1942, it transpired that the State Department had been deliberately holding the information back, and by then untold thousands were already dead.

'So much for putting our trust in princes!' The remark came bitterly from the lips of Hillel Silver, who had long scorned his brother-rabbi's apologetics for the President. All methods of rescue were now admissible, Silver asserted. The time for hypocrisy was passed; they had to loosen the British clamp on Palestine, and not shy from activities described by their enemies and detractors as 'terrorism'. Roosevelt must be publicly arraigned for his part in the Anglo-American conspiracy of silence dating from the White Paper of 1939. Furthermore – and this was a heresy to most American-Jewish ears – they should serve notice on the President that in default of positive action Jewish allegiance would be shifted to the Republicans.

Weizmann admired Silver, and looked to him to inject new life into their work in the United States. He implored the Cleveland rabbi to co-operate with Wise, whose prestige was a considerable attribute. If not, their efforts would collapse beneath the strain of internal conflicts. Silver agreed, though he was not to be deterred from his attacks upon the President, nor from making 'maximalist' demands that brought him into flirtation with supporters of the *Irgun* in America.

Weizmann himself adopted a different approach to Washington. He was summoned to the White House not as the spokesman of Zionism but as the scientist sent from England with a possible answer to the rubber shortage and the inexhaustible demand for aviation spirit. Roosevelt was impressed when he pointed to the immense quantities of grain on the American continent, given to depredation by the rats while normal export outlets were blocked by the shipping shortage. He could ferment these surpluses rotting in Canada and the U.S.A. to release substances for conversion into butadiene, and lead from there both to a very pliable synthetic rubber and to a high-octane fuel.

The strategy showed no flaw: science would also ferment support for Zionism. Unfortunately, the oil companies did not take kindly to this foreigner, who threatened to imperil the safety of solemn contracts and future demands for their products. Weizmann took his proposal to the committee, headed by Bernard Baruch, charged with facilitating such supplies. He met with hostility from the scientists there – and they were tenacious men. But Weizmann could also be tenacious, if only his health would permit him to fight it out with them. Happily, David Bergmann journeyed across the Atlantic to pursue these problems on his behalf. The young biochemist from Rehovot, whom Weizmann was now beginning to look upon as the son he had lost, took over the widespread scientific negotiations he initiated.

Weizmann sought no payment for his war-work, merely the protection of his patents against infringement once they entered into peace-time use. He had the strong support of the Vice-President, Henry Wallace, as well as of Sumner Welles, but he could not overcome the obstruction he encountered from commercial interests. He continued to resist with all the skill of a man long-experienced in the ways of governmental committees and their static concepts, for he was without equal in investing a technological discovery with its geo-political implications. He had proved his point to Britain's satisfaction when the loss of the Dutch East Indies and Malaya to the Japanese made it necessary for basic products, formerly acquired so cheaply in their natural state, to be chemically re-created in the laboratory.

Faced with difficulties from the Baruch Committee, he demonstrated the efficacy of his processes on the factory floor, in Terre Haute, Indiana and Philadelphia, where his research of earlier years was being successfully applied. Similarly, he refused to be discouraged in promoting his foods synthesised from yeast and soya products, which he claimed as the answer to feeding the hungry millions of the under-developed world. Only much later did these efforts draw from Baruch the reluctant admission that he had been mistaken in supporting American scientists against the foreigner.

The Washington atmosphere confirmed to Weizmann that Zionism as advanced on the style of the arrogant Biltmore Programme would cut little ice among the powerful. Let New York remain the parish of local spokesmen, he decided, but Washington must be separated from those men and retained as his own individual province. He entrusted his representation there to Nahum Goldmann, whose celebrated intervention had led to Weizmann's defeat in 1931 and was now back in the leader's confidence. Goldmann was to keep the less extreme position alive in State Department and White House circles, but leave the delicate Wise-Silver balance severely alone in New York.

These arrangements did not suffice to allow Weizmann to return home in the knowledge that their affairs were in the best hands in America. He dwelt dubiously upon the Zionist faithful there. How unrepresentative they were! Too many shop-keepers of the East Side, too many with foreign accents, too many rabbis, too many 'professional Jews' whose devotion was conditioned by the need for a regular wage-packet out of Zionist funds. How to bring these together with the much larger body of non-Zionists? The times were too serious for sectarian divisions.

He charged Weisgal with the task of enticing Jews of all classes and views onto a common platform. And, with his instinct for the location of power, the Jewish leader from London, who realised that in America an outsider would always remain so, impressed upon his servant that this platform was to be built round the B'nai Brith. It was as though he was asking for the union of a gypsy monarchy with the House of Windsor. The B'nai Brith was the archetype of American Jewish organisations. It had a vast membership, boasted a long tradition of community service, and was entrenched in every city of the United States. For his common platform Weizmann had as his pattern British Jewry's Board of Deputies, a community parliament of which his colleague Selig Brodetsky was President. Naturally, a parallel body in America would have greater force – ten times as many Jews lived there.

Through the creation of such an apparatus Weizmann could retain a guiding hand over American Jewry in its full spectrum, and assign to it a responsibility of its own in rescuing their people: Palestine even under a Jewish government could not become the only haven.

The war seemed on the turn at last, and he still could not find understanding, let alone enthusiasm, among his new friends in Washington for the Jewish Fighting Force. Morgenthau could not accept the necessity. Why should not the Jews enrol in existing formations in the countries of

their residence? Mostly they had done so, Weizmann pointed out. But if
they wanted recognition as a people after the war they had to fight as a
people – why was it that in Palestine it suited the British if they remained
passive like the Arabs, as though this struggle did not concern them?
Churchill understood their case, but complications rained down on him
from the Foreign Office.

The similarity with Washington was so exact it defied credence. The
State Department had its objections ready for the President whenever
Palestine was mentioned; and as to Jewish rescue, this was an attempt to
gain for them 'preferential' treatment denied to fighting Allies. One such
case was the fate of the surviving remnant of 185,000 Jews transported by
Rumania to the area of the Ukraine she occupied momentarily in the Red
Army's retreat, and which she had re-named Transnistria. The Jews were
dying on the scorched earth north of Odessa. With the fall of Stalingrad,
Antonescu, the Rumanian leader, became anxious to make amends, and
redeem himself in advance of an Allied victory. He was ready to bring the
Jews back, he declared, if funds were deposited in Switzerland against
which he could borrow for their medicines and provisions.

The sum required was $600,000 in all, and Morgenthau, as Secretary
of the Treasury, was agreeable. The Warsaw ghetto had just been liquidated, after appalling suffering. Morgenthau's efforts were resisted by the
State Department, while Weizmann's appeal to Halifax to transport the
Rumanians to Palestine likewise went unheeded. When an arrangement
was at last sanctioned for their relief only 48,000 were found to be
alive.

Now, at last, a reaction seemed to stir in the conscience of the civilised
world. Britain and America arranged a formal conference at Bermuda in
April, 1943, on what was studiously termed the 'refugee situation' as
though to specify Jewish in the title would profane it. But it was an
elaborate window-dressing exercise, conducted only to assuage the public,
and Weizmann, denied the right to attend, had to be satisfied with the
submission of a memorandum. Later, however, the Jew was invited to the
White House to put his case personally to President Roosevelt. They had
a long, friendly discussion, but the outcome was a heavy silence from the
leader of the free world.

Sumner Welles hinted at preoccupations with oil as the reason for the
President's unhelpfulness. Contrary to Weizmann's belief, Ibn Saud was
entirely unsympathetic to Jewish aspirations in Palestine; and the lord of
Arabia, who was just about to make this plain in an interview with *Life*

magazine, had decided to switch his concession from Britain to America.

With arrangements for his all-Jewish platform well in hand, and with his Washington campaign delegated to loyal friends, among them Israel Sieff and the *Washington Post* proprietor Eugene Meyer, Weizmann returned, with some relief, to London. Morgenthau, and Samuel Rosenman, and more discreetly Isaiah Berlin at the British Embassy, could be relied upon to correct the propaganda excesses spilling over from New York. They would also redress the determined hostility of people in the lower echelons of State Department service. More he could not do.

It had been a wearing, frustrating mission, and of the year spent on that side of the Atlantic complete months had to be allowed to slip by while he sought to recover his health. Vera was still numbed, 'as though in the midst of a nervous breakdown', he wrote to his brother Yehiel.

Shertok and others of the Jewish Agency in Jerusalem were imploring him to come to Palestine. They wanted to sit the chief and his lieutenant round the same table, finish off their slanging match behind closed doors and heal the rift. They needed to have Weizmann's own version of what transpired at Biltmore, which seen from Jerusalem appeared to comrades of Ben-Gurion's own party as having strengthened the hand of the detested *Irgun*.

Weizmann refused the summons. Privately, he advised Shertok of his temptation to give up the struggle against Ben-Gurion who, he complained, 'was hurtful to the best interests of the movement, undermining my authority and wasting my time'. He desired very much to be in Palestine, but not for such a purpose.

This, however, was no moment to resign, for there was scent of a Weizmann victory in the air. Discussion of the fighting force, less an army than a symbol now, was being resumed. Partition too. Churchill formed a Palestine sub-committee of the Cabinet in July, 1943, and, despite Eden's disapproval, gave a place there to Leopold Amery, now Secretary of State for India. Weizmann could not have been better served had he sat there himself: Amery, one of the draftsmen of the Balfour Declaration, was pressing for a Jewish State in a partitioned Palestine as an urgent imperial interest. Was the Prime Minister about to redeem his promise at last?

It really seemed so. Weizmann felt that all was proceeding favourably as, in the autumn ushering in the fourth year of a war that was changing both the British and the Jews out of all recognition, he was received at the Prime Minister's country residence. Still, he was dubious. Could there not be a last-minute hitch?

'You have dark forces in your Cabinet,' he reminded Churchill. But the other was now in the mood to defy anti-Zionist sentiment, particularly if it spread from the official mind in the Middle East. 'Only one in fifty of the officers returning from 'Palestine speaks favourably of the Jews,' he confessed. 'But this convinces me I am right.' The British war leader was certainly not popular with many of his immediate colleagues either, but he knew he had the nation with him, and he was ruling like a dictator.

Momentum was gathering for the final assault upon Europe, and Weizmann was sure the White Paper would not survive the war. How wrong his opponents were to belabour him for keeping faith with a country they regarded as an exhausted old war-horse! This, his unique relationship with Churchill, would be the determining factor. And how right he had been to dismiss the suggestion, put to him by Jews infuriated by British obduracy, that he work for the transfer of the Mandate to America. A naive proposition! The Americans did not want the responsibility, and would not accept it even if it were offered.

Over there, the American Jewish Conference had opened as the *Union sacrée* of his desire. No democratically-elected Jewish assembly had ever before convened on United States soil, and now the Stars and Stripes were euphorically intertwined with the Shield of David, behind a platform basking in the lustre of power. The scene was dominated by Silver. Somewhat disconcertingly for the more conservative delegates from non-Zionist organizations, the Cleveland rabbi plunged into his demand for the release of Palestine from the British yoke and the establishment of a Jewish State. Many of his hearers were not primed for such a concept, being apprehensive, as some British Jews had been in the previous war, for their personal citizen status. They demurred. Silver persevered. If the American Jewish Conference was to be anything at all, he insisted, it had to be solid for their people's national independence. He won his victory, but at the cost of keeping the conference alive as a standing institution. Much as the *B'nai Brith* wished for its survival, and despite the dramatic accretion of strength it brought to American Zionism, the apparatus had only a temporary existence, and was due to be short-lived.

Silver was not disturbed by the opposition. He now had his mandate. Dragging a half-hearted Wise along with him, and ignoring Nahum Goldmann as a Europe-reared parvenu, he attempted to consolidate the Zionist position by storming Capitol Hill. He was determined to do things his way, the true American way, not Weizmann's. Both Houses of

Congress must be made to pass Resolutions that would commit America irrevocably to making Palestine a 'free and democratic Jewish Commonwealth'. It was a tall order, but not beyond him.

Weizmann was approaching his seventieth birthday. World-wide celebrations were being planned to honour the first man in modern Jewish history who could be said to cloak his authority over this entire people. True, that authority was not evenly distributed, with local subordinates varying from the surpassing self-confidence and individualism of a Silver or a Ben-Gurion, to the desperate men in the cauldron of Europe vainly seeking to buy time through serving the Nazi purpose. But the Jews could never have an undisputed leader, and were fortunate to have this spokesman undisputed at least by the gentile world. Even in the Soviet Union his speeches were being re-broadcast; it was hint of a new Russian attitude to Zionism in the post-war settlement. Paradoxically, only in Palestine were his activities almost a closed book, for the censors clamped down on news such as the Biltmore Conference, calculated to provoke the Arabs. He could not now postpone his visit to the homeland; he determined to be with his people for his birthday.

He was engaged on a race against time in more senses than one. The very developments Weizmann feared after Pearl Harbour were in train, and beginning to shake the foundations of his office. He would not be able to control the Silver engine careering towards Washington; he was powerless to halt the deterioration of relations between officialdom and the *Yishuv* in Palestine. A mood for activism permeated the Jewish atmosphere.

His Agency colleagues were being forced into acquiescence of operations in Palestine of which they had little advance intelligence. Under the Jewish Agency's security chief, Moshe Sneh, the *Haganah* was teaming up for special exploits with the *Irgun*, and even its breakaway group the Stern Gang, two groups Weizmann classed as enemies of their cause, and regarded as such also by Ben-Gurion. The British, having penetrated all the Jewish militias, frequently closed in upon ostensibly innocent Jews engaged in modest self-defence employment but who were in reality deep in more offensive tasks. The *Haganah* developed a fine distinction between operations designed to vitiate British obstruction against the Jews, which it approved, and the sabotage by *Irgun* and Stern against the British army as an alien occupation force, which it opposed.

Could Weizmann find a means to impose restraint upon all the contrasting elements of his domain? It depended upon Great Britain. He hungered for just one tangible victory, perhaps the formal scrapping of the White Paper, or the formation of the Jewish Fighting Force. Threadbare triumphs these might now be, but they would at least betoken a new beginning. The psychological moment could well be March, 1944, when the last of the 75,000 immigrants sanctioned by the White Paper would have reached safety, and further arrivals would require the consent of the Arabs. If only Churchill would say something *publicly!* But March came and went without an announcement.

In contrast, Silver was confidently stampeding Washington. His Zionist Resolutions, sponsored as a bi-partisan measure by Senators Wagner and Taft, had almost unanimous endorsement. The Congressional hearings, under the chairmanship of a Jew, Sol Bloom, opened to a fierce background drumbeat from sympathisers throughout the United States. Lecture agencies did a roaring trade delivering politicians to fund-raising affairs supporting every facet of Zionist activity. Of course the Resolutions would be carried against only the faintest opposition.

Suddenly, America showed its British reflex. The military stepped in. General Marshall let it be known that he opposed the Resolutions. Henry L. Stimson, Secretary of War, described them as 'prejudicial to the successful prosecution of the war'. Support melted away, and the Resolutions had to be withdrawn. The Presidential Election was eight months away.

Silver might have retired in ignominy, were he not revitalised from, to him, an unexpected quarter – Henry Morgenthau. The Secretary of the Treasury personally delivered to the President a dossier proving State Department obstruction regarding the saving of Jews in Europe. Roosevelt felt he must at last say something, however non-committal, if he wished to retain the Jewish vote as the Democratic phalanx of tradition. He announced the establishment of the War Refugee Board, his first real concession to the existence of racial victims of Nazism.

More than this, he received Silver together with Wise and actually deigned to refer to the British document no Jew could think of without revulsion. The American government had never given its approval to the White Paper of 1939, he informed the two rabbis, and he was 'happy that the doors of Palestine are today open to Jewish refugees'. He promised that 'full justice will be done to those who seek a Jewish National Home'.

Well, this was progress, though as a statement of policy it bore much of the vagueness enveloping the words of President Wilson when he was urged to voice public support of Britain's intentions in the weeks preceding the Balfour Declaration. Wise was relieved at the announcement; Silver was ashamed of it.

From London, the American Zionists received Weizmann's reproof for their clumsy manoeuvre among the Congressmen. They should have ascertained the extent of the opposition before pressing blindly on with their highly-publicised lobbying. Now Zionism had been administered a gratuitous defeat just as his delicate and painful nursing of Churchill was beginning to yield fruit. He was being incapacitated not by their enemies, but by zealots within the ranks.

He ventilated his disquiet to Weisgal. 'The American and Palestine Jewish communities,' he said, 'have a great deal in common. Both are young . . . more or less provincial . . . excitable and apt to overplay their hands.' In the past this lack of balance was counteracted by the Europeans, but 'with this community gone I can see grave dangers looming ahead of us. The next Zionist Congress, should we live to see it, will consist of two great delegations, the Americans and the Palestinians. I confess I find it something of a nightmare to contemplate.'

Disconsolate at the progress of their cause under Silver, worried by the growing power of Ben-Gurion, on whom he now unjustifiably laid the blame for every terrorist exploit in Palestine, he felt ebbed of his strength. Further disappointments awaited him. His old friend General Smuts, always to be relied on in the past to use his powerful moral influence for Zionism, lost faith in a Jewish State after an extended stay in the Middle East. Finally, Weizmann's bid to save the Jews of Hungary, through a barter proposition brought by Joel Brand from Adolf Eichmann, ended in failure.

It was now August, 1944, and he was making preparations for his first visit to Palestine in five years when he received a message from the Prime Minister. Yes, the Jewish Fighting Force had won Cabinet authorisation. It would have to be a brigade group only, less than a single division. But the flag of Zion would be among the banners joined in the liberation of Europe.

Weizmann's thankfulness seems, in the circumstances, somewhat excessive. He wrote to Churchill of 'our conviction that the future of the Jewish nation is bound up with the British Empire'. Shertok and the Jewish military expert Eliahu Golomb completed their discussions with the War Office and returned home to organise the new brigade. Part of Golomb's duties were to put a stop to the growing activity that Weizmann branded as Jewish terrorism but the Palestinians ambivalently transcribed as 'resistance by dissident forces'.

Silver too had his first major achievement to report: the Democratic Party were taking note of the mood and had written strong support for Zionism into their election manifesto. The pieces were falling tardily into place, and a little sunshine was entering into Weizmann's life after a seemingly endless night. His office colleagues had promised him a celebration lunch when Pinsk was re-taken by the Russians, and they held him to it at last in October, 1944, almost six months after that happy event – or it would have been happy, were it not for the fact that many of the Jews of Weizmann's childhood home had not survived.

They coaxed him and Vera off to the Savoy Hotel just before Shertok's departure: Baffy Dugdale with Shertok and Locker, the two Palestinians of the Left who had first come to London to put some weight into the scales against 'Weizmannism', as some called it, but in the end had succumbed both to his policy and his personality. Lewis Namier came too – he was Baffy's nearest Jewish friend – and Doris May, another product of Oxford and the Chief's personal secretary. Joseph Linton, his political man of all work, completed the party. They had served him well, critically watching for every change of mood, encouraging him when his spirits drooped: a little community all its own, and made closer from having been together in Great Russell Street while the bombs fell over London. Weizmann was at his best. His memories of Pinsk were very much with him in those days, for he was making special efforts with his often-postponed Memoirs.

He had a final meeting with Churchill. They talked again of partition, and Weizmann tried to steer the conversation to a discussion on possible frontiers, but the Prime Minister refused the bait – affirming only that the solution he envisioned would enable some one-and-a-half million Jews to settle in Palestine within ten years. He expressed surprise at the opposition of influential American Jews to Zionism, specifying his friend Bernard Baruch. They needed American cooperation, said Churchill, so it was important that American Jews close to Roosevelt keep working on the President. According to the version of the discussion Weizmann forwarded to Silver, he had been assured by Churchill that 'if Roosevelt and I come together to the conference table we can carry all we want'.

Two days later a crushing blow was delivered to these hopes. Jewish assassins shot down Lord Moyne in Cairo. The former Colonial Secretary, now Minister of State in the Middle East, was personally, if not politically, dear to Churchill. Once more the guns of the Zionist terrorists had given the lie to the conciliatory words of the Zionist statesman.

Weizmann had once declared: 'If I am ever assassinated it will be by a Jew, not an Arab.' And it was with a sense of black despair that he returned to his home in Rehovot.

14

Out of Anguish, Triumph

THE MURDER OF A CABINET MINISTER, RISEN TO MINOR OFFICE WITH one government and due in time to depart with the arrival of another, exposed the pathology of a new kind of political activism among the Jews. The finger that pulled the trigger belonged to a seventeen year old youth of Oriental stock for whom the Jews of Europe were another, quite alien breed. The master-mind was East European, turned to hardness through impotence in the face of the slaughter of people close to him by kinship and culture. True, Moyne had signed deportation orders banishing terrorists to Eritrea, but he had little impress on the ultimate Jewish fate while alive, and it could only be adversely affected by his death.

Were the shots directed against Roosevelt, who refrained from exercising his power to succour the victims of Nazism, or Churchill, with his constant promises constantly postponed, or indeed Weizmann himself as a repudiated exponent of moderation, then an act of assassination would have had some frightful logic on its side. Moyne was a casualty of the Stern Gang's mystical faith in melodrama as a self-justifying doctrine.

Churchill, brought now to complete disillusionment with Zionism, stated in the House of Commons: 'A shameful crime has shocked the world and affected none more strongly than those like myself who, in the past, have been consistent friends of the Jews and constant architects of their future. If our dreams for Zionism are to end in the smoke of assassin's pistols, and one labours for its future to produce only a new set of gangsters worthy of Nazi Germany, many like myself would have to reconsider the position we have maintained so consistently and so long in the past . . .

'I have received a letter from Dr Weizmann, President of the World

Zionist Organization – a very old friend of mine – who has arrived in Palestine, in which he assures me that Palestine Jewry will go to the utmost limit of its power to cut out this evil from its midst. In Palestine, the Executive of the Jewish Agency has called upon the Jewish community, and I quote his actual words, "to cast out the members of this destructive band, deprive them of all refuge and shelter, to resist their threats, and render all necessary assistance to the authorities in the prevention of terrorist acts and in the eradication of the terrorist organisation." These are strong words, but we must wait for these words to be translated into deeds. We must wait to see that not only the leaders but every man, woman and child of the Jewish community does his or her best to bring this terrorism to a speedy end.'

The *Haganah* now recoiled from all contact with the Revisionist groups. Furnishing the authorities with hundreds of names, it directed the British to arms caches and itself kidnapped and locked away known terrorists in a frantic move to restore its position as a rational self-defence organisation solely in command. The British accepted the cooperation thankfully, though they were aware that the *Haganah* knew more than it told, and surrendered in arms less than it held.

The circumstances of war had isolated Palestine from the world. Men who might otherwise have worked together harmoniously were trying each other's nerves, like a family sheltering distant relatives in an inadequate home, so that resentments were quickly born and easily fostered. Churchill's reference to Nazi gangsters had fallen ironically on the *Yishuv's* ears: the security forces in Palestine could not themselves be exonerated from brutality. A sullen civilian population was out-witting the maladroit army in its presence, to produce an atmosphere almost automatic in such situations – it was to re-occur years later even in a home province of the United Kingdom. But at that time the Jews felt themselves the chosen target of wilful anti-semitic authority. They could quote many examples of an Arab with a gun escaping lightly while a Jew with a gun received a punitive sentence.

Outwardly, however, the entire *Yishuv* was *en fête* for its leader's arrival. Flags streamed in the wind from public buildings, and he was greeted everywhere by children's choirs and village orchestras. Every school, every social and political organisation, the *kibbutzim* of which he was so proud, all the rabbis, sent him addresses of welcome and entreated his presence for a celebration. It was as though a king were returning to his people after long exile. And Rehovot, its orchards golden with their fruit, never looked more glorious. Weizmann despatched a case of citrus, picked from his own groves, to Churchill, three days younger than himself, as 'from one septuagenarian to another'.

Perhaps this father of a nation was, like all parents, reluctant to recognise maturity in his offspring. He would not admit that this young community, just 600,000 strong, was ready for national independence. Receiving Julian Meltzer of the *New York Times* in his library, its blinds drawn to protect his eyes from the painful sun, he spoke of his fears lest, when the firing at last ceased in Europe, only a tiny remnant would have survived. And would those who did survive be able at once to take up the challenge of nationhood? He did not think so.

'We Jews will need some transitional period after this war. During that period I would like to see the beginning of considerable immigration, some 100,000 annually.' It would, he thought, take five to ten years, by political evolution, before a Jewish Commonwealth emerged. Concurrently, with the help of the United Nations, they would initiate great reconstruction projects linked with a national irrigation plan. He told Meltzer: 'The Arabs will benefit equally from such a plan. It is sheer nonsense to say that the Palestine Arabs are destined for the role of hewers of wood and drawers of water. They will be on equal footing of citizenship and responsibility with the Jewish inhabitants.'

The words could only belong to a man grown remote from his following. A handful of Jews were prepared to wait with Weizmann: a few ultra-Left *kibbutz* settlers immured in their puritanical collectives; and Judah Magnes, who was so repelled by the thought of a Jewish State on the *Yishuv's* terms that he was at that moment preaching on American platforms in company with fiercely anti-Zionist rabbis.

Thus the Second World War terminated in Europe. Churchill, by a logic understood only by the British electorate, found himself out of office. Roosevelt was dead, and when it was put to his successor that he would doubtless persuade Britain's new Labour Government to open the gates of the National Home, President Truman brushed the proposition aside: 'I have no desire to send 500,000 American soldiers to Palestine to make peace there.' Well, Hillel Silver would have something to say about that!

Weizmann's birthday present from Meyer Weisgal took the form of an undertaking to transform the Daniel Sieff Institute into an expanded Institute of Science comparable with the most advanced in the world. It would be Weizmann's legacy to the land of Israel, to the Jewish people and to the Middle East as a whole, and substantiate his Zionist philosophy of a Western movement come to partner the East in the renaissance of the Orient. The old chemist knew that with the devoted Weisgal in charge the project was bound to materialise; whether he would actually see the Institute was another question. In London the doctors diagnosed his eye complaint as glaucoma; they could stay its worst effects for a while, but sooner or later it must end in blindness.

He took the news calmly. Sickness was to be suffered, by all men equally. The agony that he bore in counting the Jewish loss in the European holocaust was of another dimension. Some estimated that six millions had died since 1939. Complete communities he once knew so well; generations of delegates at Zionist Congresses; audiences encountered by Weizmann in thirty years' campaigning on the Continent – all, with their families, gone without trace. His words of eight years earlier, to the Peel Commission, returned to him now in a threnody: 'There are in this part of the world six million people pent up in places where they are not wanted, and for whom the world is divided into places where they cannot live and places where they may not enter.' Six million plus his own son, in the Bay of Biscay; and his brother Samuel, in a Russian penal camp.

A war hesitantly begun with sporadic gun-shots across the Franco-German frontier had terminated in a Promethean challenge to the elements with atomic blasts over Japan. Some nations had been more fortunate than others, but all were altered. Chaim Weizmann's people emerged from the war as the constitutional nullity in which they entered it: without a land of their own, or a voice among the nations.

Yet that nullity mourned casualties without parallel – a third of their population, and a thousand years of civilisation lay buried in the ashes of Europe. Over half a million Jews had served in the Allied armies, some of them as generals, but those with the Shield of David shoulder-flash numbered only 5,000 of the Jewish Brigade, formed only as the war neared its close.

And whereas the conquerors, if such they were, could inspire later generations with tales of El Alamein, or Stalingrad, or Guadacanal, Jewish remembrance would know only the tragedies of Babi Yar, Auschwitz, Maidenek. At national festivities other leaders reviewed victorious regiments proudly bearing their colours; Weizmann reviewed regiments of ghosts, marching under the banner of the MacDonald White Paper. Now his people were determined never again to leave their fate in the hands of others. Zionism became a movement of Jewish revolution. Perhaps he too belonged more to the dead than to the living.

Approaching a *kibbutz* on the Sea of Galilee. Left, Teddy Kollek, later Mayor of Jerusalem.

A Press conference in Washington, 1948. Behind Weizmann, Eliahu Elath, later Israel's Ambassador.

With Lord Samuel, who had been the first High Commissioner of Palestine

Receiving, left, James McDonald, then American Ambassador to Israel, and Prime Minister Ben-Gurion.

What of the White Paper now, condemned under international law as an illegal document? The new British Prime Minister, Clement Attlee, had often declared that his Labour Party did not accept it. Ernest Bevin, his Foreign Secretary, who had supported the Zionists in the past, had dined at Weizmann's table, to listen fascinated as the latter expounded his ideas for turning the earth's natural vegetation into synthetic foods and materials for industrial progress.

The British leaders offered a monthly quota of 1,500 Jewish immigrants to Palestine, as though conceding thereby that the White Paper was annulled. To the man responsible for the survivors left stupefied in the Displaced Persons camps, it was a mockery. Were these wretched people expected to return to their old homes in Poland, or Germany? And, assuming their willingness, would they be wanted?

Restraining himself with difficulty, for he was heart-sick of this old quarrel with England, Weizmann demanded instead the formal renunciation of the White Paper, to enable the Zionists to empty the camps. Rescue teams were already on the spot, and they should begin by bringing the first 100,000 to Palestine.

Bevin seemed disappointed at what was revealed to him as Weizmann's failure to understand the facts of life. He was the first British Foreign Secretary obliged to wrestle with the new Russia, and an Arab world aflame with national feeling. Britain was now much weakened. Did the Jewish leader expect Bevin to embark upon a military pacification of the Arabs, when Truman refused to do so? One day, perhaps, after negotiations with the Arabs, the request for 100,000 might be granted. In the meantime the Jews should not try to get to the head of the queue.

This was the spark that fired the explosion. The *Haganah* ceased exposing *Irgun* and Stern members to the authorities, and instead sealed an arrangement with them by which all military operations were coordinated under its new head, Moshe Sneh. He took his authority from 'Committee X', a six-man group drawn from the Palestine Executive of the Jewish Agency, and the local Jewish Council known as the *Va'ad Leumi*. Sneh did not burden Ben-Gurion, who guaranteed to find the money to acquire arms, with exact details. Weizmann knew even less.

Soon the atmosphere of the Holy Land became acrid with the smoke of gunpowder. Naval gunboats guarding the coast were sunk, railway lines blown up, and sabotage stopped work at the Haifa oil refineries. Still more potent, however, was Silver's bombardment of the White House. Before long Truman changed his mind about Palestine, adding his own voice to

w.—16

the plea for the 100,000 – at the same time allowing just a trickle into the United States.

Truman's embargo upon immigration in quantity into his own country scandalised British officialdom; but it did not unduly disturb the Zionists, for it helped their tactics. They were turning the European camps into a Zionist domain, with educators, political parties, and all the ideological paraphernalia of the *Yishuv* itself. It was not surprising therefore that the displaced persons made Palestine their first choice for a new home. A daring process was skilfully set in train, culminating in the underground escape routes to Mediterranean ports and the dash to the beaches of the homeland. Neither Ben-Gurion nor Weizmann completely approved of it, but were powerless to interfere.

Most of the refugee boats failed to reach harbour in the Promised Land, though against this immense political capital was earned for the cause. Bevin was imaged in the world as an unfeeling, lumbering tyrant, to be burned in effigy in great demonstrations throughout America. It was a distortion of the truth, but distortions were necessary to him too, to justify his air of injured innocence at the galloping descent into anarchy in Palestine.

Ben-Gurion urged Weizmann to break off all contact with the government pending abolition of the White Paper, but the leader refused to be a party to the new, violent Zionist campaign against the Mandatory. This would spell destruction for the *Yishuv*, Weizmann retorted, for the British would bring up their tanks in an open clash. He accepted the principle of so-called illegal immigration, and the *Haganah's* measures to frustrate the blockade of the sea-lanes; more aggressive action he judged as madness. According to Ben-Gurion, the destruction of the *Yishuv* would more surely result from passivity. In his view the aged leader was now without a function, and should depart. As though to prove his point, a hurriedly-convened conference in London re-affirmed the Biltmore demand for the whole of Palestine as a Jewish State.

This placed Weizmann in a quandary. Certainly, his resignation would demonstrate the bankruptcy of Britain's policy: her most loyal Jewish ally disappearing in disgust. Doubtless such a step would not have been un-welcome to the taciturn, formidable Attlee. A Zionist declaration of war would enable him really to move in Palestine as some of his predecessors had moved against rebellious natives in the past. But if stewardship of the movement fell into the hands of Ben-Gurion, Weizmann would then have been the instrument of a change in which no one could predict the move after next. No, isolated though he might be as the only conciliator in a cause dominated by its firebrands, Weizmann felt he must not abdicate.

In the circumstances, Attlee's next step was the most astute. Determined to test Truman's good intent, he invited American participation in a new enquiry that would embrace not only Palestine but also the European refugee problem. He thereby gained time, and gave the Zionists a second target, Washington, for their attacks.

Bevin declared that, given a unanimous report by this Anglo-American enquiry, he would personally do all in his power to carry it out. So off went the new toilers in the field, out of Washington and London, to the refugee camps and to the partisans in Palestine, and finally to their writing-up session in Lausanne: eight months in all. They formed a somewhat motley committee. Only one member, the American James McDonald, had any previous experience of the subject at hand; while another, the Englishman Richard Crossman, forfeited his political career in Attlee's estimation by falling captive to Weizmann's spell. Their report was indeed unanimous, but reflected a mid-Atlantic compromise. It recommended abolition of the White Paper, immigration of the 100,000, but no partition for the present nor the departure of the British. National independence for the rival communities would, the committee decided, have to await their future reconciliation. The government spoke as though it was now burdened for all time with its reluctant inheritance. In fact, the circumstances of the Cold War had turned Palestine into a Western arsenal not to be disdained.

Attlee required the disbandment of the Jewish militias before allowing the 100,000 in, and claimed American assistance to accomplish the transfer. Both propositions were, he knew, unrealistic. As to Weizmann, he found nothing in the Prime Minister's reception of the report to enable him to restore his position in Zionism.

He was in Rehovot in June, 1946, and was summoned to a discussion with the High Commissioner, Sir Alan Cunningham. There the Englishman laid before the Jew detailed evidence of the *Haganah's* links with the other groups, one of which adhered to assassination as a policy. It was impossible, said Cunningham, that Weizmann could be in ignorance of this connection. Surely the Jewish leader did not expect the government to suffer the existence of such forces in a country under its control!

Weizmann replied: 'Our youth can no longer suffer your government's policy and keep its emotions in check.' He defended the *Haganah*, affirming that some resistance was inevitable. Nevertheless he decided to have it out with Sneh.

'Your operations are stupid,' he told Sneh, speaking in Yiddish, the favourite language of them both. 'I do not approve of them, yet I have to accept responsibility for them.' If these activities did not cease, he warned, he would resign as Jewish Agency President and let the world know that he no longer sympathised with a movement committed to such methods.

Sneh looked with compassion upon this leader, once revered, but now with his policy of moderation in tatters. He would not make Weizmann a direct reply. Shortly afterwards, six British officers were taken hostage, and only released when a number of Jews, condemned to death, had their sentences commuted. Then, on one of those sultry Palestine afternoons, when siestas were long, commotion advertised an act of violence, and silence carried a foreboding of evil, the British struck. They called it Operation Broadside; the Jews Black Sabbath – June 29, 1946.

Shertok and three of his Agency colleagues, as well as over 2,600 other Jews, found themselves in police custody. The Zionist headquarters in modern Jerusalem were occupied, and large stores of arms in the farm settlements captured. Sneh had been tipped off by his intelligence branch, and was in hiding. Ben-Gurion was safe in Paris.

It had happened as Weizmann predicted. One stupidity had begotten another. 'The Jews will not part with their arms because they remember the lessons of the past', he informed the British. 'You will have to blow up the whole of Palestine first.' And further, to the foreign Press: 'The Mufti, a war criminal and sworn enemy of Britain, sits in a palace in Cairo while Mr Shertok, who raised an army of 25,000 Palestinian Jews to fight shoulder to shoulder with Britain is imprisoned.' Indeed, Shertok was ignorant of the work of the secret Committee X, though two of its members were among the interned.

In the ensuing tension, Meyer Weisgal was conducted to Sneh's hiding-place bearing an ultimatum from the chief. All 'resistance' against the British must cease, or he would resign without further ado. The militias, Weizmann's message stated, were destroying everything achieved in two generations, and their exploits did not enjoy the formal approval of the Agency.

Two major operations were in the pipeline: the seizure of an ammunition dump and the blowing up of the wing of the King David Hotel used as Army headquarters. Sneh believed they should continue. But he was outvoted by his committee. He resigned and prepared to leave the country. Before doing so, he obeyed the committee's ruling and rescinded the order to seize the dump. The King David operation was to be an *Irgun* task, and he now called for its postponement. However, the King David blew up, with ninety-one dead, Jews, Arabs and British. The *Irgun* contended that adequate warning was given to protect life, but somewhere along the line communication had broken down. Weizmann was himself back in England by then, and he raged. But the *Haganah* insisted it was not a party to the operation, and once again he refrained from resigning.

Meanwhile, only one Zionist spokesman had been in contact with Bevin. He was Nahum Goldmann, Weizmann's chosen representative, though disavowed by Silver, in Washington. He and Bevin seemed to harmonise on essential points. The Foreign Secretary was anxious to come to terms, and was open to persuasion on partition if only America would help in its implementation. Goldmann hinted that an award of the Peel area plus the Negev would satisfy the Jews, who might then be amenable to affording military bases to Great Britain. Unofficial talks began in October, and the government released the interned Jewish leaders. Weizmann saw this as their last chance.

But first, the hurdle he had been dreading: the Zionist Congress. He needed its sanction before resuming formal negotiations. Would the Congress decide on compromise or defiance? Was he to lead the movement, or Ben-Gurion? Whom would the Americans follow? If they followed Wise, then Weizmann would win; if Silver, he would be defeated. The battle was to be fought out in Basle, where a half-century earlier, Theodor Herzl had launched the national movement.

They talked for two weeks, talked and made ever-shifting alliances and manipulated language to disguise meaning, or to cover indetermination. Some whispered of elevating Weizmann to a new office, when what they really sought was his dismissal. The leader's presence dominated the scene; his power was their problem. What was Zionism without this venerable figure, yet what would it become with him?

Silver, and his deputy Emanuel Neumann, who had just re-built the American Zionist organisation round the Cleveland rabbi, would not disguise their hostility, or rather hatred, towards this British Jew, always, it seemed to them, apologising for his hypocritical government. They would fight for Biltmore, nothing less. Not even Ben-Gurion considered this practical politics, yet he could not voice its public repudiation. He admitted to Weizmann's strength as the spiritual constant in Zionism, but when tough negotiations were required he regarded him as a weakling. Weizmann, he decided, had to go.

To dislodge their pilot, the irreligious socialist leader of the miniature nation in rebellion must make grotesque alliance with a Right-wing rabbi from the remote Diaspora. Weizmann did not believe it could be done. And if he were to depart, this Congress would be the swan-song also for so many Zionists unable to separate the cause from his leadership: Harry Sacher and Simon Marks, busy even now testing the mood on his behalf, and whipping up support among the doubters. Wise and Louis Lipsky too would have to go, for neither could endorse Silver's single-handed war against England, nor follow him in his threats of swinging the American Jews against Truman. Weizmann could rely also on Shertok, Locker, Brodetsky and Goldmann, each with a small retinue to place in the balance. When Weizmann opened the first session the diplomatic representatives of America and Russia sat among the visitors, but no Britisher: another painful symbol of the changing dispositions.

He could not forebear an 'I told you so' in the debate. The Churchill government were deliberating a partition scheme, he said, but it had soured on them with the Moyne murder. In the pre-war years the movement was ignored by influential Jews everywhere, and only now, when it was too late, and millions had been done to death in Europe, were they responding to the call of Zion.

'There are a million Arabs in Palestine,' he reminded them. 'Where an Arab builds a house a Jew cannot build; where an Arab plants a tree a Jew cannot plant, unless he uproots that tree.' Nevertheless they had no apologies to make to the Arabs: 'A nation newly-endowed with seven independent territories covering a million square miles – by what tortuous logic can our morsel be taken away and added to their feast?'

He described the glib talk of Jewish resistance as encouragement of terrorism. 'I know where it begins,' he exclaimed, 'I don't know where it ends. The Jewish Agency will not control it – it will control the Agency!' The Americans bristled beneath his taunts. Of Silver and his demand for activism, he asked: 'Has he tried it out on his Cleveland Jews? Moral, financial and political support means precious little when you send others to the barricades, to pit themselves against British guns and tanks!'

Neumann could not withstand the onslaught. 'Demagogue!' he shouted, in the only interruption of the speech. Weizmann looked up from his notes. Till then his voice had been low, and the words had come with difficulty. Now he sent out a shrill cry from the heart. 'I am called a demagogue.' He paused, then continued, 'there is a drop of my blood in every house in Tel Aviv, in every barn in Nahalal!' – the latter a Jezreel village. They sprang acclaiming to their feet.

But his magic failed him in the end. The Silver–Ben-Gurion alliance stuck. They had no difficulty in persuading the religious group to vote with them. The motion to go to London and talk with Ernest Bevin was lost.

Weizmann refused to submit himself for re-election, and the Executive was constituted without a President, responsibility being divided between the two architects of his downfall. Ben-Gurion was made Chairman for Palestine, Silver Chairman for America. Meekly, the four men he had regarded as supporters joined them. The only people to withdraw with Weizmann were those without offices to lose.

Stephen Wise declared he was quitting the movement. 'I could not believe that what had happened could conceivably come to pass,' he said, 'with England and America jointly rebuked and rebuffed by Congress and Dr Weizmann, our foremost statesman, our wisest leader – though without the support of Press agents – dropped as pilot when he was most needed. The barest majority, whipped together by election devices worthy of an American political convention at its worst, voted to make it impossible for Dr Weizmann to go to the London conference and therefore retain the leadership.'

To the triumphant Silver the movement 'has emerged from Basle stronger than ever, with a stiffer backbone and determined to halt the progressive retreat'. He had liquidated London as the headquarters. He could now operate on his home ground as an elected leader. Yet he agreed to the resumption of talks with Britain (unofficially, he insisted). So the Weizmann policy indeed prevailed, though without Weizmann.

Silver left the negotiations to Ben-Gurion. He himself returned directly to New York, to fulfil his threat of making Zionism a central issue of American politics. To judge by his rhetoric, Jewry was now at war with Britain, a situation that pained Truman but was greeted with delight by every American of Irish descent.

Face to face with Bevin, Ben-Gurion spoke an altogether different language, for he had no wish to see the British entirely expelled from the Middle East, or even from Palestine. He proffered the Weizmann formula: sovereignty in the area roughly comprising the Peel plan plus the Negev, and bases for Britain. In another room in Whitehall a new Colonial Secretary was in discussion with representatives of the bordering Arab states, and a group of Mufti-approved Palestinians. Their demand remained unchanged: complete independence.

Bevin therefore had no territory he could safely give away to the Jews. Despairingly, he produced a cantonal scheme with local autonomy (the Jews had heard it before) and a five year transitional period. Palestine would then, in the event of the two parties failing to reach agreement, be deposited at the door of the United Nations. Further, he consented to an immigration of 96,000 during the coming two years. Twenty months earlier such a proposal would have been received thankfully, for it was a full retreat by the Foreign Secretary. But it was too late now. The gap between Arab and Jew could not be bridged.

Some 100,000 British troops were now employed in what Churchill described as a 'squalid war' against the para-military forces of *Irgun* and Stern, whose excesses shocked the Jews themselves, for letter-bombs were sent through the post and water-wells poisoned. Weizmann's prophecy of a terrorism beyond control was being only too speedily fulfilled. It was now April, 1947. Martial law was imposed over a wide area, and Prime Minister Attlee admitted defeat at last. He turned the problem over to a special session of the U.N. Assembly in New York.

Having been out-played by a Congress cabal, Weizmann chose to spend these difficult days as an ordinary citizen suffering the harassments of daily life in Palestine. He would not proceed to the General Assembly, for he now regarded New York as hostile soil. Somewhat querulous, sick in heart and body, resentful at being deserted by close friends, he was nevertheless anxious to get back into the fray. When the United Nations decided on a new international enquiry to investigate the problem afresh, a delegation from the *Va'ad Leumi* nominated him to plead the Jewish case. It touched them profoundly that, at seventy-three, he was sharing their troubles. And he in turn was moved by his continued reception as a leader beyond the politicking of the party men. He still welcomed a constant stream of visitors to Rehovot, Jews and Britons. His institute was taking shape, with Bergmann recruiting scientists in Europe and America to staff it. But soon a shadow fell across the old man's relationship with the scientist he had long ago chosen as his partner and heir, and whom he loved as a son.

It happened almost by chance. Among those Bergmann selected for a post in the new institute was a young Russian biochemist, Ephraim Katchalski, trained in Palestine and America. This man (one day, as Katzir, he would be President of the State of Israel) was, like Bergmann himself, secretly working for the *Haganah*. Bergmann regarded such activity as an additional qualification for employment, but Weizmann was appalled to learn that the science he prized, and perhaps the institute that was to bear his name, were being harnessed to what he regarded as the 'war party' in Palestine – in cruder terms, placed under Ben-Gurion's control.

Weizmann reproached Bergmann with the betrayal of science, and of himself. The latter heard his chief out with dismay. Hadn't Weizmann used his scientific knowledge to assist Britain in two wars, and taken him along in the same direction? Could they conceivably deny this knowledge to their own people?

No, Weizmann replied. These so-called defence needs were reducing science to the level of cookery. He hardly had a case, but was voicing a desperate wish to keep the new institute above the storm. He visualised it as a fortress of pure research, to benefit not a partisan cause but humanity as a whole. He placed Zionism in the tradition of liberal internationalism, and his life-work had been a pledge to make Palestine a state unlike any other.

The unhappy quarrel gathered further complications, and personal vindictiveness. Bergmann felt that Weizmann was demanding his soul, with every facet of his conduct under scrutiny. He had earned his laurels in a harsh climate here in Palestine, so different from the serene optimism of Weizmann's Manchester. War with the Arabs was inevitable, of that he had no doubt. And it would be a war of survival.

He therefore resolved to serve both his masters, Weizmann and Ben-Gurion. But he knew that his future lay with the latter. Vera took the estrangement of this accomplished scientist, who had brightened her husband's life and from whom they had no secrets, almost as a bereavement. It seemed to complete their family tragedy – they were estranged also from their surviving elder son. It was a story of Old Testament pathos.

The world around Weizmann was also darkening in the literal sense. He could read, and discern the faces of his visitors, only with difficulty. But he was far from his twilight. The mental agility was still in lively evidence; a comic encounter from the past suddenly remembered, an epigram quickly formulated, a reminiscence from his early career, and he would entrance any audience.

The United Nations Special Committee on Palestine ('UNSCOP') contained eleven representatives from the smaller nations, under a Swedish Chairman. Weizmann willingly agreed to testify, but first they came to pay their respects to Jewry's world statesman in his own home. The Swede arrived with the Czech, Canadian and Uruguayan representatives, together with the U.N. Secretary-General's personal envoy, a Chinese. They sat in the shade beside the small swimming pool that divided the two wings of the house, an architectural gem of the thirties. For three hours he regaled them with stories of the old pioneering days, of Rehovot as he had first seen it in 1907, of Russia and its Pale of Settlement, of his hopes and fears for this land in the future.

Beyond the house, on the other side of Rehovot, Jews and Arabs were perpetrating acts upon each other of which both would be ashamed. Across the Mediterranean, at La Spezia in Italy, an old hulk, once a pleasure-steamer in Chesapeake Bay, was being fitted out to run 4,000 refugees through the British blockade. The boat had been rescued from the breaker's yard for 40,000 dollars, money supplied by one of Weizmann's converts to Zionism, the New Orleans 'banana king' Samuel Zemurray.

As Weizmann entertained his visitors, neither defending nor condemning unofficial immigration, for he saw it as a natural reflex of the Jewish predicament, and no less legal than the 1939 White Paper, this vessel was being transformed into the *Exodus 1947*. It was being primed, like the film scenario it was later to inspire, as an advertisement to the world. In particular it was intended to drive home, to these men of UNSCOP, the clash between British callousness and Jewish desperation.

Oblivious of the preparation at La Spezia, the old man took his guests through the collective experience that made Zionism into the only positive Jewish force produced in the twentieth century, with the revival of a language and a return to the soil. Could these ideas be enacted anywhere but in Palestine, *Eretz Israel* in Hebrew, a place unique in history for being a moral imperative, not merely a territory? Where else would the Jews shed their tribal neurosis and cease to be a problem, to themselves as well as to others?

Then, a few days later, he came to that island of neutral calm in strife-torn Jerusalem, the Y.M.C.A. building with its slender Moorish profile – outside the Old City, detached from the modern Jewish district, well clear of Government House. It was the day allocated to Weizmann's testimony to UNSCOP. He insisted that he spoke only in a private capacity, but the presence of all the Consular officers in Palestine, of British military and governmental representatives, all in their seats well before his arrival, evidenced that the only true representative voice in Jewry was about to be heard.

His first words concerned Jewish terrorism, and its origins. 'The White Paper released certain phenomena in Jewish life which I oppose with all my force. The rule *Thou shalt not kill* was given to us on Mount Sinai.

What is now occurring was inconceivable ten years ago. I bow my head in shame when I speak of it before you.' The Mandate had been rendered unworkable only because of that White Paper, but now, to produce a solution endowed with finality, and dispel some of the fears of the Arabs, they had to divide this country between the two antagonists.

'But it cannot be standing-room only!' The Jewish sovereign area he recommended would embrace Galilee with the coastal plain, the Negev and the Jewish section of Jerusalem. This would be adequate to bring in 1,500,000 people in a comparatively short period.

'Would this not cause trouble among the Arabs?' the Indian representative enquired.

'It would be foolish for me to say everything would go smoothly. Nothing goes smoothly in this world. Perhaps the Mufti will not acquiesce. Perhaps some on our side will not acquiesce. But I don't think these are insurmountable difficulties. Do not prolong our agony.'

The Indian was not satisfied. He reminded Weizmann of the Jews' discrimination against the Arabs, by refusing to employ them on their land. Did he not see that this made for hatred?

Weizmann replied: 'There are three economic sectors in Palestine, Arab, Jewish and British. In the Jewish sector, Arabs are employed; in the Arab sector, no Jews are employed; in the British sector, not enough Jews are employed. What are we to do? We are a people who are discriminated against the world over. For once, in this land, we have the chance not to discriminate against ourselves.' Two weeks later the *Exodus* passengers, at Haifa harbour, were forcibly transferred onto military transports for return to Europe. British obtuseness was steadily reinforcing the Jewish argument.

The majority report of the investigating commission recommended a surgical operation that almost completely followed Weizmann's suggested map for two separate states, except that Western Galilee was allocated to the Arab area, and Greater Jerusalem, including Bethlehem, placed under international trusteeship. But the newspapers of the world did not surrender their most prominent columns to this historic decision, for all attention was focussed on the further progress of the *Exodus* affair. British soldiers were now being employed unedifyingly in disembarking the 4,000 struggling refugees on to dry land in Hamburg. Having rotted like abandoned freight in passive resistance from one crowded vessel to another, they were now being carried back to the camps from which they had started their journey three months earlier, in May, 1947. It was two years since these same soldiers had been acclaimed the liberators of

Europe. Now some of them confessed to being ashamed of their uniform.

In New York the nations were assembling to give their verdict on the UNSCOP report. They had not only this document to consider, but the drama of the *Exodus*, the drifting situation in Palestine, and the stolid face of a declared British neutralism prophesying anarchy but playing no part in its arrest. Support for partition and the termination of the Mandate seemed assured, but would it reach the two-thirds majority necessary for its implementation?

The United States announced that it would vote in favour, as did the U.S.S.R., endorsing Zionism for the first time after numerous hints of a change of heart. Russian adherence made the votes of the Communist bloc a certainty, but doubt surrounded the Catholic states of Latin America and a France sensitive of her Moslem empire. Scattered nations, with little interest in the outcome, were likely to adopt the line of least resistance in abstention. There were fifty-seven nations in the General Assembly, and every vote was crucial.

Silver regarded partition as a solution cheating the Jews of part of their patrimony, but he now laboured zealously to secure its victorious passage through the debates; in the view of many American Jews, over-zealously. It became apparent that Weizmann's presence was necessary in New York to rescue the Zionist cause from its champion.

However, the fallen leader felt he had done enough, and he let it be known that he did not wish to see Silver, or for that matter any other Zionist spokesman, whenever they decided that their fortunes at Lake Success were in a state of crisis. The American Chairman of the Jewish Agency was bombarding Washington in a lobbying campaign without precedent.

To President Truman, Zionism seemed to intrude like an unwelcome guest whatever the subject being ventilated in the Oval Office. The un-expected espousal of the cause by Russia, coupled with the collapse of British authority in Palestine, was giving anxieties to the State and Defence Departments. Fearing the entry of the Communists into a vacuum in the Eastern Mediterranean, they planned a gesture towards the angry Arabs, who were fighting a rearguard for their sovereignty in an undivided Palestine. Secretaries George Marshall and James Forrestal hoped to save the day by switching the southern Negev from the Jews to the other side. Naturally, Silver did not take kindly to the idea. But he had exhausted his capacity to reach the President over the heads of the U.S. delegation at Lake Success.

Truman, on the other hand, was advised by his personal aides, notably his Counsel, young Clark Clifford, that his chances of re-election in 1948 would be slim unless he cultivated the Jewish vote in earnest. Both his probable opponents, Thomas Dewey and Henry Wallace, were swimming with the Zionist tide. Furthermore, Truman needed money for his election fund: rich Democrats of the Roosevelt era were defecting in alarming number, among them Jews of a previously unswerving loyalty. But the President, squeezed by conflicting persuaders, distressed at being regarded in foreign eyes as a Zionist whipping-boy, felt his office was being abused, and he decided to allow the debates at Lake Success to take their course. Only one Zionist retained any goodwill in the White House.

Reluctantly, Weizmann travelled to New York in October. Still the private citizen, he came ostensibly to raise funds for refugee relief and for his Institute of Research now nearing completion. He was fatigued, but in control. Partition had been his solution to the Arab-Jewish conflict for ten years, and he sensed in his reception the relief of American Jewry that he was once more available, to lift the cause out of the quagmire of domestic ward politics. Arrangements were at once made for him to address the nations in assembly, many of whom were still undecided. If intercession with the President were to become necessary, he could command David Niles, Truman's adviser on minorities, and Felix Frankfurter, to open the door. Both men venerated the old leader.

Intercession indeed became necessary. The Negev problem emerged in another guise. The British had their eyes on the region on behalf of their puppet in Transjordan, Abdulla, who they anticipated would absorb any new Arab state to be carved from Palestine. Bevin could use a base there; and what if that great blanket of sand were found to be rich in oil? It would give the sleeping port of Akaba, now the end of a cul-de-sac in a blind gulf, new existence as a window on the Indian Ocean. For the Jews, their state deprived of the Negev would shrink to a cabbage-patch virtually as conceived by Peel. They needed the south for living-space, to be developed with the devotion that had brought the pioneering triumphs further north. The telephone lines between Weizmann's hotel in New York and his Washington friends hummed. Clifford was in no doubt that a meeting with the President would be mutually beneficial. An invitation was despatched.

Immensely frail, Weizmann rose from his sick-bed and, accompanied by the Jewish Agency expert, Eliahu Epstein (who subsequently changed his name to Elath, biblical term for Akaba), travelled to Washington by train. Truman, in no doubt how the visit would be considered in the U.N. lobbies, insisted on absolute privacy, if not secrecy. He and the 'old doctor', as he called Weizmann, poured over Epstein's sketch-map of the area and talked for half an hour. That same afternoon, the President telephoned his chief delegate at Lake Success: the southern Negev, with its keyhole to the Red Sea, must be kept within the Jewish State. In return the Arabs were to be compensated with Beersheba and a strip along the Egyptian frontier (see map p. 266). The Russians proved agreeable, and the situation was saved. One further week remained before the final vote in the General Assembly, and Weizmann's suite at the Waldorf Astoria now became the nerve-centre of the campaign to force the partition motion through.

The list of likely opponents and abstainers was long, and gave the Zionists cause for grave anxiety. To win the required two-thirds majority, some minds had to be changed. The Jews have a way of advertising their international minority status as being a victimising weakness. In fact it can be a source of strength. Geography and economics locates them strategically in their Diaspora, granting them access to the centres of political decision. Weizmann now manipulated this power as he had long done in public life.

France was under heavy pressure from the Arab world to suppress her instinct to vote for the Jewish State. Her vote was captured from under Arab eyes by an assault from two sides. Bernard Baruch, whose war-time hostility to Weizmann had changed to admiration, advised the French representative that American aid to his country might be withdrawn in the event of a negative stand. The vote was due to be taken on November 26. The evening before, Weizmann telephoned a Zionist friend in Paris, Marc Jarblum, to transmit a message to Léon Blum, now at the end of his political and physical tether. This said: 'France's decision to abstain from voting has caused painful dismay here, and above all to the five-million strong Jewish community. For the first time, the two Great Powers are in agreement. French abstention could well lead to others following her example, and this may well wreck the entire plan. If the French government destroyed the Jewish people's last hope, it would bear a frightful responsibility.'

It was midnight in Paris. But Blum could not ignore the plea. He had the message conveyed to President Vincent Auriol, as well as to the Premier, Paul Ramadier, and the Foreign Minister, Georges Bidault. France succumbed.

Less difficult to persuade were those Central American republics whose economic life-blood depended on the United Fruit Company, for this corporation was owned by the Zionist Samuel Zemurray. The Philippines were won over when detective work tracked down an American Jew in London who had been physician and friend to the President in Manila. It was rumoured in the lobbies that Liberia was moved to a change of heart on a hint from the Firestone Rubber Company.

Passage of the resolution was still not assured, when the Arab states requested more time and Thanksgiving Day intervened. Unexpectedly, the Jews found themselves with three days grace to continue their canvass. In this interval they won over Greece, Belgium and New Zealand. November 29 was a Saturday, and Jews with religious scruples sought rabbinical dispensation to travel on the Sabbath to witness the dénouement.

Emotionally and physically spent, Weizmann remained in his bedroom while the General Assembly voted. A retinue of faithfuls constantly travelled back and forth to bring him the progress of the struggle. Suddenly, all was quiet in his suite. Weisgal, Shertok, all the others, had gone off to Flushing Meadow and he was left alone with Vera at last. For the first time in those historic weeks something snapped in the old man. He broke down and sobbed.

The spasm endured barely a few moments, and by the time he recovered the General Assembly had done its work, and Chaim Weizmann was head in everything but name of what was already virtually an independent sovereign Jewish State – restored after nineteen centuries of hope and prayer.

Weisgal returned to the Waldorf Astoria to inform his chief that the streets of New York were packed with wildly cheering people. A rally was being organised at the St Nicholas skating rink; the absence of the leader was inconceivable. Weizmann demurred. He hadn't the strength. Nevertheless he was brought there willy-nilly, and virtually carried on to the stage over the heads of the delirious crowds. He had only a brief message for them: 'The world will judge the Jewish State by its actions towards the Arabs.'

Over there, in Jerusalem, Ben-Gurion too was at the centre of scenes of excitement. He was their acclaimed national commander in the field, the peasant-warrior nurtured in the Galilean sun. But the state was not going to be established by words, nor would it be achieved by the progressive handing over of British authority. Administration ceased to function under the Union Jack, and by default the Jews took over their area, and fortified it against invasion by Arab guerillas poised to over-run the country.

Within five weeks 600 Jews and Arabs had perished as the rival armies came into the open and fought out possession of hill and roadway while the British army, not due to leave before May 15, 1948, watched from the safety of its tanks. A modern Thirty Years War had begun.

The nations observed the results of their good intentions with consternation. If the Jews persisted in the implementation of their independence, declared the Arab states, they would send in their troops. The Russians accused the British of fanning the disorders by their attitude of non-cooperation in the partition. Refugees were still being turned away from Palestine, and Jerusalem changed from a city into a beleagured nexus of fortified strong-points, with *Irgun* and Stern going their own way. Washington received this most doleful intelligence with alarm.

Testifying before the House Armed Services Committee, Defence Secretary Forrestal advanced the view that the 'unworkable scheme' would cost America her Middle East oil supply. Furthermore, suggested General Eisenhower, if America were to contribute to an international force to police the situation in Palestine they might well have to re-introduce the draft. Allied strategy in the Middle East appeared to the State Department to receive a grievous blow with every fresh casualty in Palestine. What if the plan for partition concealed a sinister Kremlin trap!

Under the force of these arguments, Truman agreed to the postponement of partition and the transfer of Palestine to the aegis of the U.N. Trusteeship Council. The Zionists foresaw a complete sell-out, perhaps the brazen return of Britain in the new, unholy guise of 'Trustee'. Once more Jewish criticism, encouraged by Silver's regular following in the Senate, was directed upon the President. But he stood his ground.

In the meantime, Weizmann had returned to London and was in the act of winding up his affairs. He was due to visit newly-independent India, and would then proceed to Palestine to be with his people in their hour of liberation. This England, of which he had been a proud citizen for nearly forty years, was no longer congenial to him. But in the conventicles of Zionism in America, and among his friends in Washington who could not abide the relentless rabbi commanding the throng there, he had no right to abdicate as yet from the struggle.

Appeals reached him clamouring for his return. Who else could perform the feat of changing Truman's mind? Yet Silver, the Chairman of the Jewish Agency, could not bring himself to admit defeat and despatch a formal summons. Weizmann hesitated. The Security Council meeting, to which the Americans were to submit their Trusteeship proposal, drew

Harry S. Truman is presented with a scroll of the Law by Weizmann on the steps of the White House, after the latter's election as President of Israel, May 1948.

Formal swearing-in of the President in the Israel Parliament after the first general election
of 1949.

near. At last Weizmann received an official cry for help. It came in the name of Abba Eban, then a junior member of the Zionist mission, and a follower of Weizmann since his student days at Cambridge. The old man left England for the last time.

The finale for Weizmann was not without its element of tragi-comedy. In New York, he wrote to the President for the interview that would have been granted as a right and common courtesy to the head of the most insignificant government. Weizmann's standing enabled him to walk with the statesmen of the world, but the Jews lacked the status of a nation and his rank was that of an insignificant individual. In a laconic rebuff the request was refused: the representative of the Jews did not merit the diplomatic niceties. Others tried on his behalf, but with no better result.

However, in Kansas City, a small-town Jewish haberdasher was enjoying minor fame among his fellow-members of B'nai Brith for having served in Truman's artillery battery during the First World War, and subsequently as the future President's partner in a short-lived business. Their store had foundered, and Truman had proceeded to higher things. But he never forgot his old friend Eddie Jacobson, to whom the door of the White House was ever open. The modest haberdasher was now enlisted to perform what was impressed upon him as an historic act on behalf of his people: he must persuade his former partner to see Dr Weizmann. A telegram went from Kansas City to the President.

The patient Truman replied that there was nothing Weizmann could tell him, and a meeting would therefore be without purpose. Jacobson, who made it a point of honour not to presume too much on his acquaintanceship with the President, was reluctant to take the matter further. Much against his will, therefore, he was bundled onto an aeroplane to bring his request in person. As always, he was ushered into the Oval Office – forewarned by Truman's aides that he had better not bring up the subject of Palestine, or the name of Weizmann.

Miserably, Jacobson kept an unreal conversation going, and found himself speaking of the President's hero, Andrew Jackson. Then he went on: 'I too have a hero, a man I never met. I am talking about Chaim Weizmann. He is a very sick man, almost broken in health, but he has travelled thousands of miles just to see you and plead the cause of my people. Now you refuse to see him just because you were insulted by some of our American Jewish leaders, even though you know that Weizmann had absolutely nothing to do with these insults and would be the last man to be party to them. It doesn't sound like you, Harry, because I thought you could take this stuff they have been handing out to you.'

This worked the oracle. On March 18, 1948, Weizmann entered the White House incognito, by the East Gate. He emphasised to the President that whatever transpired at the Security Council, his people would declare the establishment of their State on May 15. When the 'old doctor' departed, he was convinced that he had won Truman over, and that America would recognise their existence as a nation.

This did not appear likely, for the following day Warren Austin, leader of the American delegation, called for the summoning of the General Assembly to effect a temporary trusteeship over Palestine. But Weizmann would not admit to having been deceived.

The news from Palestine was bad. The *Haganah*, to keep supplies moving on the roads, was fighting pitched battles against Arab irregulars in the Judean Hills and the Negev. The Hebrew University found itself cut off on Mount Scopus, while the Jewish Agency headquarters was rocked by an explosion just as the Stern Gang planted a bomb in the Arab quarter of Haifa. Ben-Gurion saw that Jerusalem, where the British were still entrenched, could be his greatest prize, or his bitterest defeat. Jewish losses were enormous, because irreplaceable, and Zionist heroism, like Arab valour, was unevenly distributed. Moshe Sneh resigned from the Jewish Agency, announcing that he would henceforth work for a Zionism linked with the Communist bloc, whose promises remained unbroken.

In Washington, Truman, closeted with the Democratic Party bosses, his Jewish intimates and Clark Clifford, played out a stratagem to thwart the State Department while appearing to endorse its moves at the U.N. meetings. He sent Samuel Rosenman with a message to Weizmann that he would keep his word. But was his promise exactly as the latter had interpreted it? The people around Weizmann were pessimistic. He refused to be downcast, though he prudently made a long statement to the Press to remind the President of their discussion.

He was now totally restored in the public mind as the Jewish leader who could determine the outcome of events, and members of the American delegation, the French delegation, even the British Colonial Secretary Ernest Creech-Jones, beat a path to the Waldorf Astoria to win his acquiescence to trusteeship and thereby stop the waste of life in Palestine. They could not shake his faith that the man in the White House would have the last word.

By mid-April the tide in Palestine began to turn. A guerilla army was routed in the north, and Ben-Gurion forced a large convoy of food supplies and weapons along the treacherous road to Jerusalem. Many local Arabs, who had taken little or no part in the fighting, began to flee the Jewish areas. Trusteeship was now losing important supporters, and the best that Warren Austin could do was to carry a proposal through a Special Assembly for a cease-fire and further talks; there must be a renewed attempt to bring the warring parties together. Now Shertok and Goldmann also wavered. If talks could resume perhaps they should postpone the formation of the Provisional Jewish Government? It now seemed touch and go, and though in Jerusalem they bravely spoke of May 15 as the day of liberation, cautious voices around Ben-Gurion whispered that a declaration would be premature.

Ben-Gurion needed Weizmann's personal view. Direct telephone contact between Palestine and the United States had broken down. So Weisgal, on the point of leaving Palestine for New York, was instructed by the Zionist Garibaldi to stop off in Nice and consult his master. Weizmann's reply left no doubt: Ben-Gurion must go ahead. Weisgal reported back accordingly. On May 14 Truman received a communication from Weizmann requesting prompt recognition by the President of Ben-Gurion and his immediate colleagues in Palestine as the Provisional Government of a state that had not as yet been given a name.

It was just before the Sabbath in the tiny Tel Aviv museum that afternoon. David Ben-Gurion had summoned a meeting of his Provisional State Council, and there he proclaimed Jewish sovereignty in a state to be called Israel. The miracle, for such it was, demanded one further act for its consummation, and it came immediately afterwards. The United States granted Israel recognition as an independent state, and was followed almost at once by the U.S.S.R. Weizmann heard it on the radio.

The following day Weizmann received a message from Ben-Gurion and his principal colleagues at the front line. 'On the establishment of the Jewish State,' it stated, 'we send our greetings to you, who have done more than any other living man towards its creation. Your stand and help have strengthened all of us. We look forward to the day when we shall see you at the head of the state established in peace.'

He was elected First President of the Council of State. The long journey to Zion was ended. And it was to be ended also, far from the scenes of strife, for one other, who had dreamed and toiled and suffered with him. In a remote corner of Scotland, on May 15, Baffy Dugdale, niece of the author of the Balfour Declaration, gently breathed her last.

15

The Last Phase

FROM ITS MOMENT OF BIRTH AS AN INDEPENDENT STATE, ISRAEL WAS locked in a struggle to survive. But President Weizmann passed his last years tormented by the knowledge that he was a bystander.

David Ben-Gurion filled the stage. Many of his prophecies of the preceding decade were now being fulfilled, some according to his warnings, others according to his desires. War had come; immigration was made free; the Jews' capacity for organisation, meticulous planning, single-minded dedication to the ultimate Zionist aspiration, won the struggle for mastery of the territory against everything the invading Arabs could pit against them. In the humiliation of their collapse, the Arab states descended into a long night of introspection and unrest. Abdulla of Transjordan acquired land he had long coveted, with Old Jerusalem the jewel of his crown. His readiness to forget the past and make peace with the Jews cost him his life.

Revealing great strength of decision, Ben-Gurion set about eliminating the factionalism, a heritage from the British occupation, that challenged the rule of law in his country. He would not consider the return of the hundreds of thousands of departed Arabs except within the terms of a formal peace, a decision that was to fuel smouldering fires. He invited Zionist leaders abroad to share in his government, but only if they came as citizens of the State. Even the religious forces saw Ben-Gurion now as the man of destiny. Weizmann was the man of history.

Nothing was written into the statutes of the powers of Israel's President, and Weizmann found, to his dismay, that he had none. Ben-Gurion did not invite him to a single Cabinet meeting, and moreover denied him access to its Minutes. To have done so would have been apposite as an act of brotherhood, which was a quality the Prime Minister lacked. While the President had no wish to direct the government, nor to turn his home at Rehovot into another White House, he visualised a place for himself as the Thomas Masaryk of the Jews; indeed, the pattern of democratic Czechoslovakia was before him when he received notice of his election as Head of State.

Neither his frailty nor his years disqualified him for such a role. His mind retained its full vigour for almost two years after independence was won, and his long experience as unofficial Prime Minister, Foreign Minister and Treasurer of the nation in the making made it inconceivable that his counsel should be ignored. But the state was established in the reflection of its battle commander, his virtues, his determination, his failings.

Thus for the man in Rehovot, the last phase fell into a realm of agonising might-have-beens. He was severe towards the government's hasty identification with the West, considering this to be a gratuitous rejection of Russia's hand of friendship, and all the more damaging given the Soviet Union's contribution to the creation of Israel. Zionism, Weizmann maintained against Ben-Gurion, was not dead. It could be a movement of mediation between the capitalist and socialist worlds, between Europe and Asia, between modernity and traditionalism. He was eager to play his part in healing the conflict with the Arabs, but the months went by and he was not called.

Ben-Gurion could not share his powers. His Foreign Minister, Moshe Shertok, now Sharett, developed as a moderate in the style of Weizmann, but his functions fell short of policy-making. In December, 1949, the United Nations passed a resolution for the internationalisation of Jerusalem and while Sharett deliberated Ben-Gurion defied the order and moved his capital from Tel Aviv to his section of the divided city. Russia's displeasure with Israel, roused by its tutelage to the United States and Ben-Gurion's longing glance towards Soviet Jewry as candidates for Israeli nationality, hardened thereby into hostility. Weizmann failed to recognise how the era of statehood forced the Jews into painful decisions of Realpolitik, whereas in their stateless condition they could afford grandiloquent generalisations that were resonant of noble but unreal intent.

While Rehovot was growing into a scientific bridge to the world, it simultaneously shrank into a St Helena for the President. David Bergmann finally left the great Americanised campus in 1951 to serve Israel's new leader at the Ministry of Defence and assume a Chair at the Hebrew University. It was as though Weizmann had relinquished his last contact with active life. He was now almost blind, and rarely left the house, so that Yehudi Menuhin, appearing before great audiences all over the country, interrupted his tour to play to him and Vera privately in their drawing-room.

The panoply of Presidential office had little appeal for him, and he referred sardonically to the role he was fated to play in the orchestra of government. 'They tell me I am a symbol,' he would inform his visitors, 'so here I am cymballing away.'

To the younger generation of Israelis, exalting in their freedom, he was a figure to be equated with Jewish weakness and apologia, survivor from a period when their people received insults without protest, and were slaughtered unresisting. May 14, 1948, marked for them the resumption of time after their many centuries suspended in a vacuum, and Weizmann had no part in this glory of re-birth because, when the hour struck, he had stood with the Diaspora in New York, not with the *Yishuv* in the front-line. This reflected less on the forgetfulness of the young than on Israel's education system, which was heavily laden with the ideology of a territorial nationalism.

The Declaration of Independence, drafted by an all-party committee and given its final polish by Ben-Gurion himself, bears the signatures of thirty-seven Jews, many of whom participated only insignificantly in the struggle for statehood. Weizmann's name is not among them. He took this as a personal slight, and his friends regarded the omission as Ben-Gurion's last gesture of disapproval against the aged leader. It was not so. The names constituted the Provisional State Council, made up of the Palestine members of the Jewish Agency together with the internal *Va'ad Leumi*. Brooding over this as a symbol too, Weizmann frequently spoke of resigning the Presidency. But he refrained from making his disappointments public, for the nation's devotion to its Prime Minister was an index of its courage in defying its enemies. When Weizmann's Memoirs appeared, in 1949, they contained not a breath of reproach against Ben-Gurion.

His last two years passed with Israel's dramatic strides reaching him as distant echoes. New cities mushroomed, the population more than doubled, and great expanses of neglected land came under the plough, to foster a new sense of identity among Jews everywhere that transcended Zionism. A retrospective view would judge the self-confidence of those days as excessive, for once the refugee camps were cleared and Jews from Moslem lands were brought out of their hostile environments, immigrants were hard to come by. But faith was then the vital ingredient of a nation engaged on tasks which by any rational calculation were impossible.

When Chaim Weizmann's end came, at the age of seventy-seven on November 9, 1952, Prime Minister Ben-Gurion spoke of him as a man 'taking his place in the eternal history of the Jewish people alongside the great figures of the past – the Patriarchs and Kings, the Judges, Prophets and spiritual leaders who have woven the fabric of our national life for four thousand years'.

He was mourned in England, the country that won his love equally with the Holy Land, as one of its own. Winston Churchill was addressing the Lord Mayor's Banquet in London when he received the news. Departing from his prepared text he said: 'Those of us who have been Zionists since the days before the Balfour Declaration know what a heavy loss Israel has sustained in the death of Chaim Weizmann, who was famed and respected throughout the free world, and whose son was killed fighting for us. Weizmann led his people back to the Promised Land, where we have seen them invincibly installed in a sovereign state.'

He was laid to rest in a simple grave, inscribed only with his name, in the garden of his beloved Rehovot. His monument is around him, in the institute dedicated to the spirit of enquiry, in the fields made to blossom in the desert, in the reunion of his people with their soil, in the end of the Exile.

Havens for Jewish Refugees 1933-1945

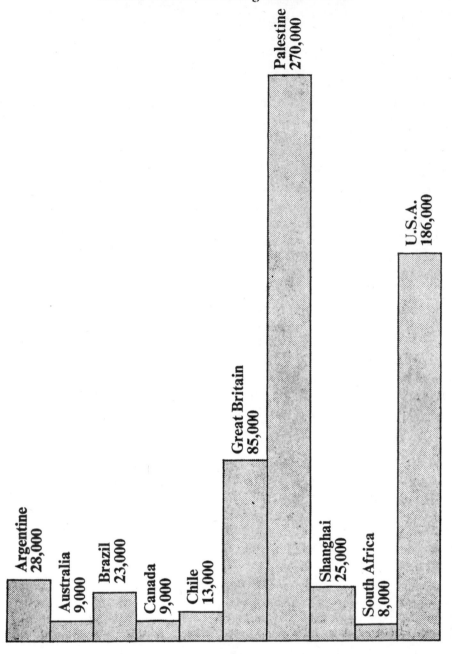

Note: No figures are given for the U.S.S.R., as many fleeing from Eastern Europe were either overtaken by the German invaders and perished or returned subsequently to their homes, mainly Poland and Rumania. The Palestine figure excludes 'illegals', about 100,000. Peak figures for U.S.A. were in 1939–42. Figures for France are not available, as many refugees were either in transit or perished in deportation. The British total includes about one-third who moved to other countries. Shanghai admitted Jews without visa, but the total includes some 3,000 deported there by Japan.

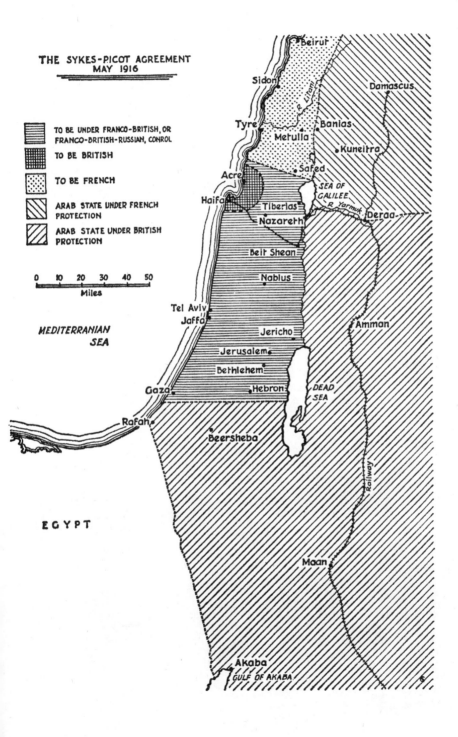

THE SYKES-PICOT AGREEMENT
MAY 1916

TO BE UNDER FRANCO-BRITISH, OR
FRANCO-BRITISH-RUSSIAN, CONTROL

TO BE BRITISH

TO BE FRENCH

ARAB STATE UNDER FRENCH
PROTECTION

ARAB STATE UNDER BRITISH
PROTECTION

0   10   20   30   40   50
Miles

MEDITERRANIAN
SEA

EGYPT

Beirut
Sidon
Tyre
Metulla
Acre
Haifa
Tel Aviv
Jaffa
Gaza
Rafah
Beersheba
R. Litani
Banias
Kuneitra
Safed
SEA OF
GALILEE
R. Yarmuk
Tiberias
Nazareth
Beit Shean
Nablus
Jericho
Jerusalem
Bethlehem
Hebron
DEAD
SEA
Damascus
Deraa
Amman
Maan
Railway
Akaba
GULF OF AKABA

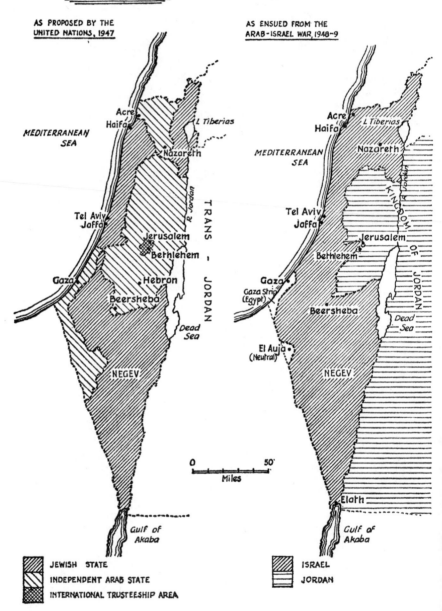

PALESTINE'S FRONTIERS

AS PROPOSED BY THE
UNITED NATIONS, 1947

AS ENSUED FROM THE
ARAB-ISRAEL WAR, 1948-9

MEDITERRANEAN
SEA

Acre
Haifa

L. Tiberias

Nazareth

R. Jordan

TRANS - JORDAN

Tel Aviv
Jaffa

Jerusalem
Bethlehem

Gaza

Hebron

Beersheba

Dead
Sea

NEGEV

MEDITERRANEAN
SEA

Acre
Haifa

L. Tiberias

Nazareth

KINGDOM OF JORDAN

Tel Aviv
Jaffa

Jerusalem

Bethlehem

Gaza
Gaza Strip
(Egypt)

Beersheba

Dead
Sea

El Auja
(Neutral)

NEGEV

0   50
Miles

Elath

Gulf of
Akaba

Gulf of
Akaba

JEWISH STATE
INDEPENDENT ARAB STATE
INTERNATIONAL TRUSTEESHIP AREA

ISRAEL
JORDAN

Glossary

Alliance Israélite Universelle   Founded in Paris, 1860. Largely, though not exclusively, an educational philanthropic organisation.

Ashkenazim   Jews mainly originating in Northern Europe, most of whom spread eastward in modern times.

B'nai Brith   Founded 1843, an American organisation originally consisting of Jews of German cultural origin.

Bund   Founded 1897 as a confederation of Jewish workers in Lithuania, Poland and Russia, affiliated to the Russian Social Democratic Party. Though upholding the national identity of the Jews, it was strongly anti-Zionist.

Diaspora   The Jewish dispersion.

Fellah   Arab peasant.

Goy   A gentile.

Haham   Term applied to Sephardi rabbis, particularly, as in England, a principal rabbi.

Hatikvah   The Zionist hymn, later Israel's national anthem.

Haganah   Jewish defence force in Palestine accepting Zionist Organisation control.

Hilfsverein der deutchen Juden   Founded in Berlin, 1901, as a non-Zionist philanthropic and educational organisation.

Histadrut   The General Federation of Labour in Palestine, founded 1920.

Irgun Zvai Leumi   Revisionist (right-wing) military organisation founded in 1930s and outside official Zionist control.

Kibbutz   Jewish collective settlement.

Maskil   Followers of the Enlightenment (modernisation) movement in Jewry in late 18th and 19th centuries.

Mizrachi Orthodox religious party in Zionism, founded 1902.

Sephardim Strictly, Jews emanating from the Iberian Peninsula, but taken to embrace also those of Mediterranean and Oriental provenance.

Talmud Body of teaching comprised in Jewish oral law and literature, with commentaries, codified in the fifth century of the Christian era.

Va'ad Leumi Jewish National Council of Palestine during Mandate.

Yishuv The Palestine Jewish community.

Yom Kippur Day of Atonement.

Select Bibliography

To list all the works consulted, including general histories of the Middle East, books by or about world statesmen, and the publications of Zionist and non-Zionist bodies, would diminish the usefulness of this bibliography. The author wishes particularly to acknowledge his indebtedness to the following:

Weizmann, Chaim, *Trial and Error*. London and New York, 1949.
Weizmann, Chaim, *Letters and Papers*, Vols. 1–7, individually edited by Leonard Stein, Gedalia Yogev, Barnet Litvinoff, Camillo Dresner, Hanna Weiner, Shifra Kolatt, Evyatar Friesel, Dvora Barzilay, Nehama Chalom. London and Jerusalem, 1968–75.
Weisgal, Meyer W., Editor, *Chaim Weizmann, Statesman and Scientist*. New York, 1944.
Weisgal, Meyer W., *So Far*, an Autobiography. London and New York, 1971.
Weisgal, Meyer W., with Joel Carmichael, Editors, *Chaim Weizmann: A Biography by Several Hands*. London, 1962.
Goodman, Paul, Editor, *Chaim Weizmann:* A Tribute on his 70th Birthday. London, 1945.
Weizmann, Vera, *The Impossible Takes Longer*. London, 1967.
Herzl, Theodor, *The Complete Diaries*, edited by Raphael Patai. London and New York, 1960.
Krojanker, Gustav, Editor, *Reden und Aufsätze:* Speeches by Chaim Weizmann. Tel Aviv, 1937.
Stein, Leonard, *The Balfour Declaration*. London, 1961.
Kisch, Fred H., *A Palestine Diary*. London, 1938.

Bentwich, Norman, *For Zion's Sake:* A Biography of Judah L. Magnes. Philadelphia, 1954.

Wilson, Trevor, Editor, *The Political Diaries of C. P. Scott.* London, 1970.

Clark, Ronald W., *Einstein.* London, 1973.

Dugdale, Blanche, *Arthur James Balfour.* London, 1936.

Rose, Norman A., Editor, *Baffy:* The Diaries of Blanche Dugdale. London, 1973.

Sieff, Israel, *Memoirs.* London, 1970.

Antonius, George, *The Arab Awakening.* London, 1938.

Samuel, Herbert (Viscount), *Memoirs.* London, 1945.

Jabotinsky, Vladimir, *The Story of the Jewish Legion.* New York, 1945.

Schechtman, Joseph, *The Jabotinsky Story.* New York, 1956, 1961.

Simon, Leon, *Ahad Ha'am.* London, 1960.

Rabinowitz, Oskar K., *Fifty Years of Zionism:* A Critique of *Trial and Error.* London, 1952.

Brodetsky, Selig, *Memoirs.* London, 1960.

Ruppin, Arthur, *Memoirs, Diaries, Letters.* London, 1971.

Goldmann, Nahum, *Memories.* London, 1969.

Crossman, Richard H. S., *Palestine Mission.* London, 1947.

Ben-Gurion, David, *Rebirth and Destiny of Israel* (Essays and Addresses). New York, 1954.

Ben-Gurion, David, with Moshe Perlman, *Ben-Gurion Looks Back.* London, 1965.

Ben-Gurion, David, *Letters to Paula.* London, 1971.

Silver, Abba Hillel, *Vision and Victory* (Addresses). New York, 1949.

Barbour, Nevill, *Nisi Dominus.* London, 1946.

Manuel, Frank E., *The Realities of American-Palestine Relations.* Washington, 1949.

Klausner, Joseph, *Menahem Ussishkin.* Jerusalem, 1942.

Wise, Stephen S., *Challenging Years.* New York, 1949.

Sacher, Harry, *Zionist Portraits and other Essays.* London, 1959.

Lipsky, Louis, *A Gallery of Zionist Profiles.* New York, 1956.

Index

Index

Jm 11/1/77